PELICAN BOOKS

A 784

THE DEATH OF JESUS

Joel Carmichael was born in New York City in 1915 and educated at Columbia University, the Sorbonne, and Wadham College, Oxford, where he was holder of the Hody Hebrew Exhibition and winner of the Pusey and Ellerton Hebrew Scholarship. He was also a Fulbright Fellow in Islamic studies at the Sorbonne.

He is also the author of *An Illustrated History of Russia*, *A Short History of the Russian Revolution*, and *A Short History of the Arabs*. He has also edited and translated Carl Brockelmann's *History of the Islamic Peoples*, Sukhanov's *The Russian Revolution 1917*, and Theodor Dan's *The Origins of Bolshevism*.

Joel Carmichael now lives in New York.

D1420115

THE DEATH OF JESUS

JOEL CARMICHAEL

PENGUIN BOOKS

Penguin Books Ltd, Harmondsworth, Middlesex, England
Penguin Books Pty Ltd, Ringwood, Victoria, Australia

—

First published by Victor Gollancz 1963
Published in Pelican Books 1966

—

Copyright © Joel Carmichael, 1962

—

Made and printed in Great Britain
by C. Nicholls & Company Ltd
Set in Linotype Granjon

CONTENTS

PREFACE

In this book I suggest a theory to explain the discrepancies in the Gospel narrative that still perplex scholars and laymen alike.

Simply put, these discrepancies revolve around the enigma of why a seemingly peaceful prophet was put to a cruel death by the Roman authorities, with the connivance of or indeed through the instigation of his own people, the Jews.

The thesis of the book is at variance with traditional views. It undertakes to prove that Jesus thought of himself as no more than the herald of an imminent material transformation of the world (the Kingdom of God), that his message was addressed to the Jews of his own time and to no one else, and that upon the failure of the Kingdom of God to appear he embarked on an altogether different course of action, which led to his violent death. My discussion of what this course of action might have been is the most radical part of the book, and of course the most speculative.

The explanations I have suggested of the various discrepancies in the Gospels would be agreed to, I think, by most independent scholars. The plausibility of my hypothetical reconstruction of Jesus' activity will be judged by the reader for himself. The final chapters, in which I explain the extraordinary transformation of Jesus' memory into a new religion, are hardly more than a summary of authoritative opinion, but I hope they will be of interest to the general reader.

Though the bibliography required for the study of the New Testament, the life of Jesus, and the origins of Christianity generally is well-nigh boundless, I have encumbered this book with scarcely any scholarly references. I thought it sufficient to refer to several works I have consulted for various interpretations, though these, to be sure, are generally such as can be arrived at by any unbiased person through independent study of our sources, which, when all is said and done, remain almost exclusively the New Testament and more particularly the four Gospels.

My attitude throughout is purely historical. While brought up with no formal religious instruction, I developed an early interest in the mysteries of the ancient Middle East; this led me to the study of a number of classical languages at the university – Hebrew, Aramaic, Arabic, and Greek – and ultimately to a sustained concentration on the Bible and on the origins of Christianity, a problem of singular fascination. The ambiguity I have referred to above as underlying the genesis of Christianity seems to me to have survived with undiminished vigour down to our own day; it goes far beyond the confines of denominational religion.

I hope that the problem of Jesus' life on earth, discussed for the past hundred and fifty years with so much anguish, can be approached from a different angle, in accordance with the temper of our times.

J.C.

New York City
1962

I

THE APPROACH

THE birth of Jesus Christ is the starting point of all real history for more than one third of the human race, and it is a strange fact that he remains, humanly speaking, obscure and enigmatic. It is even stranger that until the last few generations there was scarcely any interest in the earthly aspect of his career : he was worshipped only as a divine being, and for some eighteen hundred years no serious attention was paid to his life on earth.

Admittedly, it would have been difficult to find much material for a biography of Jesus the man. Our knowledge, after all, is confined almost entirely to the contents of the New Testament, and for all practical purposes to the four Gospels. The information given us there is extremely scanty; what we read in the Gospels, in fact, covers no more than a small fraction of Jesus' life. The fourth Gospel, the most theological, or least historical, spans no more than three years at most; the other three add up to a few months or less, and in any case not more than a year. Indeed, estimates have been made of the time it would actually have taken Jesus to utter all the discourses attributed to him and to perform all the actions reported : they amount to a few weeks all told.

We can see now, in short, that the outlook was never very promising for any of the biographers of Jesus. But we can see that only now; at the beginning of the nineteenth century, as a historical attitude towards all subjects spread throughout the scholarly world, a movement was launched to apply to Jesus, and more broadly to the origins of Christianity itself, the same historical methods of research that had been so fruitful in other fields. Beginning in Germany, among liberal Protestant theologians, a movement of what came to be called 'criticism' busied itself so zealously with all the materials bearing on Jesus' life that in the space of a few generations an immense number of biographies of Jesus was produced, estimated at some sixty thousand!

It is obviously the very scantiness of the material that has enabled so many books, expressing so many divergent views, to be written: an abundance of information would have restricted the possibilities. As it is, scholars have been in the relatively happy position of having in fact nothing more to cope with than the biographical fragments in the Gospels; it is this that accounts for the enormous variety of these 'Lives of Jesus', most of which have been no more than portraits of Jesus projected in terms of the biographers' own ideals. It became fashionable to contrive highly speculative and fanciful accounts, of varying degrees of erudition, into which the odd fragments contained in our Gospels could be made to fit as deftly as possible, depending on both the skill and the bias – romantic or theological – of the biographer.

Now that an enormous amount of spadework has been done and all potential themes in the biography of Jesus have been experimented with, what should have been evident from a cursory glance at the Gospels is more evident than ever – it is impossible to write an adequate life of Jesus. The extraordinary meagreness of the information concerning Jesus as a human being is actually a foreshadowing of the kind of interest taken in him throughout the whole history of Christianity. In the very earliest accounts we have, Jesus the man is already submerged in the divine Christ: the narrative given in the Gospels is swallowed up by the ritual or doctrinal interests of their authors and editors. Still more importantly, it is told from an altogether different point of view – that of the Resurrection and Glorification of the Saviour. This new perspective is plainly independent of Jesus' human existence, yet it completely dominated both the recording and the interpretation of his life. The impression is unavoidable that Jesus as a historical personage was almost entirely obliterated by his transformation into the devotional lodestone of the early Christian community.

We are naturally so steeped in our own tradition that the Gospels and the New Testament as a whole are difficult to approach without bias. It is almost impossible to read the Gospels as it were naïvely – as a mere story of something that *happened*. Our tradition blocks our own approach to it: we see these texts, which in many ways look so simple, through a glass darkly. The whole of the New Testament has been so thoroughly absorbed into our patterns of thought, it has been accepted with such completeness, that quite apart from the sort of bored familiarity with it that characterizes so many of us, it requires an active and unflagging effort of the mind to study it as we would any other written account.

Yet surely such an effort is needed. The preoccupation of untold millions of people with the figure of Jesus on the Cross is constant, indeed growing. The interest in the Old and New Testaments that began with the Reformation is still going on, and is being pursued with greater zeal than ever. The feeling that something of immense importance happened in Palestine some nineteen hundred years ago is not only the conviction of more than eight hundred million believing Christians, but many whose ancestral faith has been lost as a doctrine have, doubtless for that very reason, come to regard Jesus as all the more significant for the temporal world.

The discovery some years ago of what has come to be known as the Dead Sea Scrolls has stimulated an even greater interest in Jesus' historical background, hinted at so meagrely in the Gospels. Most people will recall the discovery of these Scrolls in 1947; it unleashed one of the most violent controversies in scholarly history. When the Scrolls finally percolated through the cloisters of academic erudition, the huge lay audience they reached was fascinated by the hope of some illumination to be cast – for the first time in history – not merely on the historic facts of Jesus' life, but on what might have been his specific cultural or, for that matter, organizational background.

From this point of view the Scrolls have proved a disappointment. Even assuming their antiquity, still vigorously contested in certain authoritative circles, they have shed no light at all on Jesus personally, nor have they added in any way to our knowledge of his immediate milieu.

There is no consensus, even among the scholars who believe in the pre-Christian dating of the Scrolls, about just what information may be derived from them concerning the world of contemporary Judaism as a whole; it is much too soon to attempt an assessment of their data.

All that may be said about the Scrolls at this point, assuming them to be as old as some scholars think, is that they have increased the density, so to speak, of the general Jewish background of Christianity. The entire epoch is so empty, so deserted, as far as we know, by ancient chroniclers that we are confronted by an almost total dearth of specific factual information concerning the birth of the religion that revolutionized the world. Hence, no matter how obscure, fragmentary, and elusive these Scrolls may be, they are bound to remain precious as a means of piecing out the mosaic of the turbulent Jewish world that engendered Christianity, and of disentangling some of the strands that later went into the composition of the early Church.

Thus, though we may possibly know more about Jesus' background from the Dead Sea Scrolls, we do not know more about him. We are still dependent on the New Testament, and though, as I have said, no genuine biography can be based on the skimpy information contained in the Gospels, there are many fascinating possibilities suggested. A candid reappraisal of the Gospels will lend support to a reconsideration of Jesus' tragic career.

As we shall see, the Gospel account is not only scanty as a source of historical information; it is curiously contradictory. To extract an intelligible account of what might have happened, it is necessary to embark on a radical reconstruction of the sequence of events; such a reconstruction, based on but not subservient to the material available, has long been possible, though seldom ventured.

Let us look at the story of Jesus once again.

2

THE ENIGMA OF JESUS' DEATH

IF we force ourselves into a naïve attitude towards the Gospels, what an extraordinary impression they make! What a fascinating jumble of puzzles, contradictions, gaps, hints, and suggestions!

The story is about an individual, but actually it never tells us anything personal. The narrative is so barren it baffles us. Jesus seems to be moving in a vacuum; we cannot see what his day-to-day life was like, nor understand his relations with his companions. For that matter their behaviour is scarcely reported at all. In spite of the occasional circumstantial atmosphere there is a fog of obscurity and timelessness about the events that blurs their interconnexion: the rationale of Jesus' activities escapes us. The individual anecdotes that make up the substance of the story all seem to hang in the air, as do Jesus' parables and sayings. Even when the symbolical point of all these is clear, their framework in life varies significantly from one account of the same incident to another. In any case the parables seem so remote from real life that they illuminate neither Jesus' character nor the situation they might be relevant to. Personal motives are seldom indicated, except with a childlike and obviously contrived simplicity. Not only do we not see what Jesus' inner thoughts or feelings were, but even his aims are obscure. He is, in fact, like a statue, fixed in one pose or another. Even his suffering remains on a somewhat nonhuman plane: without a perception of his aims or thoughts what can it mean to us?

It would seem that, though the Gospels are intent on telling a story, it is one that is not meant to convey a portrait of a personality, but to build up a theme.

And there are so many contradictions in the presentation of that theme! Jesus is presented to us throughout as the quintessence of goodness, yet he arouses an incomprehensible malevolence in his own people that brings him to a cruel death. He is called eternal and divine, yet detailed genealogies are given connecting him with the Jewish royal house. He even has a family, including a mother, four brothers, and at least two sisters, who far from regarding him as divine think him out of his mind. His Judaism is conventional, yet he seems to be intermittently both friendly with Jews and hostile to them *as such*. He has disciples who are supposed to teach, but the disciples themselves are taught in parables they not only find unintelligible, but also are forbidden to communicate. At different points Jesus seems to be appealing to Jews exclusively, then to the world at large. He seems to be meek, yet claims to be greater than Solomon, and for that matter to be at the right hand of God. He forbids the use of invective, yet he is constantly excoriating his opponents. Baptism is made much of, yet we are told Jesus never baptized anyone himself. Multitudes acclaim him on one day and reject him on the next. When his disciples call him the Messiah he cautions them to keep silent, though his public behaviour clearly cries out for some such explanation. His disciples are forewarned of his doom, yet 'forsake him and flee' when it takes place. And so on.

The more all this is looked at, the more puzzling it becomes. With information so scanty it is difficult to establish a scale of plausibilities. We seem to be lost without a compass.

But in fact a compass can be found. At the very core of the entire Gospel narrative – the climax itself – there is a conundrum. The crucifixion and the reasons for it are curiously enigmatic; in unravelling the conundrum we shall find ourselves facing a solution of the problem as a whole.

The puzzle is this: though Jesus is evidently a pious Jew, as he shows by many of his remarks (which we shall look into below), he falls out with other Jews on apparently religious grounds. They hate him, we are told, and plot his undoing. But he is finally executed, not by the Jews, as we might expect, but by the Romans.

Summed up, a Roman governor crucifies a Jew who is politically inoffensive for what is, at one point, said to be an offence against the Jewish religion. At another point an offence against Rome is also mentioned, but this is expressly declared to be imaginary. Yet it is ultimately for just this offence against

Rome, as a pretender to power ('King of the Jews'), that Jesus is crucified.

This contradiction at the very crux of the Gospel account is an indispensable signpost for the reconstruction it clamours for.

Now, let us disregard for the moment other discrepancies in the account, and proceed in reverse. Let us take as our starting point the tragic end of Jesus' life and go as it were backward through the Gospels. We shall try to see whether we can arrive at an alternative to the traditional view of Jesus' career, and grasp what it meant to the people of his time.

We shall, in fact, be paralleling the historic genesis of the Gospels: just as the crucifixion and its interpretation brought into being and shaped the accounts of Jesus' career, so it will provide us with a clue to a reinterpretation of that career.

For this process of reverse analysis we shall have to establish two facts:

First, the above-mentioned transformation of perspective of the earliest chroniclers, based on the glorification of the divine Saviour through his Resurrection.

Second, the atmosphere in which the Gospels were compiled and edited. This was done when the newly evolving Christian sect was definitively splitting off from the parent body of Judaism, with which it had been identified during the first couple of generations of its existence. While growing increasingly self-conscious, the Christian community kept colliding more and more with the hostility of Jewry, especially of the learned Jewish scholars who throughout the period of the formation of early Christianity were its chief opponents. Jewish elements in the early Christian faith were dislodged or swamped by elements drawn from the Greco-Roman world. The writers and editors of the Gospels shifted to the lifetime of Jesus their own disputes with the Jewish rabbis. This process was reinforced by the Romans' destruction of the Jewish state in A.D. 70, which substantially wiped out the small community of Jews who believed in Jesus' personal singularity, though not his divinity, and left the new sect to develop wholly under the influences of the Greco-Roman world.

The perspective created by the progressive magnification of

Jesus dominated the writing of the Gospels; it has remained the basic focus of all Christian thought. Paul himself has given us the formula epitomizing this process of cultic transfiguration: his sole concern was with 'Christ crucified' (I Cor. 1:23). This concise summing-up explains not merely the point of view of the first Christian generations but also the rapidity with which the authentic recollections of Jesus' life were subordinated to the transcendental tendency Paul's phrase expresses so succinctly.

Indeed, if the Gospels had been systematically and intelligently screened we should know nothing *at all* about Jesus the man. When one recalls the sweeping powers assumed by the Church when Christianity became a state institution under Constantine the Great, and the severity of the censorship authorized under him and applied with vigour ever since the fifth century, the survival of the few scraps of information we have is astonishing. We owe them to an indifference to history compounded by inefficiency and subordinated to a reverence for traditional texts. This left a great many holes in a web of piety that was ideally intended to exclude all mundane facts in the interests of Jesus' glorification.

The internal cultic transformation of perspective involved in the magnification of Jesus was accompanied by the external, historic change of perspective due to the growing and ultimately unbridgeable schism between the new sect and Judaism.

This theme is basic in any study of Christian origins; it will be reverted to often as our inquiry proceeds.

We shall examine the multiple, disparate elements woven into the Gospels under the influence of this double shift in perspective – theological and historical.

This will give us our cardinal criterion:

Anything that conflicts with this transformation of perspective is likely to be true.

That is, any fragment we can manage to isolate that runs counter to the prevailing Gospel tendency of exalting Jesus, of preaching his universality, and of emphasizing his originality, will be regarded as *ipso facto* probable (other things, of course, being equal).

Now, the very first Gospel – *Mark* – was not written down,

even in its most primitive form, until a generation after Jesus' death. The other Gospels were composed still later, and the final harmonizing and editing of the earliest traditional elements incorporated in our present Gospels did not take place until this much later time. Jewish hostility forced the universal mission of Christianity to find its arena, not among the Jews, but in the broad reaches of the Roman Empire.

Keeping in mind the positive factor of the new perspective of the divine Jesus, and the negative factor of the hostility between the Jews and the newly evolving Christian Church, we shall be able to see to what an extent the clear-cut expression of this anti-Jewish feeling, especially in *Matthew* and *John*, lies behind the enigmatic character of the crucifixion.

It is because of the rancour embedded in the Gospels that an impression has become quite common, and is in fact taken by many people for granted, that it was the Jews who were primarily responsible for Jesus' undoing. For that matter this has been a leitmotif of the Christian world, with varying degrees of intensity, ever since its inception. The impression is unmistakable that the venom of the Gospel writers was directed at the Jews; the Romans are referred to in a quite innocuous way. Indeed, it is also obvious that an attempt is occasionally made, before our eyes, so to speak, to whitewash the Romans and exonerate them as far as possible of any active role in the execution of Jesus. The Gospels put the Roman authorities in the position of being innocent tools of a Jewish plot: we are actually told in so many words that the Roman procurator, Pontius Pilate, was really opposed to Jesus' condemnation but was forced by Jewish pressure to consent to it.

In the climate of the Gospels this is surely the prevailing wind.

Now, why should a Roman functionary intervene to save a poor Jewish visionary? Conversely, why should Jesus' fellow Jews insist on having him killed by the Romans?

We shall see that there is a more or less conscious *desire* to blame the Jews and exculpate the Romans; it is this anti-Jewish rancour of the Gospel writers that, while partially explaining their friendliness to the Romans, makes it all the more significant that in the last analysis the actual execution of Jesus is neverthe-less laid at their door.

If the Gospel writers were so hostile to the Jews, and took such pains to blame them for the crucifixion of Jesus, why is it that in spite of the absence of *detail* in the narrative, which would obviously make all sorts of inventive fancies possible, all four Gospels report that it was the Romans who *in fact* sent-enced Jesus to crucifixion and carried out the sentence them-selves?

The crucifixion is in itself decisive: it was a characteristic Ro-man execution and was never used as a capital punishment by Jews. The capital sentence that the Jewish authorities would have been authorized to carry out was strangulation, stoning, burning at the stake, or decapitation. The mere fact of Jesus' crucifixion thus involves the direct authority of the Romans.

Crucifixion was, furthermore, while apparently of Oriental origin, the ignominious death *par excellence* by the time it came to the Romans, who learned it from the Carthaginians as the Greeks had learned it from the Persians: it was originally re-served for slaves, and later extended to thieves, criminals in the provinces, political offenders, and so on.

But it was not merely the mode of execution that was Roman; the charge itself that justified Jesus' crucifixion was a charge that was of interest primarily to the Romans: he was executed as *King* of the Jews, that is, as a contender for power. This was not a religious matter at all, but it was of direct concern to the Roman state.

It is true that another charge was laid against Jesus before a Jewish tribunal, the Sanhedrin, where we are told that Jesus was accused of claiming to be the Messiah, that is, the (Anointed) One Who Was to Come – the Herald of the cataclysmic change from the reign of evil to the reign of good. But if we look at the account more closely, we are struck by the singular coincidence that of the various perplexing and contradictory charges sup-posed to be laid against Jesus by the Jewish authorities the charge of claiming Messiahship was the *only* one that would have ap-peared to the Romans to have had any political significance. But claims of being the Messiah did not constitute an offence against

Judaism. The Roman authorities would inevitably have disregarded the otherworldly trappings of the Jewish Messiah and have interpreted the title as a mere circumlocution or euphemism for King. The identity in the Jewish mind of these spiritual and material functions would have interested the Romans only in respect of the material claim to power, since the purely religious views of the Jews had no interest for them.

In any case, even if a claim to Messiahship was a charge laid against Jesus by the Jewish authorities, and even if claiming to be the Messiah was blasphemy in the eyes of the Jews (which it definitely was not), the actual sentence was handed down and carried out by the Romans, on a *Roman* charge (Kingship) and by a Roman execution.

Thus, while there is no doubt that a systematic effort has been made in the Gospels to create an entire framework of *Jewish* judicial procedure around the capture, trial, and execution of Jesus, and at first this framework gives an impression of coherence, this impression lasts only a moment. A closer look will indicate that the entire structure of Jesus' trial is highly insubstantial, contradictory, and above all tendentious.

Let us look at the events leading up to the arrest and trial of Jesus, and see what may be made of their broad outline.

The general impression that emerges from the Gospel account is that Jesus' career was ended by the Jewish religious authorities, aided by the treachery of Judas. There is of course no reason to question the probability that Jesus was not in harmony with the conservative individuals we may assume were in charge of the Jewish Temple. In the normal course of events they might easily have been irritated by a reformer's zeal. It is not this *general* disharmony that seems implausible, but the specific objectives and methods the Gospels describe in mock-detail.

We are told that the Temple authorities were chary of arresting Jesus in the midst of the Passover feast, when Jerusalem was filled with great multitudes of people, *'lest there be a tumult of the people'* (Mk 14:2). Thus the reason for the Temple authorities' hesitation was fear; Jesus' enemies were afraid of simply stopping his agitation.

But on the face of it this is inadequate: if there really was enough public sentiment in favour of Jesus to intimidate such an immensely powerful institution as the Temple, the second seat of authority in Palestine after the Roman power, what was there to be gained by delay? Jesus' followers would presumably have been infuriated by the fact of his arrest, not by any diplomatic ruses on the part of the authorities.

And why, in fact, should they have been afraid? Was Jesus' agitation directed at them? If it was, why didn't they make specifically Jewish charges against him, and deal with him themselves?

Above all, why are the Romans not reported as also having been alarmed, since their régime depended on the local institutions that collaborated with them? Why doesn't Pilate make his appearance at once?

If the Jewish plotters have been unable to use their own police against Jesus, why haven't they already notified Pilate, and involved the Roman authorities immediately?

This would clearly have been the natural thing to do, since, if what they were afraid of was Jesus' popularity among the Jews, nothing could have been simpler than shifting the entire blame on to the Romans, who were sufficiently hated in any case.

The real point here is the difficulty of understanding why a humble and devout Jew from the provinces would have so aroused the fury of the wealthy, conservative, and powerful Jewish aristocracy. If, on the other hand, Jesus' popularity was not so great, and granted the absence of Jewish sympathy for whatever his teaching was, why should they have hesitated, and clutched at various ruses to avoid appearing in a disagreeable role?

All this is curious and puzzling. The contradictions in detail are made still hazier by the style of narration, which though psychologically arid seems grounded on the most intimate and unknowable thoughts, feelings, and intentions of the conspirators. In the first three Gospels especially (called 'Synoptic' because they share the same general viewpoint, though the discrepancies between them are interesting) the narrator sounds as though he were wholly in their confidence; otherwise there would be no way of knowing what he appears to know. I shall show further on that this atmosphere of intimacy is really a sort of mock deduction from the two fundamental factors mentioned above – the crucifixion itself, and the transformation of Jesus, by the time the Gospels were reduced to writing, from a simple Galilean condemned to death into the Saviour, the Light of the World, whose agony, the cardinal mystery of the newborn religion, was being institutionalized during a period when the enmity between Jews and Christians was congealing.

Jesus' arrest has some enigmatic features about it. Its actual mechanism is described as being set in motion by the treachery of Judas Iscariot, which is puzzling in itself.

For generations attempts have been made to penetrate into the meaning of Judas's treachery; the moral problem it poses has rightly been considered beyond comprehension, and it has generated a vast amount of pseudo-psychological speculation concerning his motives.

We are bound to believe it actually took place, for it was an extraordinary embarrassment for Christianity both in the beginning and afterward: how could the Lord's prescience be reconciled with his admitting a traitor to the circle of his intimates?

The Gospels themselves – which contain all we know about it – tell us practically nothing. *Mark* attempts no explanation at all, while *Matthew* simply advances as the motive Judas's greed (Mt 26:15): he is recorded as bargaining for thirty pieces of silver, an amount that as such is of course absurd, and is doubtless to be taken as nothing more than an emendation of the parallel passage in order to give a greater show of accuracy. But, if Judas were interested in money only, it would obviously have been far easier for him simply to have absconded with the treasury of Jesus' followers than actually to sell his Lord. For that matter the actual figure of thirty is doubtless taken from *Zechariah* 11:12, and is in line with *Matthew's* general preoccupation with Old Testament references.

The fantasy of scholars has run riot in the attempt to extract a believable motive from the aridity of the Gospel narrative. The most extravagant, ingenious, and subtle hypotheses have been elaborated to make Judas's betrayal intelligible. Goethe, for instance, developed a theory based on the assumption that Judas was determined to push Jesus into action, and have his claims put to the test just *because* he believed in him: he wanted to trap him into realizing his aims. Judas's deed was, that is, tantamount to an act of faith; after realizing how mistaken he had been he felt obliged to commit suicide.

Ambition and jealousy have also been advanced as explanations for the betrayal; but it is impossible to say what Judas could have been ambitious for, or whom he could have been jealous of – how could his jealousy be satisfied by betraying his Lord?

The fact is that all these theories are mere speculation, and, with no facts to go on, extremely implausible to boot. Perhaps the likeliest of the non-psychological explanations is that which takes Judas's act, incomprehensible on the human plane, as a mere personification of a legend that sprang up later, and is indeed the leitmotif of the Gospels taken as a whole. Judas is simply the Jew *par excellence*; hence the whole story is a legendary way of expressing the Christian tradition as it becomes embodied in the New Testament, that is, that Jesus was undone by the Jews.

There is another, ingenious explanation that is considered plausible by some scholars, to the effect that the word Iscariot is actually a sort of sobriquet meaning the Deliverer: taken from a Hebrew root (*skr*) meaning 'to deliver', in reality it represents the sentence of *Isaiah* (19:4) 'I will give over [deliver] the Egyptians into the hands of a hard master.' This same word is supposed to have been used by Judas himself in his offer to the priests: 'What will you give me if I deliver him to you?' (Mt 26:15), and is also mentioned by Paul (I Cor. 11:23).

Of course, for such a word to have been used by the writers of our Gospels without their understanding it must mean that it goes all the way back to the primordial Aramaic-speaking background of Jesus' immediate circle. This is actually the best argument for the historicity of the event.

But all such explanations are bound to sound farfetched; they founder primarily on the sheer absence of data, and also on the stubborn and unintelligible element of baseness that clings to the deed like a miasma. No theory, however plausible, can actually persuade us to believe in the Judas story *as it now stands*; it is inherently senseless, for the simple reason that aside from Judas's motivation (which there is no reason for the intimates of Jesus to have been familiar with or to have transmitted to some later chronicler) the betrayal had no *objective* purpose.

The Gospels tell us that the Temple authorities were alarmed by the simple fact of Jesus' popularity, by the dimensions, presumably, of a popular movement they disliked.

This obviously implies that Jesus was a celebrity whom thousands of people must have known about. If he was such a well-known public figure, who had preached to multitudes in the enormous Temple courtyard, and was the leader of a movement large enough to arouse the hostility of the authorities, both Jewish and Roman, why was Judas needed simply to point him out to his captors?

Quite apart, that is, from Judas's inexplicable baseness, just what information was he supposed to be selling? What, in short, was it worth to anyone?

Thus, with respect to Judas, there is a curious incoherence and contradictoriness in the present Gospel account that has led many scholars to deny any historicity at all to the episode and to regard it as either entirely unintelligible or as a reflection of some later legend.

I shall try to show later on (Chapter 8) that there is another, and to my mind more plausible, reason both for Judas's defection and for the later suppression of the explanatory facts.

Going on from Judas's 'delivery' of Jesus to his captors, the next question is: Who were these captors? Who actually carried out the arrest?

The Synoptic Gospels give the impression that Jesus was arrested by a disorderly throng at the behest of the 'chief priests and the scribes and the elders' (Mk 14:43), that is, in the service of the Jewish authorities, who had been informed by Judas.

Perhaps the point about the Synoptic account that is so striking at first glance is just this fact of the disorderliness of the arrest: although Jesus was later, presumably, to be taken to the Jewish Sanhedrin and put on trial, the Synoptic narrative does not give the impression of a regular act but of something impromptu. Theoretically, it is conceivable that if Jesus had been a troublemaker some private citizens prominent enough to arrange a sort of kidnapping might have had him seized and brought to the Romans; but the overwhelming likelihood is, after all, that if it was the Temple authorities who were going to try him on a relevant charge they would have had him arrested normally and brought before their tribunal, since Roman soldiers would never have arrested him merely in order to bring him before a Jewish court competent only in religious affairs.

It is here that *John*'s divergence from the Synoptic account is of special significance. For in the fourth Gospel Judas is reported to have procured a band of men and officers from the chief priests and Pharisees (Jn 18:3) and then brought them to where Jesus was staying. The colourless or misleading word used here, 'band', is extremely significant, for the word in Greek (*speira*) means a 'cohort', and refers to the Roman force garrisoned in the Antonia Tower of the Temple: a little later (Jn 18:12) its commander is called *chiliarchos,* translated in Latin and English by the word *tribunus* (tribune) or captain, and making it unmistakable that if the 'band' of people was disorderly it was at any rate 'accompanied' by Roman troops.

In short, it was a Roman cohort that arrested Jesus, and the mention of it here is the most convincing proof of the Roman responsibility for the arrest of Jesus: since the whole early Christian tradition tended to take the blame away from the Romans it is a detail that could never have been invented after the event.

But how could Judas possibly have had the authority to summon a Roman cohort? Obviously he could not have. This point – the relationship between the Jewish and the Roman authorities – remains obscure.

Like all the many other obscure points in this story, it has received an enormous amount of critical attention. Most scholars have agreed that, since the fourth Gospel generally goes furthest in exculpating the Romans and blaming the Jews, the mention of the Roman cohort must, by its retention in the text, represent a fact.

It is a graphic illustration of the complex origins of the Gospels. Clearly, two traditions concerning Jesus' arrest are involved. One was to the effect that Jesus was arrested by a mixed force of

Roman troops and Temple police; the other simply mentioned a 'band'. It was the second, later tradition that was embodied in the Synoptic account, which discarded the other. The compilers of *John* combined the two. Since obviously Judas could never have been a commander of Roman troops his name must have been interpolated after the primitive account had been written down in a stable form. And despite *John*'s general anti-Jewish tendency the discrepancy survived.

Some commentators have suggested that since the point of all four Gospels is not only the allocation of blame but even more the magnification of the Saviour in the face of his persecutors, both Jewish and Roman, it is conceivable that the fourth Gospel simply built up its story from a dramatic point of view. The detail about the Roman cohort was to heighten the effect.

This is improbable, primarily because in its net effect the fourth Gospel, in its present state, does not emphasize in any way the presence of the Romans: they seem as it were to have slipped into the stream of the narrative almost unconsciously. The dramatic effect of the mere words *chiliarchos* and *speira* is negligible; while vital as historical evidence, once they are looked for, they contribute nothing to the exaltation of Jesus at this crucial moment.

It is far more sensible to accept them submissively as a detail, ultimately founded on fact, that somehow remained firmly interwoven with an early strand of the tradition, which for the most part was busily engaged in cutting out all hostile references to the Romans – *wherever possible*.

But let us abandon these general impressions for a moment, and look at the actual treatment of the trial.

3

THE TRIAL

THE question of what happened at Jesus' trial, and why, is of course the crucial point. It must be reduced to its main elements: What were the charges and who were the judges?

The Gospel account implicates both the Jews and the Romans in Jesus' trial, though in contradictory and ambiguous ways; both the procedure and the content of the trial are deeply confused. The charges laid against Jesus are not those he is condemned on; we are told that the Romans, who actually condemn him, consider him innocent, while the Jews, who do not carry out the sentence, seem determined to undo him for reasons that either do not concern them or have no validity from a religious point of view.

The attempt to implicate the Jews, in the teeth of contrary evidence that somehow survives the manifest manipulation of the texts, reaches a great pitch of concentration in this, the climactic episode of Jesus' career. It illustrates in miniature the basic theme of the Gospels as a whole.

The following is the general outline of the trial narrative, or rather the framework of the Synoptic account based on *Mark* (and followed by *Matthew*):

Jesus is supposed to be taken to the High Priest's house by the band that has arrested him. The Sanhedrin assembles there at once, in the middle of the night. Jesus is interrogated by the High Priest, confronted by witnesses, ill-treated, and finally condemned to death for blasphemy.

The following morning there is *another* meeting of the Sanhedrin, which decides to take Jesus to Pilate: we have been shifted to the Romans.

The trial is reopened before Pilate. The charge – made explicit only in Luke 23: 2–4 – is that of inciting the people to revolt, forbidding them to pay tribute to the Caesar, and putting himself forth as the Messiah.

This charge is incontestably of Roman concern; it is also completely *different* from the charges of blasphemy, and so on, that are supposed to have been heard during the Sanhedrin trial.

The purely judicial portion of the trial before Pilate boils down to nothing but a brief interrogation, the showing of both Jesus and a certain Barabbas to the multitude, the sentence of death extracted from Pilate by Jewish pressure, and the scourging of Jesus prior to the crucifixion.

With the exception of the transformation of the charges, this general outline hangs together, but only for a moment. It is actually no more than a global impression that depends on disregarding the manifest disagreement in fundamental details between the various Synoptic accounts; *Luke* stands outside it altogether.

Luke not only gives a different order of events, but makes an entirely different impression. It speaks of only one meeting of the Sanhedrin (the morning one), does not mention any witnesses, and refers only to Jesus' Messianic claims. In addition, no judgement is actually expressed; Jesus' confession is sufficient. The Sanhedrin is passive: it does no more than take Jesus before Pilate, without having either judged or condemned him.

Generally speaking, *Luke*, far more than *Matthew* or *Mark*, gives the impression of a case that involves the Romans only, or at any rate has only been tried by them, though no sentence is actually indicated as having been passed by Pilate: Jesus seems to have been left for the Jews to deal with.

When we look at the fourth Gospel, still another impression is given. Despite the greater antipathy to the Jews that is shown in *John*, there is never really a question of the Sanhedrin at all.

According to *John*, Jesus is simply

led to Annas; for he was the father-in-law of Caiaphas, who was high priest that year [Jn 18:13].

This is puzzling: it seems to indicate that the early tradition was unsure of the actual name of the High Priest who was supposed to have presided at Jesus' Jewish trial. Caiaphas is not mentioned in *Mark* at all, though the name recurs in *Luke* (3:2) as well as in *Acts* (4:6). The awkwardness of the passage in *John* seems to imply that the original text that was incorporated into our present Gospel may have read simply 'to Annas', and that the name of Caiaphas was inserted later in order to harmonize with *Matthew* (26:57).

In any case, Annas simply asks Jesus 'about his disciples and his teaching' (Jn 18:19), surely the vaguest of formulas. Upon an innocuous reply from Jesus, Annas sends him off to Caiaphas, where oddly enough nothing actually happens either. Jesus is simply taken from Caiaphas to Pilate in the early morning. Thus, it is Pilate who is to try Jesus after all, and – by implication (Jn 19:16) – to condemn him; the Sanhedrin itself plays no effective role in the actual trial.

Of the two charges laid against Jesus in the fourth Gospel – that he is King of the Jews and that he claims to be the Son of God – the first is obviously of moment to the Romans, while the second is a matter of indifference, implying as it does some parochial conflict within Judaism. Yet when Pilate refuses to deal with the matter, the Jews parade Jesus' Messianic pretensions (a version of his being 'King of the Jews') (Jn 18:29–31), but then unaccountably insist on his being an 'evildoer' – and it is on *this* point that Pilate yields!

And when Pilate asks Jesus whether he is King, and Jesus admits that he is, Pilate thereupon goes out to the Jews and tells them he doesn't find him guilty of anything!

Then Pilate proposes, as a compromise, releasing Jesus for Passover grace. The Jews refuse: they demand Barabbas. Pilate goes further by way of concession: he suggests flogging Jesus, presumably to save his life at least, while giving the Jews satisfaction in principle.

But this fails: the Jews persist in demanding Jesus' death because he had made himself Son of God (Jn 19:5–7).

Pilate interrogates Jesus on this *new* accusation and again finds him innocent (19:8–11), though the charge is obviously outside his competence or interest.

Then the *Jews* take up the political charge again and by threatening Pilate with a denunciation at Rome as no friend of

Caesar manage to persuade him to take his place at the tribunal and pronounce sentence. Although the passage

Then [Pilate] handed him over to them to be crucified [Jn 19:16]

seems to indicate that Pilate gave Jesus *back* to the Jews for crucifixion, it is instantly contradicted:

Pilate also wrote a title and put it on the cross; it read, 'Jesus of Nazareth, the King of the Jews' [Jn 19:19].

In the fourth Gospel, accordingly, Pilate is plainly the focus of the essential action.

If we compare the account of the Sanhedrin trial in the fourth Gospel with those in the Synoptic Gospels, we see that the Sanhedrin trial in *John* basically tells us nothing. In the Synoptic account the two elements emphasized are Jesus' remark about the destruction and rebuilding of the Temple, then his statement about the Son of man coming on the clouds of the skies (generally taken, in this instance, to be a synonym of the Messiah). In *John* the first element is transposed to the beginning of Jesus' career, where it is unintelligible in terms of the Sanhedrin trial, while the second is altogether omitted. The omission is doubtless to be explained by the subsequent theological development of Jesus' life in a way that conflicted with the notion of the Son of man coming on the clouds. This is a very ancient formula and, since it makes no reference to the Resurrection or Glorification of Jesus, evidently precedes this later hub of the nascent cult. For the same reason it is also likely to be authentic; perhaps it is a recollection of Jesus' essential belief concerning the Kingdom of God (Chapter 6).

I have given a bird's-eye view of the general incoherence of the Gospel account of the trial. Now let us glance at its development in greater detail.

One of the first things to make us restive about the rationale of the present trial narrative is the way in which the Jews, in all four Gospels, simply summon Pilate to deal with a case that presumably concerns only themselves. In *Mark* for instance, we are told:

And as soon as it was morning the chief priests, with the elders and scribes, and the whole council held a consultation; and they bound Jesus and led him away and delivered him to Pilate. And Pilate asked him, 'Are you the King of the Jews?' And he answered him, 'You have said so.' And the chief priests accused him of many things. And Pilate again asked him, 'Have you no answer to make? See how many charges they bring against you.' But Jesus made no further answer, so that Pilate wondered [Mk 15:1-5].

The presumption seems to be that Pilate was holding himself at the disposition of the Jews, even though, as we shall see, it was during a festival, when he must have known there could be no trial. He then simply asks Jesus a straightforward question involving the capital charge – Has Jesus claimed to be the Messiah? Roman justice must surely have had far more protocol. The absurdity of it is capped by Jesus' straightforward reply to the question, in the affirmative – 'You have said so.' Since Jesus had always forbidden his disciples to put it about that he was the Messiah, his own admission of it, at this moment, must surely be thought badly timed.

There has, naturally, been a great deal of discussion about the nature of the statement – 'You have said so,' or, more colloquially, 'You're the one who says so.' But as far as the Gospel writers are concerned the sense can only be affirmative, for we have been prepared for it by the same unequivocal answer Jesus has already given at his supposed trial before the Sanhedrin, when the High Priest asks him whether he is the Messiah:

And Jesus said, 'I am; and you will see the Son of man sitting at the right hand of Power, and coming with the clouds of heaven' [Mk 14:62].

Jesus has evidently acknowledged *in advance* the charge made against him before Pilate as well as before the Sanhedrin.

The curious parallelism between the two appearances before the Sanhedrin and Pilate is deeply suspect: we cannot help feeling that the same data are being duplicated in a quite unrealistic way. In the account of the trial before the Sanhedrin, for instance, what is stressed by the Synoptic Gospels is the crime of claiming to be the Messiah, which though it is no religious crime *per se*, is the only crime that could have interested Pilate:

The high priest asked him, 'Are you the Christ [that is, the Messiah], the Son of the Blessed?' [Mk 14:61].

The trial section in *Mark* is organized so as to emphasize the following three episodes:

the deposition of the witnesses (14:55 ff.);
the interrogation of Jesus (14:6 ff.);
the abusive treatment of Jesus by the audience and guards (14:65 ff.).

Now, the identical episodes are merely *repeated* in *Mark* in the account of the trial before Pilate, in the form of

the testimony of the Jews,
the questioning by Pilate, and
the insults of the soldiers.

The same facts, whatever they were, are clearly duplicated, and since the actual core of the matter is evidently Jesus' condemnation and execution by the *Romans* on a political charge, we are led to believe that the arbitrary parallelism is due to the redundancy of the Sanhedrin trial.

The trial before the Sanhedrin, in fact, appears to be nothing but an artificial device; it was introduced in order to make the Jews responsible for the death of Jesus, just as the celebrated episode of Barabbas, which we shall come to in a moment, was put in for the purpose of making the Roman procurator the guarantor of Jesus' innocence. (It is a minor though perhaps intriguing question how the original narrator could have known what had been going on in the alleged nocturnal session of the Sanhedrin, since Peter, the only disciple physically close enough to the scene to have learned something of this, was busy denying his Lord at cockcrow [Mk 14:53–72].) If one wishes to, one can, of course, speculate on the possibility of the informant having been Joseph of Arimathaea, or some other member of the Sanhedrin who was converted after the Resurrection, but only a pious apologist could resort to this; it was never thought of by the Gospel writers themselves.

A juxtaposition of the Gospel passages concerning Pilate's relation to Jesus is enough to make the progressive tendency towards the inculpation of the Jews apparent at once:

Mark (15:9–15)
Pilate asks the crowd whether they want him to release Jesus; sees that it was 'out of envy' that the 'chief priests' had delivered him up. The priests stir the crowd up to demand Barabbas; the crowd insists that Pilate crucify Jesus; Pilate 'delivered him to be crucified', 'wishing to satisfy' them.

Matthew (27:11–19, 24–26)
Pilate insists on freeing Jesus; asserts the Jews are acting out of envy; his wife's dream; washes his hands of it; the Jews accept their responsibility.

Luke (23:2–25)
Pilate sends Jesus off to Herod; it is Herod and his soldiers who insult Jesus, not Pilate's; Pilate says unequivocally that Jesus is innocent: he does not condemn him, but on the insistence of the Jews hands him over to them.

John (18:38, 19:4, 19:6, 12–18)
Pilate proclaims Jesus's innocence three times over, and out of personal fear of his own of a denunciation to the Emperor abandons Jesus, but does not, in fact, condemn him formally, though he hands him over to the Jews for crucifixion.

It is clear that the Gospel account is straining at some unchallengeable tradition in order to evade the embarrassment of Pilate's role. In *Mark* and *Matthew* his behaviour is crucial, though he says nothing. In *Luke* he acts only on behalf of the Jews. *John* says that the Jews were given Jesus to crucify. This contradiction is especially blatant, for not only is it Pilate who actually writes the words on the cross (Jn 19:19) but a moment later (Jn 19:23) it is said, with no explanation, that Jesus was crucified by the Romans (the soldiers). Also, it is Pilate who has to be petitioned for Jesus' corpse (in all four Gospels), and has to give permission for the burial. *John* is particularly contorted in its attempts to implicate the Jews, since it lacks even a Jewish trial of Jesus; in fact the Jews explicitly disclaim any judicial powers (Jn 18:31).

We are obliged to conclude that there is a cumulative momentum in the attempt to establish Jewish culpability. If we take this unmistakable tendency in the inverse sense, our certainty increases, as we survey the gradual building up of the case against the Jews (between *Mark* and *John*), that the earliest Christian records must have considered the Romans, *not* the Jews, responsible for Jesus' execution.

The general theme of Jewish guilt is given a piquant though somewhat mystifying highlight in the celebrated episode of Barabbas. This is very peculiar.

Here it is, as given in *Mark* :

Now at the feast he used to release for them any one prisoner whom they asked. And among the rebels in prison, who had committed murder in the insurrection, there was a man called Barabbas. And the crowd came up and began to ask Pilate to do as he was wont to do for them. And he answered them, 'Do you want me to release for you the King of the Jews?' For he perceived that it was out of envy that the chief priests had delivered him up. But the chief priests stirred up the crowd to have him release for them Barabbas instead. And Pilate again said to them, 'Then what shall I do with the man whom you call the King of the Jews?' And they cried out again, 'Crucify him.' And Pilate said to them, 'Why, what evil has he done?' But they shouted all the more, 'Crucify him.' So Pilate, wishing to satisfy the crowd, released for them Barabbas; and having scourged Jesus, he delivered him to be crucified

[Mk 15:6–15].

The first thing that arrests the eye is the idea of the custom itself, that the Roman authorities were *compelled* to release a tried and convicted criminal at the mere command of a Jewish mob. Not only is there no other evidence for this in any classical record; it is inherently extraordinarily unlikely. It is either entirely legendary or the sole hangover of a vanished state of affairs. Lawyers have exercised their talents on this as on all the other aspects of Roman judicial procedure, but though instances of clemency have been found they do not apply to the case of Barabbas. A free pardon might have been thinkable, but that would presumably have been dependent on the Senate, and even if the emperor himself had had the right to exercise it independently of the Senate it is far from likely that his procurator would have exercised it in his place. Even if that were possible, why on earth should Pilate have wished to do so, in favour of a Jewish rebel against the Roman power? He even has to remind the Jews of their own national custom, of which there is no Jewish trace!

In all probability the formation of the belief in the Roman *custom* of releasing a prisoner to a mob on demand was purely literary, as the juxtaposition in sequence of the relevant passages indicates:

Mark 15:6–8
Now at the feast he used to release for them any one prisoner whom they asked. And among the rebels in prison, who had committed murder in the insurrection, there was a man called Barabbas. And the crowd came up and began to ask Pilate to do as he was wont to do for them.

Luke 23:17 (absent in best MSS)
Now he was obliged to release one man to them at the festival.

Matthew 27:15–16
Now at the feast the governor was accustomed to release for the crowd any one prisoner whom they wanted. And they had then a notorious prisoner, called Barabbas.

John 18:39
'But you have a custom that I should release one man for you at the Passover; will you have me release for you the King of the Jews?'

The historical absurdity of such a Jewish privilege is balanced by the abrupt reversal of the mood of the populace, which the Gospels elsewhere indicate to have been enthusiastically in favour of Jesus.

The Barabbas episode in its present setting, in short, has a theatrical, tendentious effect, well in line with the general anti-Jewish and pro-Roman tendency of the Gospels but flagrantly contrary to probability.

But 'probability' here simply means historical probability, or fact, a notion alien to the writers and editors of the Gospels, who were interested solely in discovering occasions for edification. The Barabbas episode fits admirably into the moralizing tendency of the Gospels in yet another way: it symbolizes the *choice* the Jews had been offered between the Way of God and the Way of Satan: they *chose* Barabbas, the son of their father Satan, and not the Son of God:

'You are of your father the devil, and your will is to do your father's desire' [Jn 8:44].

Perhaps the most interesting substantive element in the whole Barabbas episode is the use of the word 'insurrection' in the above-mentioned passage from *Mark*, which must surely be of great significance. In the parallel account in *Luke* it has been softened to '*an* insurrection started in the city' (Lk 23:19); this also makes an odd impression, since no further mention of such an insurrection is made and Barabbas is otherwise referred to as a mere 'murderer'. (I shall return to this in Chapter 8.)

The casual reference to Pilate's wife (Mt 27:19) scarcely calls for comment. If not much is known about Pilate, nothing at all is known about his wife: the only other references to her are in the countless apocryphal legends that often purport to tell us more about what happened than the Gospels, with far less authority.

Perhaps the most revealing detail in this whole strangely contorted version of Roman judicial procedure is the language ascribed to Pilate in Matthew 27:24 above; his unaccountably favourable attitude towards Jesus is expressed here in an unmistakably Jewish manner: in the symbolical gesture of 'washing one's hands of something'. Not only is the gesture Jewish, as well as what it symbolizes (Deut. 21:6 Ps. 26:6), but Pilate's answer to the mob, in fact, as he 'washes his hands' of Jesus' blood, actually contains a quotation from the Old Testament, where David is supposed to have said: 'I and my kingdom are forever guiltless before the Lord for the blood of Abner the son of Ner'; adding 'May it fall upon the head of Joab, and upon all his father's house' (II Sam. 3:28, 29).

It need hardly be said that the traditional Gospel account is not concerned with reporting Pilate's cowardice, but with condemning the Jews. The Gospel writer is so indifferent to mundane history that he actually has a Roman governor express himself in a purely Jewish manner, with what amounts to a quotation from the Jewish scriptures, and in a version that in fact comes from the Greek translation of those Scriptures (the Septuagint) since that was the version the writer and editors of the Gospels themselves were familiar with. The mob naturally gives the counterpoint in its own fashion by completing the Old Testament reference:

'His blood be on us and on our children' [Mt 27:25].

It is ironical to reflect that this sentence, which has wrought so much havoc through the ages, is due to nothing more than an editorial insertion!

None of these above-mentioned oddities can be reconciled except by dint of painful contortions; hundreds of scholars have broken their teeth on various rearrangements or violations of the text, generally chronological, in an attempt to restore a logical sequence. But, aside from general questions of plausibility, the specific difficulties are too great. I shall outline the principal ones.

It was against Jewish custom to begin a trial on Passover day. The arrest of Jesus and his appearance before the Sanhedrin are recorded in *Mark* as having taken place on the Passover night, so that we are to presume that instead of celebrating the great Passover festival in a normal way, all those in authority were milling about the city involved in a criminal case.

John, it is true, has a different chronology (oceans of ink have been spilled over this point too), but if anything it makes this difficulty more insurmountable. The crucial point remains that in *John* too the Sanhedrin sits in judgement at night, though Jewish custom did not allow nocturnal judgements, nor could a sentence of guilt be handed down on the same day as the interrogation itself.

Further, there is some question about the Sanhedrin's having had the right in general to pronounce a capital sentence. This has been much debated, like everything in the Gospels, but the real point in any case lies elsewhere. Whether or not the Sanhedrin could inflict capital punishment for religious crimes, Jesus was not *in fact* condemned on a religious charge.

This point about the Sanhedrin's inability to inflict death sentences has been given undue importance in scholarly discussion. It is the scholarly consensus at present that the Sanhedrin was perfectly competent to do so, but aside from this it is clear that the authors of *Mark* took the Sanhedrin's power for granted. They would surely have mentioned any restriction on it, since that would have given them a quite convincing explanation of why the Jews did not kill Jesus in spite of their desire to.

In any case the Sanhedrin is quickly disposed of in the Gospel account. When Jesus is handed over to Pilate a completely fresh trial begins, as though the whole matter were entirely outside the Sanhedrin's competence, as though, in fact, the Sanhedrin had neither tried the case nor decided it. Moreover, the charges themselves, as well as the character of the sentence, make the whole procedure quite different from the mere transfer of a heretic by a religious tribunal to the secular authority. Jesus was not remotely under the ban of the Jewish Law (Chapter 7); nor were the charges levelled at him in different parts of the Gospel narrative relevant to the Jewish religion. He did not, in fact, blaspheme, even if it is true that he told the Jews he was the Messiah. Announcing oneself as the Messiah might be a criminal matter, as part of raising an insurrection, but it was not blasphemy, since the Messiah was expected to be a perfectly normal man inspired by God. In short, in spite of the use of the word 'blasphemy' none of the specific charges laid against Jesus in fact involved blasphemy, and so did not concern the religious authorities.

But the claim of Messiahship was, of course, very much the concern of the secular authority – the Roman procurator.

It is the mode of execution that is the most convincing demonstration of the Romans' decisive role in the execution of Jesus. For if Pilate had merely *confirmed* a decision made by a Jewish tribunal, the punishment would have had to be Jewish too – stoning, the stake, strangling, or decapitation. But *Matthew* and *Mark* indicate unmistakably that the real condemnation, whose punishment was execution, was pronounced by Pilate and was, in fact, the characteristic Roman punishment of crucifixion.

The bringing in of Herod, which is an episode peculiar to *Luke*, is from a historical point of view very farfetched; it must be taken to be an alternative way of dissipating the guilt of the Romans for Jesus' undoing, and establishing that of the Jews. In *Luke* Herod simply represents the Jewish authorities. Historically, it is hard to imagine that Pilate would have renounced his own jurisdiction in a matter that if it meant anything at all must have been regarded as affecting the security of the state.

There is also a reference to Herod not only in *Acts* (4:27), which is not surprising in view of the identity of authorship between *Acts* and *Luke,* but in the apocryphal *Gospel of Peter,* where Herod is represented as one of Jesus' judges, who actually orders Jesus to be removed for execution. Without going into the usual thorny questions of scholarship concerning the authorship, date, and so on, of the *Gospel of Peter*, we may simply take it for granted that there was an early legend somehow implicating Herod in the crime and finally putting the entire blame on him. It corresponds to the fiction of the trial before the Sanhedrin; it is another way of rearranging the recollections of historical fact in the light of the much later perspective of the Gospel writers.

If Pilate's interrogation were a genuine one, its lack of precision would be baffling. Those who maintain that the Roman trial was a parody of justice fall into an absurdity – why should a Roman official have parodied his own justice? If Jesus had been proscribed and searched for before his arrest, he must have been charged with something perfectly definite; why then should there have been any hesitation about the charge when he appeared before Pilate?

Indeed, the whole portrait of Pilate is completely artificial. It is altogether out of accord with other accounts of him. The Alexandrian Jewish philosopher Philo, for instance, a contemporary of Jesus, refers to him as exceptionally unbending and cruel. He was also full of antipathy to Jews, whom he found incomprehensible and stubborn. There is actually a slight hint of this trait in the Gospels too:

[Some] told [Jesus] of the Galileans whose blood Pilate had mingled with their sacrifices [Lk 13:1].

This is suggestive, especially since it is independent of the trial itself and in its present context is actually very obscure.

But even apart from these indications the futile leniency and passivity ascribed to Pilate by the Gospels is obviously unreal. Though he doubtless would not have been moved by the plight of a visionary or religious reformer, such as Jesus seems to be in the Gospels, it is even less likely that he would have been prompted to make a legal decision under the pressure of a Jewish mob. If we take the Gospel accounts of the trial at their face value, we are bound to come to the conclusion that if

38

Pilate had thought Jesus innocent he would simply have acquitted him; if he had thought him guilty, he would have condemned him. But for reasons peculiar to the Gospel writers' perspective, they would not admit that Jesus was a genuine danger from the Roman point of view, and at the same time were equally incapable of saying, in the teeth of a firmly established fact, that Pilate had freed him.

In short, the Gospel narrative of the trial gives us a general impression of incoherence, which is reinforced by a study of the details. Nor is this merely the incoherence of an imperfectly remembered event; the incoherence is the result of dynamic factors – it is *tendentiously* incoherent.

Perhaps the most striking thing about the trial material relating in all four Gospels is the extreme barrenness of the information given. On examination all we can say with any assurance is that Jesus was arrested, tried, and condemned by the Romans, perhaps with the support of the Jewish Temple authorities, and crucified by the Romans on a capital charge of sedition.

In all probability the writers, and editors of the present Gospels knew nothing beyond this. When the Synoptics tell us, for instance, that the Jews made a great many accusations against Jesus, the vagueness of this remark makes it clear that the chroniclers did not know what those accusations were. One thing is obvious from the stylized, fragmentary way the trial is reported in the Gospels: the last thing that crossed the minds of any of the chroniclers was the idea of reproducing an actual Roman, or for that matter Jewish, trial with any accuracy. Their perspective was altogether different.

It was not a mere matter of either forgetting or suppressing facts. By the time the Gospels achieved their present form the Christian community had already taken shape. The ritual and cult were established; the process of dogmatizing the religion had begun. Jesus' earthly career was only *understood* in the light of transcendental factors. In the eyes of the Gospel writers their Saviour had been crucified as the result of an utterly appalling sacrilege that was, simultaneously, no more than the mysterious working out of God's will. For the Gospel writers could not, after all, have been interested in a mere *historical* account. Their whole perspective was that of the Resurrection and Glorification of their Saviour; the historical elements of his actual life on earth were of interest to them only insofar as they conformed not only with this perspective but doubtless even more with the ritualistic forms of the cult that was already established by the time the Gospels had been reduced to writing and were being editorially harmonized.

By this time the quarrel with Judaism had long since become embittered: regarded in the early first century or two after Jesus as mere Jewish sectarians, the early Christians had the burden on the one hand of differentiating their cult from that of Judaism, and on the other of making it perfectly clear to the Hellenistic world that they had nothing in common with the Jewish troublemakers who had in any case been crushed by Vespasian in A.D. 70, when the Jewish Temple was destroyed and the Jews substantially dispersed. Hadrian, who crushed the second Jewish insurrection of A.D. 133, merely put the finishing touches on the Roman campaign to liquidate the Jews as a political community.

The silence of *Mark* particularly, on the Roman role in Jesus' execution, is doubtless due to its having been composed in Rome, according to scholarly opinion, some time after Vespasian's successful enterprise. The most natural thing to do was to play down the Roman share in the trial, foreshadowing the more general tendency throughout the Greco-Roman world. For *John*, on the other hand, written somewhere in the Middle East, the written tradition implicating the Romans, one strand of which was used in the fourth Gospel, must have been irresistible, while the counter-pressure of a specifically Roman environment was missing.

The entire inculpation of the Jews, accordingly, must be viewed in terms of a later perspective. The trial of Jesus by the Sanhedrin, as recorded in the Gospels in its present form, was obviously the most demonstrative available evidence of the pernicious role of the Jews in furthering Satan's intention of undoing the Saviour in the divine drama of the redemptive crucifixion.

In Chapter 7 I shall discuss the possibility of whether there might be some historical explanation of a Jewish role in the frustration of Jesus' enterprise. At this point I should like to indicate merely that on the basis of the present Gospel account the role of the Jewish authorities is unintelligible; in its present form it can only represent a much later editorial reworking of whatever the facts might have been.

The discrepancies in the present Gospel narrative are irreconcilable. Any attempt to stitch them together by subjective projections of one kind or another is bound to fail. The present texts have of course been studied from a legal point of view any number of times; the most these quasi-juridical studies have produced is the unintelligible claim that every form of justice was violated and that Jesus was the victim of a judicial murder. That is, though given the punishment reserved for political insurrectionaries (which all scholars would agree to), he was in fact something quite different.

Such explanations, which ultimately revolve around the notion of a 'misunderstanding', might have some weight if they provided us with some theory of *why* he was murdered, *why* justice was travestied, *why* his message was misunderstood, and so on; but that is where they fail us. If there was a misunderstanding, our present texts were the first victims of it, and since they are our chief evidence we can only get at the nature of the misunderstanding through them.

There must have been *some kind* of trial. Something *did* happen.

It is the very silence on this point, which is so resolutely though unsuccessfully cloaked by the Gospel account, that may give us a hint: if Jesus was tried he must have been tried for something; he must even have defended himself, or had a defence of some kind. Our present tradition, by obscuring his real defence and replacing it by vagueness, contradiction, and stylized moralization, must be a later, secondary growth. Jesus' authentic defence, whether in court or in life, must have been repugnant to the earliest Christian tradition; this doubtless led to the suppression or omission, conscious or not, of the actual events, and to the creation of the present, essentially theological account of Jesus' behaviour.

Beginning with the perception that the Jews had no reason for executing Jesus, and in fact did not do so, we must ask: If the Jews did not kill Jesus, why did the Romans?

4

JESUS' ORIGINS

THE Jews had no reason to kill Jesus, and they did not. The Romans did.

But did they have a reason?

This question leads us into the heart of the problem. Taking as our starting point Jesus' crucifixion, one of the few undebatable facts in the Gospels, let us follow the thread of its implications through the maze of the events it brought to a climax.

Let us go backward from the crucifixion and fix our minds on the manner in which Jesus presented himself to his contemporaries. Let us consider his origins, his nature, his message, and the career that led him to his death.

Here a word of caution is essential: the point has already been made that when the Gospels themselves were put in writing, that is, when what had been a purely oral tradition was first transcribed, a generation at least had already elapsed since Jesus' death. The crucifixion and the belief in the Resurrection – facts that were to dominate the entire genesis of Christianity and its evolution through the ages – had already intervened between the memories of Jesus, whatever they were, and the current devotional interests of the first Christian generations.

Recalling our cardinal criterion that anything that conflicts with this perspective is likely to be historical, we may actually see the magnification of Jesus progressively taking place in the very text of the New Testament, a palimpsest in which each of five stages has left unmistakable traces:

First there is Jesus' humble birth in a poor family – the point farthest removed from his ultimate glorification;

Then there is his assumption to the Messiahship, after a biologically natural birth;

His royal descendance;

His supernatural birth (without human father);

And finally his divinity, which is described in two different ways by Paul and the fourth Gospel.

43

The springboard for this progressive development may be considered to have been a belief in the Messiahship of Jesus on the part of his immediate disciples. This may have been kindled by the belief in his Resurrection, or it may have developed concomitantly. The question of whether Jesus himself thought he was the Messiah is, of course, more elusive; we shall return to it later (chapter 10).

Let us leave the Gospel terrain now for a moment and see what Paul himself has to say about Jesus. Though Paul does not seem to have known him personally, he was his contemporary, and his *Epistles* preceded the Gospels by many years.

The first thing that strikes one about Paul's comments on Jesus the man is their skimpiness, which is far greater than that of the Gospels. This is all he tells us:

Jesus was a Jew born of a woman 'under the [Jewish] Law'.	Gal. 3:16, 4:4
He was descended from David.	Rom. 1:3
He preached only to Israel, according to the promises (made by God to the Jews).	Rom. 15:8
He obeyed God to the point of accepting death on the Cross.	Phil. 2:8
He chose Apostles.	Gal. 1:17, 19
He was reviled and crucified.	Rom. 15:3, I Cor. 15:3, Gal. 2:20, Gal. 3:13, etc.
Through Jewish malice.	I Thess. 2:15
He rose on the third day.	I Cor. 15:4
He showed himself to Peter, the Apostles, and others, including Paul himself (in a vision).	I Cor. 15:5–8

This (with the exception of a reference to Jesus' having instituted the Eucharist on the night of his betrayal [I Cor. 11:23], and to his now sitting on the right hand of God, awaiting the Great Day when he will come again [Rom. 8:34]) is all Paul has to tell us of Jesus the man.

I emphasize Jesus the *man*, for the striking thing about these meagre details of Jesus' life is the arresting contrast they offer to the very full Christology, that is, the elaborate, indeed over-whelming abundance of material on the transcendental Christ. In short, this is evidently what Paul means when he speaks of his interest in Jesus solely as the Christ 'crucified and glorified'. Paul, in fact, seems to take it for granted that the details of the man Jesus and his life are of no consequence at all except inso-far as they serve as necessary but sufficient points of departure for his real interest, namely, Christological doctrine.

Thus, as far as Paul is concerned, we are no better off with respect to Jesus' earthly career than we are with the Gospels. The Gospels, of course, display the same tendency, but they are a much later attempt to put in order all that was known about Jesus after the death of the first generation of those who had known him, and after, more significantly, the above-mentioned destruction of the Jewish community of believers in Jesus in the wake of the Jewish national catastrophe of A.D. 70. Thus, though the material about Jesus in the Gospels is also subordinated to the perspective of the Risen and Glorified Christ, there is a far greater abundance of detail.

Let us return to the Gospels.

Because of their somewhat deceptive narrative form, there is a curious intermingling of the information (confirming Paul's) about Jesus' purely human life and what may be called the theological, or at any rate non-biographical, elements that are woven into the same narrative.

With respect to Jesus' birth, we find a number of discordant elements in the Gospels. It was doubtless the conviction of Jesus' Resurrection that sufficed to establish or reinforce the faith of his disciples in his Messiahship whatever their attitude to this had been beforehand, and independently of what Jesus thought of his own activity. Hence there was no reason for Jesus' disciples, even if they thought he was the Messiah, to think him anything but a man. Nor did a belief in his Resur-rection alone imply that Jesus had not been an ordinary human being to begin with. In those days resurrection was not con-sidered a world-shattering miracle, and, since the Messiah was a man like another, distinguished only by his divine vocation, it was perfectly possible for the disciples to believe that Jesus had been both a man born of woman and the Messiah too.

It is thus not surprising to find unmistakable evidence of Jesus' ordinary human birth recorded in what must be the oldest stratum of tradition in the Gospels – that is, the point farthest back from his ultimate glorification and hence doubtless the historical fact.

It is evident that in the oldest Gospel, *Mark*, we are expected to believe quite simply that Jesus was one of a number of children born to a family in humble circumstances:

'Is not this the carpenter, the son of Mary and brother of James and Joses and Judas and Simon, and are not his sisters here with us?'
[Mk 6:3].

Here the humanity is plain and unadulterated.

The second stage, as indicated above, lay in Jesus' assumption to the Messiahship, after a biologically normal birth.

A glance at the Gospels tells us that Jesus' public career is contained within the relatively brief period of time spanned by his baptism at the hands of John the Baptist and his death. This is the account of his baptism given in *Luke*:

And the Holy Spirit descended upon him in bodily form, as a dove, and a voice came from heaven, 'Thou art my beloved Son; with thee I am well pleased' [Lk 3:22].

Without discussing the supernatural details of the above, we may take this as the embodiment of a tradition, evidently ancient, that Jesus' career as Messiah was launched on that day, more especially since the most authoritative manuscript (the so-called Codex D of the Western Text) replaces the phrase 'with thee I am well pleased' by 'this day I have begotten thee'. In any case, while his vocation is miraculous, in that God is reported as having spoken to him directly, it does not affect the circumstances of his birth, which are still regarded as perfectly normal.

The third stage of progressive magnification lay in the establishment of Jesus' royal status. In accordance with a prophecy in the Old Testament, the Messiah was supposed to come from the House of David; this was accepted throughout Israel at this time as an indispensable prerequisite for any pretender to Messiahship. The claim to royal descent is established in the Gospels by means of two lengthy genealogies in *Matthew* and *Luke*, which connect Jesus with King David by direct descent. As indicated above, Paul concurs in this.

The purpose of the genealogies is perfectly clear; we are still on the plane of humanity. For that matter there is nothing *inherently* impossible in an actual kinship of Jesus with the illustrious Hebrew royal family. There must have been many impoverished descendants of the House of David still alive at the time; it would have been perfectly possible for Jesus to be one of them.

But while possible, it is doubtful for other reasons, as we shall see.

In any case, whatever we may think of Jesus' davidic claims, when we take a close look at the proof that is adduced in *Matthew* and *Luke* we are instantly disturbed by the intrusion of a third element into this secondary stage of *human* exaggeration – the beginning of Jesus' glorification on a supernatural level.

This is the legend of the Virgin Birth, the initial and decisive stage in the development of the theory of Jesus' supernatural status.

The legend of the Virgin Birth retrojects a divine element into the circumstances of Jesus' birth, though not as yet into his own personality. It is evidently a culminating stage of a faith in Jesus that had not yet progressed to the point of making him divine, and for the time being demanded merely that he be the Messiah authorized by God.

Before looking in detail at the genealogies, which represent Jesus' maximum promotion, so to speak, within the framework of humanity, we shall find it instructive to see how the Virgin Birth is, regardless of the cost to common sense, placed in simple conjunction with the train of thought designed to establish Jesus' human lineage.

In the genealogies in *Matthew* and *Luke*, for instance, it is obvious that the Virgin Birth has been forcibly injected into the sequence leading from King David to Jesus.

This is the crucial sentence in *Matthew*: after enumerating who was the father of whom in a lengthy genealogical list, leading to Jesus from David, the chronicler ends up with:

... Matthan the father of Jacob, and Jacob the father of Joseph the husband of Mary, of whom Jesus was born, who is called Christ [Mt 1:15-16].

Here great pains have been taken to link David and Jesus, and all goes well – we shall see discrepancies later – until the final, crucial transition between Jesus and his parents; a sudden hiatus emerges – Mary's name is interpolated into the list with unprepared-for abruptness, nullifying the whole of the preceding passage. The pains taken in the following sentence to give the proper number of generations are still more futile, since if Mary is given out as the mother of Jesus, and Joseph is not the father after all, there can be no point in enumerating all the generations of *Joseph's* ancestry.

We are obviously confronted by a process in the development of an idea, the gradual magnification of Jesus, in which a prior layer of tradition has actually been pried up by the wedge of another, later tradition, and instead of replacing it has simply been juxtaposed. The clumsiness – from our own, naturalistic point of view – is demonstrated still more strikingly in *Luke*, where the impressive enumeration of Jesus' forebears, this time as far back as Adam, through King David, is marred at the very outset (Lk 3:23) by the incomprehensible interpolation of a parenthetical phrase: 'Jesus ... being the son (as was supposed) of Joseph', and so on.

This simple-minded ('as was supposed') cancels the whole point of the lengthy genealogy, which is then given in detail anyhow!

The editors who copied out the list establishing Jesus in the Jewish line of royal succession were evidently active in a milieu that believed in the later story of the Virgin Birth. They simply inserted the parenthetical phrase to cancel what would otherwise be normally conveyed by the presence of the genealogy – the perfectly natural sonship of Jesus. That it also cancels the point of the entire list must have seemed negligible to the devout believers who were making an attempt to harmonize equally 'valid', that is, equally sacrosanct, pieces of devotional tradition.

It should be mentioned that the genealogies themselves, which have an impressive look of exactitude, are demonstrably nothing more than contrived: this is even admitted implicitly in the last verse:

So all the generations from Abraham to David were fourteen generations, and from David to the deportation to Babylon fourteen generations, and from the deportation to Babylon to the Christ fourteen generations [Mt 1:17].

That is, the number fourteen is arbitrarily used as a sort of harmonizer, either because of its magical significance or out of a desire for symmetry. The second series in *Matthew*, beginning with 'David begot Solomon', comprising the Kings of Judah, has left out four names. In *Matthew* 1:8, Joram did not beget Uzziah, but was his great-great-grandfather. Nor did Josiah, in *Matthew* 1:11, beget Jechoniah; he was his grandfather. This cannot be called a mere casual forgetfulness; the compiler of this pseudo family tree simply left out anything that did not fit into his harmonious list, which was designed to prove simply that Jesus had accomplished the sacred destiny of the House of David by realizing the divine promises made to his ancestor Abraham.

Luke's genealogy illustrates the same point, but in reverse. It contains seventy-seven names, beginning with Jesus, and going through David and Abraham to God. The inclusion of the name Cainan (Lk 3:36) which is not in the Hebrew text of the Bible, but in its Greek translation, indicates its source. *Luke*'s list is the same as *Matthew*'s from Abraham to David, but after David it takes a different turn, tracing the descent not through Solomon, but through Nathan, still another son of David, mentioned only in the Old Testament in II *Samuel* 5:14, and nowhere else.

Beginning with Nathan *Luke*'s list is basically quite different from *Matthew*'s; only two names are the same – Salathiel and Zerubbabel – otherwise the list in *Luke* is characteristic down to Joseph. *Luke* gives us fifty-six generations from Jesus to Abraham, while *Matthew* gives us only forty. *Luke*'s Hellenistic original (taken as certain by all scholars) is further indicated by its carrying the list back to Adam, thus intimating the universality of salvation, as well as by its dependence on the Greek Bible. The convergence on the two names of Salathiel and Zerubbabel is obvious, since both names are inextricably linked to the return of the Jews from the Babylonian Exile, but today it is quite impossible to determine the reasons for any specific divergence. This is further complicated by the fact that *Matthew*'s list of what should be forty-two names (fourteen times three) actually amounts to only forty, while *Luke*'s list of fifty-six is not given uniformly in all manuscripts.

Two traditional answers have been made in defence of the accuracy of both genealogies: one answer is based on the assumption that while one list represents the real line of descent the other represents a *possible* line of descent by way of the institution of the so-called levirate, an ancient Jewish custom that laid it down that if a man died childless his nearest relative was called upon to marry his widow for the sake of the posterity he had not had. This defence founders on an inherent absurdity, which becomes evident if we compare the lists once again: we should have to assume that the levirate affected *all* the generations between David and Joseph except those two – represented by Salathiel and Zerubbabel – that are common to the two lists. This would further imply that through the levirate the generations sprung from Solomon somehow fused with those sprung from Nathan. This would reduce the numerical discrepancies by only a trifle, at the cost of an obviously absurd assumption.

A later explanation attempted to retain the plausibility of the traditional interpretation in the teeth of the differences between the two lists by claiming that *Matthew*'s list applied to Joseph and *Luke*'s to Mary. This theory collapses completely under the impact of a number of objections; two are enough to establish the point.

The Jews did not reckon birthright through women; consequently Mary's genealogy would be useless as a proof of Jesus' decent from David. Further, it is Joseph's lineage that *Luke* also tries to establish, not Mary's, since even the present text reads that Jesus was supposed to be the son of *Joseph* (Lk 3:23).

We are left with an ineradicable discrepancy between the lists. In fact, the only thing they have in common is the same object of 'proving' that Jesus was really the 'son of David' expected by the Jews. It is this tendentious aim that explains why it was that no one ever tried to deduce Jesus' Messiahship from his davidic descent, but just the opposite: after the belief had grown up that he was the Messiah it was simply inferred that he was, necessarily, a scion of the house of David.

A further indication is given in *Mark*:

And as Jesus taught in the temple, he said, 'How can the scribes say that the Christ is the son of David? David himself, inspired by the Holy Spirit, declared, "The Lord said to my Lord, 'Sit at the right hand, till I put thy enemies under thy feet.'" David himself calls him Lord; so how is he is son?' [Mk 12:35–37].

This passage evidently establishes a contrast between a davidic, or human, Messiah, and a transcendental Messiah. Jesus is evidently explaining *away* here the indispensability of davidic blood for the Messiah. Theoretically, of course, from a purely logical point of view, Jesus might have meant that it was possible to be a davidic descendant and *still* deal with the transcendental aspect of the Messiah implied in the above passage. But it is easier to arrive at the plain meaning of the text by assuming that Jesus was answering those who objected to his Messiahship because he was not a descendant of King David. Taken alone, the passage does not indicate any way of *resolving* this contrast, and it is most sensibly interpreted as implying non-descendance from the Jewish royal house.

Perhaps the real point about Jesus' descent, whether davidic or otherwise, was that to Jesus himself it did not matter. Though as indicated above he might theoretically have been one of the doubtless thousands of individuals with David's blood in their veins, the fact is that neither Jesus himself nor any of his disciples actually made this claim.

In the Synoptic account the question never arises as being discussed either by himself or by them. It is true that it is mentioned on two occasions, in *Mark* 10:47:

And when [the blind man] heard that it was Jesus of Nazareth, he began to cry out and say, 'Jesus, Son of David, have mercy on me!'

and in *Mark* 11:9–10 (the Messianic welcome):

And those who went before and those who followed cried out, 'Hosanna! Blessed be he who comes in the name of the Lord! Blessed be the kingdom of our father David that is coming!'

but it is obvious that the blind man is simply supposed to have guessed that Jesus, passing by, was in reality the Messiah and was merely giving him his proper name, whereas the crowds hailing Jesus were in reality acclaiming the advent of the Great Day.

These two passages would seem to have no weight as against the insurmountable silence of Jesus and his companions. This negative conclusion is reinforced by the fact that the descendants of the Judeo-Christians of the very earliest times, the so-called Ebionim, rejected all the genealogies and their opinion seems founded on the oldest tradition.

Further, the writers of *John*, although they must have been aware of the early belief in Jesus' davidic descent, did not believe in it. In *John*, after some admiring comments made about Jesus at the conclusion of one of his sermons, an objection is raised:

When they heard these words, some of the people said, 'This is really the prophet.' Others said, 'This is the Christ.' But some said, 'Is the Christ to come from Galilee? Has not the scripture said that the Christ is descended from David, and comes from Bethlehem, the village where David was?' [Jn 7:40–42].

The fact that this claim is not refuted is surely significant; it can only mean that, as far as the author of the fourth Gospel was concerned, Jesus was far *more* than a descendant of David; he was already his Lord, the World Saviour. Otherwise he would presumably have stated at once that Jesus was in fact one of

David's descendants, and had been born in Bethlehem. His silence must mean that in the circle that gave rise to the fourth Gospel this claim had no weight.

The same impression is given by the following passage:

Again Jesus spoke to them, saying, 'I am the light of the world; he who follows me will not walk in darkness, but will have the light of life.' The Pharisees then said to him, 'You are bearing witness to yourself; your testimony is not true.' Jesus answered, 'Even if I do bear witness to myself, my testimony is true, for I know whence I have come and whither I am going, but you do not know whence I come or whither I am going' [Jn 8:12–14].

If Jesus had wished to convince the Pharisees, he would surely have claimed descendance from David; they might have demanded corroboration, but the claims as such would have been bound to make some impression on them.

All this shows that the belief in Jesus' davidic claim to Messiahship, while it had some currency among his earliest followers, did not survive them.

Not only are the genealogies in *Luke* and *Matthew* irreconcilable even chronologically by as much as four centuries (between David and Jesus *Luke* has forty-two names and *Matthew* only twenty-six), and are actually irrelevant to and contradictory of the Virgin Birth, which cancels them, but there is also a curious silence about the Virgin Birth elsewhere, both in *Mark* and throughout the rest of the New Testament. This is surely conclusive proof of the lateness of this motif. It failed to win the belief of even the latest editors of *Mark*, who must have known of the tradition of the Virgin Birth; if they failed to add it to their version of *Mark* it could only have been because they did not accept it.

The devotional problem presented by the magnification, that is, divinization of Jesus, of which one solution is given by the legend of the Virgin Birth, is dealt with in a similar but far more exalted way in the fourth Gospel.

The point of view of the writers of *John* is quite different from that presented in *Matthew* and *Luke*, and there is no reason for *John* to adhere to their version of Jesus' birth. In *Matthew* and *Luke* the story of the Virgin Birth was merely designed to prove that God had specially created a child to be his Messiah; this special act of creation was naturally accomplished by a miraculous process, an infallible 'sign' of divine activity.

But in *John* the whole point is that Jesus is the incarnation of the *Logos*, the Word, and hence coeternal with God himself. According to this point of view Jesus was nothing *but* the Christ, and hence not human at all. Not only was there no need for him to have had an earthly father, but an earthly mother was equally superfluous. This must be the meaning of:

... who were born, not of blood nor of the will of the flesh nor of the will of man, but of God [Jn. 1:13].

But the fact that Jesus was the incarnation of the Word does not mean that insofar as he was a *man* he was not subject to the ordinary laws of human generation. The author of *John* believed that it was at the Baptism that the Word infused Jesus, making him the Christ. Thus while exalting *Mark*'s earthly presentation of Jesus, there was no reason for the author of *John* to change its external framework; in fact he refers repeatedly to Jesus as the 'son of Joseph', completely contradicting the tradition represented by *Matthew* and *Luke*.

Perhaps the point is made most clearly if we recall that Paul's *Epistles* are to be interposed, from the point of view of the genesis of doctrine, between the Palestinian tradition (generally conceded as the background of the Synoptic Gospels) and the fourth Gospel. On this point the *Epistles* are clearly closer to the truth about Jesus' family circumstances; they were written during the lifetime of the earliest generation and in contact with men who must have known Jesus and doubtless his family too, or something about them.

Paul does not refer to the Virgin Birth either; he has his own version of the Christ as the incarnation of the Holy Spirit: 'The Lord is the Spirit' (II Cor. 3:17).

Paul may have believed, like the author of *John*, that the Christ was co-existent with God before the beginning of time:

'Yet for us there is one God, the Father, from whom are all things and for whom we exist, and one Lord, Jesus Christ, through whom are all things and through whom we exist' [I Cor. 8:6; also II Cor. 8:9, Gal. 4:4, Col. 1:15, etc.].

But this again had nothing to do with the man Jesus being born in a perfectly normal way, as indicated in:

'But when the time had fully come, God sent forth his Son, born of woman, born under the law' [Gal. 4:4].

where the word 'woman' in conjunction with the rest of the passage merely indicates the normal birth of a Jewish child, since otherwise there would have been no reason for Paul not to say 'virgin'. Paul, moreover, as we have seen above, believed in Jesus' davidic descent, that is, in his human antecedents. To drive the point home, the prologue to Romans makes a simple statement that Jesus Christ 'was descended from David according to the flesh' (Rom. 1:3), which is quite unequivocal.

For that matter the Synoptic Gospels themselves, with the exception of the specific passages in *Luke* and *Matthew* that play up the point, are otherwise quite unfamiliar with the Virgin Birth. In the celebrated passage in *Mark* (3:33) where Jesus asks, 'Who are my mother and my brothers?' when they try to call him, there is obviously no inkling of his having been conceived by the Holy Ghost: otherwise the whole passage and its implications become nonsense. In an equally striking passage (Mk 3:21) Jesus' friends (possibly = family) come to take him away because they think him out of his mind.

It seems clear that the story of the Virgin Birth, super-imposed on the earlier Palestine story of Jesus' davidic origins, was originally intended as an argument to combat the scepticism of those Jews who did not believe Jesus was the Messiah. But once having begun as a reaction to Jewish scepticism it developed and condensed, as it were, on Greco-Roman soil: it was an argument that was attractive to early Christians because of a perhaps unconscious desire to invest their own Saviour with the same miraculous privileges possessed by all the other Lords, Saviours, Redeemers, and so on, that the ancient world teemed with. Christianity, as it developed in the Hellenistic world, did not simply obliterate the belief in Jesus' Messiahship that had grown up in Palestine and was later to be wiped out almost entirely by the Roman destruction of the Jewish Temple in A.D. 70. It merely added its own new and characteristic elements to the older, traditional Jewish substratum, leaving us with the resulting confusion to disentangle.

The Hellenistic colouring of the Virgin Birth legend is unmistakable. It is true that Palestine, together with the whole of the Semitic Orient, was familiar with the related myth of the Mother-Goddess, sometimes the Virgin-Goddess, and that a cognate myth of the virgin birth of the King, the Son of God and the Saviour of his people, had also been an element in the ancient Semitic religions, but – aside from the fact that some points do not wholly correspond to the Virgin Birth of Christ – it seems that by this time these religions had altogether died down in Israel. The Jews, to be sure, believed the birth of the Messiah would be accompanied by miraculous 'signs', but there is no evidence that they thought his mother could remain virgin throughout the act of conception, or for that matter that the Messiah himself would not be born of a woman normally. On the contrary, it was held that he would be a man like other men, and since he was to be descended from David, and since Jewish tradition reckoned lineage only through men, he could not be born of a virgin.

Thus, a virgin birth, as a 'sign', was non-Jewish. It is really in the Hellenistic world that parallels abound. In the legend of Perseus born of Danae, for instance, we hear of a virgin who was impregnated by a shower of gold: in the story of Attis, her mother, Nana, became pregnant by eating a pomegranate, and so on. In one way or another, great men in general were linked to gods in an actual filial relationship, such as Pythagoras, Plato, and Augustus himself. In the second century the similarity between the Virgin Birth and the Perseus legend was maliciously exploited by the Jews to such effect that in their embarrassment the Christian fathers were forced to maintain that it was a lure of Satan designed to confuse people.

It was doubtless not through any conscious imitation that the story of the Virgin Birth took shape, but simple through the congeniality of the cultural milieu. The Christians naturally tended to assume, while championing their newly forming faith, that Jesus was surely not inferior to other august personages.

Once fixed on Hellenistic terrain, Jesus' transcendental status developed swiftly in the directions of both Pauline and Johannine conceptions: their analysis would evidently take us far afield. (See Chapter 12.) For our purposes it will be enough to have flaked off the accretions of legend after Jesus' death, and obtained a glimpse into his home surroundings.

With what we may call the doctrinal aspects of the Gospels laid aside, we may feel on firmer ground with respect to Jesus' earthly family. The dominant impression in the Gospels – indeed, the point is stressed over and over, despite the clash with the loftier versions of his origins – is quite simply that Jesus came of very humble beginnings. Both he and doubtless his father before him were carpenters or in any case obliged to earn their bread by manual labour.

This has nothing to do with an ancient Jewish custom in which even the most learned of rabbis was expected to follow a trade while applying himself to the Law: Jesus was simply an artisan, one of the many in the settled Jewish population of the time. Socially speaking, his simplicity may be hinted at in a passage from *Matthew*, where he seems to think a royal court is a place where people wear fine clothes:

'Behold, those who wear soft raiment are in kings' houses'
[Mt 11 :8].

This explains the celebrated passages recording the amazement of his family and friends at what must have been the inception of his career:

And when his friends heard it, they went out to seize him, for they said, 'He is beside himself' [Mk 3 :21].

And his mother and his brothers came; and standing outside they sent to him and called him [Mk 3 :31].

And on the Sabbath he began to teach in the synagogue; and many who heard him were astonished, saying, 'Where did this man get all this? What is the wisdom given to him? ... Is not this the carpenter, the son of Mary and brother of James and Joseph and Judas and Simon, and are not his sisters here with us?' And they took offence at him. And Jesus said to them, 'A prophet is not without honour, except in his own country, and among his own kin, and in his own house.' . . . And he marvelled because of their unbelief

[Mk 6:2–6].

There is not the slightest reason to doubt this tradition, both with respect to his family's amazement at his activities and, perhaps even more significantly, with respect to the authenticity of this mention of his brothers and sisters, which comes as a surprise to so many people. The tradition is embedded in the oldest Gospel, *Mark*, and precisely because of the other magnifying tendencies that have governed the composition of the Gospels as a whole, including *Mark* itself, its historical probability seems assured.

It is true that orthodox critics have uniformly found it unpalatable for the Saviour's mother to have given birth to other children, but if this is a problem it is one for theology, not for history. Any unbiased student can see that the orthodox critics have plainly found the texts intractable. In their attempt to rescue at least a shred of the Virgin Birth theory, they have maintained that whether or not Jesus had brothers or sisters, at least he himself, as the firstborn, had been born while Mary was still a virgin.

If we forget the Virgin Birth here and simply consider the possibility of Jesus' having been the oldest child, there is certainly no way of disproving this. He might very well have been. There is nothing about it in the Gospels one way or the other. Even the earliest tradition confines itself to a bare, almost parenthetical remark about his brothers and sisters. Nothing is known about these with the exception of Jacob (James), who in spite of his apparent initial disbelief in his brother's singularity went on to become the head of the first Jerusalem community of Jesus' followers (*Acts*), though it is true that we remain in great uncertainty as to just what this community believed and how its beliefs were related to the 'Pauline' branch of Christianity that after the destruction of the Jewish Temple in A.D. 70 expanded independently in a non-Jewish milieu. (See Chapter 13)

To return to the problem of Jesus' siblings, some orthodox critics have gone so far as to maintain that Jesus was Mary's only child; they have sometimes linked this contention to the parallel claim of Mary's perpetual virginity. Ultimately the defence of this comes down to the statement that the words translated by 'brother' and 'sister' are in reality to be taken in the sense of 'cousin' (male or female), on the theory that in Aramaic and Hebrew there is an inevitable equivalence.

While this is true in a limited way, it is, of course, altogether farfetched : both Aramaic and Hebrew, as indeed all languages, are perfectly capable of making a distinction between 'cousin' and 'brother' or 'sister'. If such a misunderstanding had been possible, precautions would obviously have been taken to avoid it when making the translation into Greek.

The oddity perhaps is that, even after the belief in the Virgin Birth was solidly established, there was nothing offensive to the earliest Christians in the suggestion that Jesus had brothers and sisters. Mary acquired devotional interest much later, when, indeed, she became the object of a cult. As far as the early Christians were concerned, there was no reason why she should not have reverted to the status of an ordinary woman as soon as her divine mission had been accomplished. For that matter the very insistence on Jesus' having been the firstborn *implies* the existence of younger children.

It was the growth of asceticism in the Christian Church that led to an attempt to make Mary a perfect example of perfect continence; the Church became concerned with the elimination of Jesus' brothers and sisters despite both tradition and common sense. Some critics have gone even further and attempted to make the same claim of perfect continence on behalf of Joseph – surely a self-defeating effort, since if successful it would imply by definition that he could have had nothing to do with Jesus at all, as far as davidic descent is concerned.

In any case, there is no more historical foundation for this than for the similar claim, sometimes advanced by a number of scholars who believe that Jesus never even existed, that the words 'brothers' and 'sisters' were used in the sense of 'brethren' – that is, members of the mystical fraternity of early Christianity. This assumption is also quite groundless, especially when Jesus' brothers are actually refererd to by name : when 'brethren' does occur in this sense it is quite unmistakable, as in *Matthew* 28 :10, where Jesus is supposed to have said, 'Tell my brethren to go to Galilee,' and so on.

A curious instance of the way legend operates may be seen in the use that was made of a Biblical passage to 'prove' that Jesus' birth had been in accordance with prophecy. There is a passage in *Isaiah* (7:14) in which the prophet reassures King Ahaz of Judah, who is anxious about an attack to be launched against him by a coalition of the King of Syria and the King of Israel, by saying that a 'virgin' will conceive and give birth to a son called 'Immanuel' (God with us) and that before the child can tell the difference between good and evil the country of the two enemy kings will be abandoned.

Because of an accident in the Septuagint, the ancient Greek version of the Old Testament, this passage gives a word as 'virgin' that in the Hebrew original simply means 'young woman'. This was seized on as a prediction of Jesus' Messianic birth and mentioned in *Matthew* 1:23, even though the sentence as a whole is plainly a rhetorical way of indicating a certain passage of time with no thought of anything Messianic at all. At a time when the early Christians were still preoccupied with establishing Jesus' claim in order to impress potential Jewish converts, the passage was seized on as one more validation of his Messianic status.

As for Jesus' actual birthplace, the two contradictory stories that sprang up concerning it must be considered part of his Jewish, or terrestrial, magnification, as it were; they were aimed at making this detail, too, conform with prophecy.

The very earliest tradition locates Jesus' birthplace in Galilee, probably Nazareth, but from very early times on the belief in Jesus' Messiahship seems to have given rise to a quite different story. This was to the effect that Jesus was born in Bethlehem (some five and a half miles south of Jerusalem) in order to 'fulfill a prophecy' of the Messianic redemption of Israel, in the Old Testament (*Micah* 5:2).

Matthew and *Luke* both say explicitly that Jesus was born in Bethlehem, while *Mark* is quite definite in favour of Nazareth; the fourth Gospel seems to imply the author's acceptance of the view in *Mark*:

Others said, 'This is the Christ.' But some said, 'Is the Christ to come from Galilee? Has not the scripture said that the Christ is descended from David, and comes from Bethlehem, the village where David was?' So there was a division among the people over him

[Jn 7:41–43].

That is, if the compiler of *John* thought Jesus had been born in Bethlehem he would not have missed an opportunity to refute the sceptical Jews. On the other hand, by the time *John* was set down the whole question of the Messiahship was outdated; it was no longer of interest to writers of the fourth Gospel.

Perhaps the simplest way of summing up the discrepancy on this point, which has also, of course, given rise to a vast literature, is to say that while it is quite certain that Jesus was *not* born in Bethlehem it is not at all certain that he *was* born in Nazareth. The accounts in *Luke* and *Matthew*, while fundamentally in complete disagreement – *Matthew*'s is tragic, *Luke*'s idyllic – are in agreement on the one point of the fulfillment of the davidic prophecy. In *Matthew* especially, almost everything that happens is in fulfillment of prophecy: Jesus is born at Bethlehem to bear out *Micah* (5:1), he goes to Egypt to bear out Hosea (11:1): the cries of the bereaved mothers are Rachel weeping for her children; Jesus' family goes to Nazareth to vindicate the prophecy that 'he shall be called a Nazarene'. Thus the account in *Matthew*, while independent of that in *Luke*, is equally in the grip of non-historical considerations, and this point may be disregarded.

The oldest tradition, in *Mark*, does not mention Bethlehem. In *Mark* all the evidence points to Jesus' having been born in Galilee. Though Nazareth is definitely mentioned as the actual town he came from, the mention alone is not entirely satisfactory, since it may well be that the rivalry between the two towns, Bethlehem and Nazareth, arose because of the necessity of fulfilling two prophecies, one that he had to be born in Bethlehem, to bear out *Micah*, and the other that he had to be born in Nazareth, to 'be called a Nazarene'. This may have led to the contradiction.

Thus, from a historical point of view, Nazareth is likelier to have been Jesus' birthplace only because it is in Galilee; originally the word Nazarene itself probably did not mean someone from Nazareth, but was related to the Old Testament prophecy. The name is used as though it had an aura about it derived from the power of names in the ancient Middle East and elsewhere. In general the ancient nations, especially the Jews, thought that names expressed a special, mystical power; it seems likely that the word 'Nazarene' was not a mere geographical reference, more particularly since the earliest tradition plainly shows very scanty interest in the mundane details of Jesus' life before his career began. On the other hand, it is possible that a name with some significance in Aramaic was passed on uncomprehendingly into Greek, where it became congealed as a special title and still later was explained in a simple way by editors ignorant of Aramaic, who linked the word 'Nazarene' phonetically to a town in Galilee whose name sounded similar.

The point is not of great consequence in relation to Jesus' actual career; the traditions concerning his origins are of interest primarily insofar as they contain those unintegrated deposits of homely fact that clash with the more glamorous elements in the Gospel tradition. These homely details – his humble origins, his family's astonishment at his activities, and so on – must be taken as proof that his career was never anticipated in his immediate surroundings. This is simply another way of saying that as far as we can see, Jesus' initiative – with the exception of his relationship to John the Baptist – originated with him in a milieu alien to all the various myths and legends that arose after the transformation and obliteration of Jesus' own character and beliefs by the crucifixion, the Resurrection, and the Christology in general.

5

JESUS IN PUBLIC

In the apparently straightforward beginning of each Synoptic Gospel, Jesus is presented as a Herald – a Herald of the Kingdom of God that was at hand. He is announcing the final transformation of the world that was looked forward to by pious Jews, when the reign of evil would be replaced by the reign of good.

The words sound simple enough, but they imply many conundrums that have been mulled over with great zeal for the past five generations.

This is Jesus' formula summing up this proclamation of the Kingdom of God:

'The time is fulfilled, and the Kingdom of God is at hand; repent, and believe in the gospel' [Mk 1:15].

It is what launches the Synoptic Gospels. It is a formula, arresting in its simplicity, that would seem both ancient and authentic, more particularly since as we shall see, it is profoundly at variance with the great structure of dogma that has been erected over it.

Before discussing what the formula means, let us consider it as a link to Jesus' immediate background. It leads us at once to John the Baptist, whose sombre, enigmatic figure looms over the very threshold of Jesus' public career; the formula epitomizing his teaching is practically identical with Jesus'.

'Repent, for the kingdom of heaven [God] is at hand' [Mt 3:2].

The figure of John the Baptist, though profoundly involved in the launching of Jesus on his career, remains hopelessly obscure. The only information we have concerning him is contained in the four Gospels and in Josephus (A.D. 37–A.D. 95), the celebrated Jewish historian who was in the service of the Romans and is our sole external source for this whole period. There are about fifteen references to the Baptist in the Gospels and one in Josephus (*Jewish Antiquities*, Book 18).

Josephus refers to the Baptist as a 'good man', whose message to the Jews consisted only of some excellent advice concerning virtue, justice, and piety. He accounts for the Baptist's death at the hands of the Tetrarch Herod Antipas as being due merely to Herod's incomprehensible fears that John's ethical counsel might somehow have led to a movement to unseat him, which he forestalled by seizing, jailing, and killing John. Josephus makes a special point of the Baptist's harmlessness: according to him all the Baptist wanted was to purify by baptism the bodies of those whose virtuous living had already purified their souls and thus made them welcome to God; it was the Baptist's eloquence, according to Josephus, that made the people flock to him and alarmed Herod.

In the Gospels, John's message is recorded only as the simple exhortation to 'repent', and the statement that a great purification by fire would precede the fulfilment of this promise (which like the Kingdom of Heaven itself was part of conventional Jewish belief). What he was urging his listeners to do was simply to have a change of heart that would enable them to live according to the will of God; this 'repentance' would prepare both body and soul for the advent of the Messiah who was to herald the establishment of the Kingdom of God.

Thus John's addition to the doctrine of the advent of the Kingdom of God was the threat of punishment as well as the mere announcement of the Good News of this advent (the original meaning of 'Gospel').

There is a possibility that John's stark summons to 'repent, for the kingdom of heaven is at hand' should be interpreted as meaning 'repent *so that* the Kingdom of God may come,' that is, that his baptism was also a dynamic means of bringing the Kingdom about, as well as a way of securing access to the Kingdom for the individual penitent. Just how this was to work out is also obscure.

At various times the notion has become popular that the Baptist was connected with the Essenes, a monastic sect that believed in daily ritual ablutions, lived in seclusion, and had its chief monastery, as now seems likely, near the Dead Sea. (The Essenes are considered the authors of some of the 'Dead Sea

Scrolls'. For that matter, Josephus clearly implies their connexion with John, but there are some basic differences that make this doubtful. John's baptism seems to have been a rite that was undergone only once; it was a permanent initiation of the converted, the 'repentent', not a mere daily ablution like that of the Essenes. If he had any sectarian similarities with the monastery, or monasteries of Ein Gedi or Qumran, with their communal life and their ritual, then our Gospel texts conceal them from us, a possibility that is, of course, altogether conceivable.

Otherwise John, in terms of the general impression made on us by the sources, was not an unconventional phenomenon of the time. Josephus himself claims to have spent three years with a certain hermit called Bannos (which means a 'baptist') who dressed and ate what the trees supplied him, and bathed frequently in order to keep 'pure'.

In those days the so-called 'wilderness' was a favourite rendezvous of the disaffected. It was not the mere waste of sand we tend to imagine. The wilderness referred to, for instance, in *Mark* is the lower valley of the Jordan near the Dead Sea. This has dense vegetation, including real trees, and at the very spot where the Christian tradition locates Jesus' baptism by John the Jordan River looks, or at any rate must have looked in those days, like a turbulent American or European river. 'Wilderness' merely meant that it was largely uninhabited, except for a monastery, some pilgrims' stations, and so on.

As for John's dress and diet, he 'was clothed with camel's hair, and had a leather girdle around his waist, and ate locusts and wild honey' (Mk 1:6). This was traditional for prophets. Locusts and wild honey are perfectly good food and are still eaten by many people as a matter of course. Elijah, the Old Testament prophet, 'wore a garment of haircloth, with a girdle of leather about his loins' (II Kings 1:8).

In short, as John appears in the Gospels and in Josephus's works he seems to have been in the prophetic tradition of classical Judaism; he gave his message because God had inspired him to.

As far as the rite of baptism itself was concerned, the Gospels themselves show that it had three qualities: it was a purification rite like other Jewish ablutions; it was a ritual of initiation, presumably into a real fraternity of penitents awaiting the Kingdom of God, and it was also a Jewish baptism of converts: just as baptism introduced non-Jews into the Jewish community, so John's baptism also restored the quality of a son of Abraham to those who had lapsed into sin.

Nothing is known about how John performed the ritual of baptism, or his personal role in it. Though Josephus and the Gospels agree on the fact of the baptism, they differ on everything else. Josephus writes as though it were no more than a symbol of a moral event, while the Gospel writers, doubtless thinking of Christian baptism in their own time, ascribed to it a practical efficacy against sin. The fact is, however, that such details elude us.

In any case, what we are most concerned with is John's relationship with Jesus. I shall discuss the inception of that relationship now, and its outcome later (Chapter 9).

The Gospels are unanimous in linking Jesus' emergence as a prophet in his own right to his having been baptized at the hands of John. This association is not a mere chronological sequence; we are meant to believe that Jesus actually assumed his Messianic status as a consequence of John's baptism, but we are left in a quandary with respect to its meaning.

It is obvious that though Jesus' career is, in this sense, dependent on John, there is a systematic effort made in the Gospels, whenever the question of John comes up, to harmonize all accounts in favour of Jesus' primacy, while at the same time respectfully according an honoured status to John as Jesus' 'forerunner'.

It is in fact just this contradiction – as we may now begin to expect – that guarantees the actuality of Jesus' baptism by John, and also illuminates its historic, or pre-theological meaning.

The problem of Jesus' baptism by John was obviously of the greatest delicacy in the formation of the earliest tradition. For since the whole of Christian tradition was engaged in confirming John's 'validity' only as a forerunner of Jesus, his baptizing Jesus must have been a tremendous hurdle for the early chroniclers. It was a problem that was given particular urgency by the fact that John was survived by a sizeable group of followers, and it was doubtless the aim of this Christian propaganda, which was in favour of John, but of a John subordinate to Jesus, to attract them into the fold.

John's rite of baptism, after all, was a 'baptism of repentance for the forgiveness of sins' (Mk 1:4); if Jesus had been baptized by him it could only have implied either that Jesus was a sinner like everyone else, or that he had become Messiah as a result of the baptism. Both these notions were repugnant to early Christian thought, and because of this the attempt to lessen the implicit importance of John's baptism gave rise to characteristic ambiguities, obscurities, and contradictions in the Gospels.

Put simply, the baptizing of Jesus by John could not have been invented by Christians, who were interested not in heightening the Baptist's originality but in eradicting it altogether. Nevertheless, despite all the attempts to veil this fact, or tone it down, it emerges in the Gospels with great clarity.

According to *Mark* and *Luke* it was not until the Baptist was arrested by Herod Antipas that Jesus actually began his own preaching. *Mark* reports the Baptist's arrest as taking place during the period of Jesus' withdrawal and meditation, when his consciousness of his mission presumably matured.

Mark thus makes it clear that it was when the voice of the 'one crying in the wilderness' had been put a stop to that Jesus launched himself on his own mission of proclaiming the Kingdom of God and his own role as Herald, in which he simply repeated John's theme (Mk 1:14, 15).

Thus, according to the Gospel account, John was the triple cause of Jesus' career: (1) it was his fame that drew Jesus to the banks of the Jordan; (2) John's arrest propelled Jesus into a public career in order to carry on John's role; (3) Jesus became aware of his calling after being baptized by John.

The version in *Mark* is the simplest Gospel account:

Jesus ... was baptized by John in the Jordan [Mk 1:9b].

This statement is so bald it defies adornment. The contortion of the narratives in the remainder of the Gospels is evidently due to the attempt to explain away this plain and simple fact.

The *Matthew* account, for instance, is far more complicated; since the chronicle makes Jesus' Messiahship dependent on nothing but his actual birth, *Matthew* is compelled to report Jesus' baptism as a mystery of God's will.

This is how the narrative refers to John's baptism, while blurring its meaning:

John is reported as expressing surprise at being asked to baptize Jesus, saying Jesus ought to baptize *him*; Jesus merely says,

Let it be so now, for thus is it fitting for us to fulfil all righteousness [Mt 3:15].

By which is meant, to carry out God's plan. Afterwards, it is implied, they can carry on as before; that is, Jesus can resume his inherent superiority.

The problem for Paul and the writers of the fourth Gospel is of course even thornier because Jesus is identified by them with a pre-existent Word, the ultimate stage in his magnification.

The account of the Baptist in the fourth Gospel is revealingly obscure and contradictory: Jesus has more disciples than John (Jn 3:26; 4:1), yet no one receives his testimony (Jn 3:32); he baptizes (3:22; 4:1) and does not (4:2), and so on.

These curious discrepancies do not imply a mere awkwardness on the part of a writer or editor. The actual source material must have been heterogeneous; there must have been some other historical document that the Gospel writer had to accommodate with his own material. This could only have been a document or memory deriving from a Baptist milieu, from a community still distinct from the Christians and doubtless being wooed by them.

In any case the attempt made in the Synoptic Gospels to pretend that Jesus' contact with the Baptist was brief is clearly artificial and collides with common sense. The simple statement in *Mark*, after the report of Jesus' baptism by John: 'The Spirit immediately drove him out into the wilderness' (Mk 1:12), which with its 'immediately' implies that there were no further personal relations between the two, is plainly at odds with every other indication in the Gospels. The Baptist and his followers were of great interest to the early Christians, who borrowed many things from them, including baptism itself and probably fasting, common prayer, and so on.

As with the varying methods of explaining Jesus' personal status, the editorial difficulties of coping with the problem of the Baptist can be best shown by the juxtaposition of texts.

In the original tradition Jesus was simply baptized by John. He was a follower, disciple, collaborator, or in any case a subordinate of some kind, though possibly an intimate one. This simple relationship was gradually both attenuated and distorted by the later doctrinal requirements that displaced Jesus' Messianic status first to his birth (the Holy Ghost), then to his pre-existence as the Word, and so on. The fact that the fourth Gospel omits any specific mention of Jesus' actual baptism, while at the same time reporting other circumstances indicating Jesus' dependence on John, must be taken as a sort of doctrinal correction of the Synoptic accounts.

Looked at functionally, so to speak, the legend of the Baptist as forerunner essentially implies that the older Baptist tradition was simply absorbed by the Christian community. Further, we must believe that in the oldest tradition Jesus was subordinate to John, and doubtless baptized by him. The concession can be made, to be sure, that the actual act of baptism is perhaps to be understood as merely an indication, by means of a symbol taken from later Christian practice, when baptism was already solidly established, of the hierarchical relationship between John and Jesus.

Because of the growth of Christian doctrine, the Baptist has been unfairly dealt with by history. Just as he is mentioned by Josephus only in connexion with something else (the reign of Herod Antipas), so the Gospels mention him only in connexion with the baptism of Jesus. Because of the lopsidedness, for different reasons, of both these accounts, we remain in ignorance of the Baptist himself and of his movement.

At this point let us consider the message they both proclaimed – the imminence of the Kingdom of God.

What did this mean?

6

THE KINGDOM OF GOD

If we go by the Gospels and assume that the proclamation of the imminence of the Kingdom of Heaven was the starting point of Jesus' career, as a sequel to John's, we are instantly led into the thick of the problem concerning his message and his role. As Jesus never explains what he means by the 'Kingdom of God', we are left to assume he was using a phrase or an idea that was part of current Jewish thought, and thus could be understood by anyone in his audience. We must accordingly deduce its meaning from the general background of his time and in conjunction with various hints in the Gospels. The coming Kingdom of God is a part of conventional Judaism; it is repeated even nowadays by pious Jews three times daily (in the prayer called *Shemoneh Esreh*, No. 17).

Now, though some aspects of contemporary Jewish thought on the subject are elusive, since in the nature of things prophetic spirits enlarged on conventional themes in a highly personal way, we can nevertheless form a general enough view of this notion to see what it was that Jesus could assume his audience would understand him to be talking about.

In Jesus' day the general Jewish view of the Kingdom of God was roughly as follows:

The Kingdom of God (sometimes called the Kingdom of Heaven because of the Jewish taboo on the mention of God by name) was conceived of as a new order, installed on earth through the power of the Almighty. It constituted a total transformation of the whole world and the initiation of a new life in which the righteous and pious, from the past as well as from the present, would prosper; the righteous who had died would be resurrected to share the new order.

Thus the Kingdom of God was just that – a divine work accomplished at a moment chosen by God, and through the exercise of his power.

More importantly, it was not a divine work accomplished

71

within the soul of the individual; it was not a spiritual reformation of the individual, but was something put into effect *outside* the individual: it was a *material* transformation of the universe.

It is just this point around which a lively controversy has revolved for a long time: if Jesus preached that the Kingdom of God was at hand, and the Kingdom of God has never appeared, what is to become of Christian doctrine?

This is the basic reason for the zeal with which the debate about the meaning of the Kingdom of God has been carried on ever since the investigation of Jesus' life and the origins of Christianity began towards the end of the eighteenth century. Official religion has a great deal at stake, indeed its very existence. If Jesus was *mistaken* in his estimate of when God was going to institute his Kingdom, obviously the churches' claims to authority are substantially weakened.

The debate has been made possible not by any genuine ambiguity in the idea of the Kingdom of God, either in the Jewish world at large or in Jesus' view of it as implied in the Gospels, but because the Kingdom of God has a moral significance *also*. It is the *righteous* who are to come into their own; consequently, the idea of entry into the Kingdom has a moral content. People are called to repentance so that they may have the right to enter; they are called upon to effect a complete change of heart, which if accomplished in time will permit them to enter the Kingdom.

It is because the Kingdom is accompanied by these moral accessories that many scholars have felt justified in developing a spiritual interpretation of the whole matter. The debate on this theme, central in Jesus' religion, has been carried on along the following three lines, which broadly speaking sum it up:

1. The first view is as above: the Kingdom is a material reality to take place in the future, near or remote;

2. The Kingdom is a spiritual reality of the present; it consists of the victory of virtue in the human heart – justice, compassion, and the love of God and of one's fellows. Its establishment will not depend on a celestial cataclysm, but on the progressive conquest of the human heart by these virtues. According to this view, Jesus was not merely the Herald of the King-

dom, but actually established it around himself by his very being.

Thus the Kingdom is to be considered, not a state of affairs, but a state of mind.

3. The third class of views combines the two mentioned above: while the Kingdom is fundamentally a reality of the future, the Gospels are a sort of anticipation of it. The inception of the Kingdom is conceived of as taking place gradually as a result of Jesus' words and of the consequent repentance they bring about.

Those who wish to remain constant to the traditional Christian faith are plainly bound to believe in some combination of the last two interpretations: it is difficult to reconcile most forms of Christianity with a view of the Kingdom that leads to the conclusion that Jesus simply blundered.

But a look at the Gospels themselves is illuminating. Because of the complex process of the establishment of the present Gospel text, and, above all, of the perspective of the post-Jesus generation, which had its eyes fixed on his crucifixion and Resurrection, all three schools of interpretation mentioned above can find one verse or another that confirms, or seems to confirm, their characteristic views. But I think it can be convincingly demonstrated that the 'spiritual' interpretations of the Kingdom, as opposed to the material, are basically apologetic; they correspond to the religious demands of the Church after Jesus and cannot possibly have represented the point of view of Jesus himself.

To begin with, it should be recalled that the Kingdom of God itself formed part of a still more general Jewish conception of the world, which it cannot be detached from without wrenching it meaninglessly out of context.

This general conception of the world, from the Jewish point of view current in Jesus' time, was that of a division between the 'world to come' (*Ha-Olam Hab-Bah*) and 'this world' (*Ha-Olam Haz-Zeh*).

These two worlds are radically contrasted and, even though one moral state of the individual as distinct from another might be required to pass into the Kingdom once it was established, the essential difference between the two worlds cannot be reduced to a mere contradiction between the two moral states of individual souls. The spiritual *character* of the new divine order must be distinguished fundamentally from its material *framework*. They are related to each other, but for that very reason they are obviously not the same thing.

It is true that Jesus might also have had an auxiliary conception of the Kingdom of God. He might have conceived of it not only as a material transformation of the world but as implying another type of Kingdom as well. There is a famous passage in *Mark* that seems to combine the two conceptions of the Kingdom:

'Truly, I say to you, whoever does not receive the kingdom of God like a child shall not enter it' [Mk 10:15].

There are clearly two points of view in this apparently simple passage. Those who believe that the Kingdom of God is *only* a spiritual transformation of the individual must find them irreconcilable, for the first part of the sentence implies a future state of being, while the second half implies a present state of mind. The great question is to decide which of the two is, in Jesus' mind, the essence of the matter, and which is a subordinate element.

The disentanglement of this simple sentence contains in essence the various points of view that theologians of all shades of opinion have been compelled to mingle, modify, qualify, and so on, in their attempt to interpret Jesus' conception of the Kingdom in a spiritual sense.

In the ensemble of the interpretations that have been offered, the nuances are endless; I shall confine myself to a few observations that I hope will shed some light on the question as a whole.

The first point has been mentioned already: since Jesus is not recorded as having given any definition of the Kingdom at all, it would seem evident that he shared, at least in broad outlines, the view of the Jewish community on this question. Otherwise his failure to explain a different view would be incomprehensible.

Further, the very first Christians seem to have been altogether given over to eschatological expectations, that is, a feverish waiting for the Great Day that was to inaugurate the 'Final Things' of this world. If Jesus had really taught something quite different, why were they still dominated by this eschatological fever?

Finally, the Gospels, by and large, have too many passages that can only be explained by this material view of the Kingdom; precisely because they fail to conform with the other elements in the Gospels they must be taken, in accordance with our cardinal criterion, as the most primitive layer of the tradition.

For instance, the Kingdom is compared to a feast of the righteous, and those who are unworthy of it are cast 'into the outer darkness; there men will weep and gnash their teeth. For many are called, but few are chosen' (Mt 22:1–14, and Synoptic parallels).

After their resurrection, the righteous are said to form a company similar to that of the angels (Mk 12:25), in which the wicked have been eliminated. None of this is remotely equivalent to a gradual progression of the forces of good in their conquest of human hearts; it must refer to an instantaneous action on the part of the Supreme Judge, who puts the righteous on one side and the wicked on the other.

The Kingdom, then, is a gift of God – it is not the same thing as those who will inhabit it. Jesus may have regarded himself as the Herald or even the pastor of the righteous flock out of love for them, but he was leading them into something that might very well exist without them. The Kingdom itself, though it may be there for the benefit of the righteous, does not *depend* on their existence.

In other words, the Kingdom of God is not a sort of parimutuel totalisator of individual repentances: the Kingdom is present and available for all those who can enter, but it would exist regardless of their number, and once the righteous have entered, the last one in will be given the same wages as the first (Mt 20:1–16).

All the most relevant passages bear out this interpretation.

If the Kingdom were not an extrapersonal manifestation of the power of God, why should the Gospels insist so much on the swiftness of its arrival, without forewarning? 'Take heed, watch; for you do not know when the time will come' (Mk 13:33 ff).

This idea of the suddenness, and of the unexpectedness *at any given moment*, of the Kingdom's advent recurs throughout the Gospels and throughout the earliest Christian documents as well, where the point is made over and over that the Lord 'will come like a thief' (Rev. 3:3; 16:15, also II Peter 3:10), or 'as travail comes upon a woman with child' (I Thess. 5:3).

There have been many scholars and theologians, as well as independent thinkers like Tolstoy, who have maintained the exclusively spiritual quality of the Kingdom, that is, its present realization in the hearts of men. However, after interpreting various parables such as that of the Feast (Mt 22:2–14, Lk 14:16–24), that of the Talents (Mt 25:14–30 and Lk 19:12–27), and that of the Wise and Foolish Virgins (Mt 25:1–13), they have found themselves reduced, because of the inconclusiveness of their interpretation, to a famous passage in *Luke*, in which men of the most divergent opinions in all other matters have come to see the most fundamental, indeed the essential teaching of the Gospels.

This is the passage:

Being asked by the Pharisees when the kingdom of God was coming, [Jesus] answered them, 'The kingdom of God is not coming with signs to be observed: nor will they say, "Lo, here it is!" or "There!" for behold, the kingdom of God is in the midst of you' [Lk 17:20–21].

This thorny passage has given rise to endless debate. The first phrase, translated as 'signs to be observed', makes use of a Greek word drawn from astronomy, concerning the signs of something like an eclipse, or the interpretation of the movements of the stars in order to foretell the future. Thus it is another way of saying that there is no way of knowing just when the Kingdom of God will come about.

The second phrase is the kernel of the whole debate. If the word here translated as 'in the midst of' (*entos*) is given the variant translation of 'within', the difference is evidently profound. It is this really basic and unbridgeable difference that has given rise to such a torrent of ink; copious evidence of a purely linguistic kind has been brought into play by all those preoccupied with this cardinal question.

In brief, the Greek word variously translated as 'in the midst of' or 'within' in fact has been used in both senses; there is accordingly a perfectly good case to be made out, on a *purely linguistic basis*, for translating it as 'within' and thus salvaging a spiritual interpretation of the Kingdom. Some authorities even consider that general Greek usage tilts the balance slightly in favour of this.

The difficulty that hampers interpreting this Greek word as 'within' is not linguistic at all: it is a question of general probability.

If Jesus is addressing himself to the Pharisees, for instance, with whom he is presumably debating doctrine, it seems quite senseless for him to tell them that the Kingdom of God is already within *them*. Even disregarding the Pharisees, and assuming for the moment Jesus' doctrinal differences with them, how could Jesus have said this to any other Jews at all, including his disciples? What could it have meant to them? Quite apart from the fact that this interpretation of the notion of the Kingdom has no echo at all throughout the Gospels, how could such an isolated remark, so pregnant with novelty for the Jews of the time, be taken as summing up Jesus' teaching, or as its central tenet?

It is obvious that the purely linguistic possibility, in any case dubious, is nullified by common sense, more especially since in this case common sense is fortified by the whole context of the passage, in which Jesus is, after all, using this remark as a sort of prelude to a general exhortation of his disciples, for he goes on at once to say that the Son of man will come 'as the lightning flashes and lights up the sky from one side to the other' (Lk 17:24).

If he is announcing the lightning-like advent of the Kingdom of God, how can he simultaneously be saying that it is already present in the hearts of his audience? How can he be telling them that it will come unannounced like the lightning, when no one expects it, and at the same time that it is already there?

The meaning of the passage is thus made clear by its very content: the phrase 'in the midst of' is evidently a future event, and in this sense what Jesus is saying is perfectly clear; there will be no difficulty in telling when the Kingdom of God is here, for it will be 'in the midst of you', quite suddenly, or it will be in your hearts, in the functional sense, as it were, in which those whose hearts will have been prepared will be able to enter the Kingdom that will be accessible to them at that time.

In short, a reading of the sentences immediately following the passage that says the Kingdom of God is 'in the midst of' Jesus' audience indicates beyond question that Jesus, or more probably the Gospel writer recalling one of the most powerful feelings of the first Christian generation concerning the Return of Christ (which is what the Kingdom came to mean to the first generation *after* Jesus), was not referring to an existent or even potential state of affairs, but to a state that was to be brought about, without forewarning, by the majesty of God.

Thus the most it seems possible to say about Jesus' view of the Kingdom of God is that it conformed in its essentials with current Jewish belief: it was to come as God's gift. If there was any difference at all in his own belief, it could only have consisted in the view that since his mission was that of Herald of the Kingdom, a belief in this mission might, conceivably, have been regarded by him as a prerequisite for entry into the Kingdom once established. In this sense it might have been believed that a faithful follower was potentially in possession of the Kingdom. Nevertheless, this is not to be confused with the forgiveness of sins or with God himself or with the justice and mercy of God as functioning within the heart of individuals. The private acts of individuals, their moral reform, and everything this concept implies, may guarantee the individual the Kingdom of God when it is established, but they are not the Kingdom, which, to repeat, is nothing but the material transformation of this world.

Some attempts have been made to interpret the expression used predominantly in *Matthew*, 'Kingdom of Heaven', as referring to a future *celestial* realization of the Kingdom; but as indicated above, the phrase 'Kingdom of Heaven' is merely a pious euphemism for the Kingdom of God. In any case, the celebrated saying ascribed to Jesus in the Sermon on the Mount, 'Blessed are the meek, for they shall inherit the earth' (Mt 5:5), simply refers to the earth now dominated by violence and evil, which an act of God will transform so that the righteous, the meek, will come into their own. Hence the conception of the meek inheriting the earth, when added to the installation of the Kingdom among those still alive, manifestly excludes the notion of a purely celestial reward.

Another passage from the Sermon on the Mount has sometimes been used to fortify the 'celestial' interpretation of the above. This other passage reads, 'Rejoice and be glad, for your reward is great in heaven . . .' (Mt 5:12).

Since it is evident, however, that this reward in heaven simply means that the origin of the Kingdom is divine and transcendental and that the good actions of the 'meek', and so on, in this world are being carefully toted up to be rewarded when the Great Day comes, this passage is also a cul-de-sac for the 'spiritual' interpreters.

Summing up, it cannot seriously be doubted that what was in Jesus' mind when he referred to the Kingdom of God was a terrestrial, material transformation of the world, instituted by divine power and terminating the present sinful order of human affairs.

The question involved in the time of the arrival of the Kingdom is somewhat subtler, since varying estimates are given. Jesus is supposed to have said that the Kingdom was 'at hand' (Mt 10:7), that is, imminent. But the notion of 'imminence' is, after all, inherently elastic.

Perhaps the point is that though Jesus regarded the advent of the Kingdom as being imminent generally, he expressly states that it was impossible to know the precise moment of its arrival, since it was dependent entirely on the will of God, as his gift. Its unexpectedness is thus inherent in its nature:

79

But of that day or that hour no one knows, not even the angels in heaven, nor the Son, but only the Father [Mk 13:32, also Mt 24:36].

This does not contradict the imminence of the Kingdom, but merely makes the precise moment of its installation unpredictable.

There are two passages that make the conviction of general imminence, so to speak, unavoidable:

As they heard these things, he proceeded to tell a parable, because he was near to Jerusalem, and because they supposed that the kingdom of God was to appear immediately [Lk 19:11].

The second passage that indicates the same thing, without going into detail, is the following:

Truly, I say to you, I shall not drink again of the fruit of the vine until that day when I drink it new in the kingdom of God

[Mk 14:25].

Such a day must clearly be fairly close in point of time, and in any case cannot be longer than a year: it is made more precise by the following:

For I tell you I shall not eat [the Passover – at most a year later] until it is fulfilled in the kingdom of God [Lk 22:16].

These passages are given here not in order to claim that Jesus actually uttered the words they contain (a precision that eludes us), but to indicate that the very earliest tradition clung to them despite what would have seemed their inappropriateness to the actual deeds of Jesus. Hence they are at least authentic in the sense that they reflect the conviction of the earliest disciples.

Indeed, it is obvious that the event did not in fact justify these words, and so the early generation of Christians was bound to extend their significance at least to make them refer to the Second Coming of Jesus: when that was also postponed, or adjourned *sine die*, the Church was forced to alter the entire conception that lay behind the words, so simple in themselves, and content itself with an altogether spiritualized interpretation of Jesus' message. It may even be said that it was just this failure of the Kingdom to materialize that generated the Christian Church, which filled up, so to speak, the vacuum of Jesus' disappointment.

Some light is shed on the elasticity of this continuing disappointment of the early Christian generations by the fact that the imminence of the Kingdom, while unquestioned, is given in three or even four stages, which may reflect either Jesus' changes of mind in accordance with his shifting fortunes, or else the attempts of the earliest chroniclers to harmonize his remembered sayings with the recalcitrant facts.

The briefest approximation of the advent of the Kingdom is seen, for instance, in *Matthew,* in a passage reporting what Jesus says to the apostles before dispatching them on their mission:

Truly, I say to you, you will not have gone through all the towns of Israel, before the Son of man comes [Mt 10:23].

Now, it may well be (as we shall see below) that there was no apostolic mission as referred to in the Gospels, and that consequently Jesus never used such words: but there can be equally little doubt that the earliest tradition believed that he had, and believed it in spite of the fact, which the earliest authorities must have been well aware of, that the apostles perforce returned without having seen the Great Day come.

Mark gives us the second postponement:

And [Jesus] said to them, 'Truly, I say to you, there are some standing here who will not taste death before they see the kingdom of God come with power' [Mk 9:1].

Some independent scholars even believe that the word 'some' in this sentence may be a correction of what was originally 'all those'; that is, it was one of the very earliest textual changes in the original tradition, introduced to explain the *first* delay in the appearance of the Kingdom, or, in the minds of the evangelical generation that followed Jesus, in the Second Coming of Jesus himself.

The appearance of the Kingdom is postponed still further in another passage in *Mark*:

Truly, I say to you, this generation will not pass away before all these things take place [Mk 13:30; also Mt 24:34].

It is true that for obvious reasons various theologians, confronted by the brutal fact that that generation *did* pass away without seeing the accomplishment of anything forecast by Jesus, did their utmost to expand the sense of the word 'generation' to vindicate the accuracy of Jesus' prophecy. It was a futile effort: the sense of the word is all too plain, not merely in the Greek in which it has come down to us, but in the logic of the whole speech. When such a figure as St Jerome enlarges the focus of this plain and simple prediction to make it refer to the entire human race, thus ensuring the target of the prophecy for all foreseeable time, we may admire his imagination and fortitude, but must surely differ with him on the meaning of Jesus' words.

The fourth postponement referred to above may be indicated by a different interpretation of the passage from *Mark* in which Jesus says that 'of that day or that hour no one knows' except God (Mk 13:32): if this does not mean merely the unpredictability of the Kingdom's advent, it sounds almost like the beginning of a note of despair, as though Jesus were beginning to suspect the failure of his career. I shall discuss further on what conclusions he might have drawn from this.

It is of course perfectly legitimate to doubt the authenticity of all the above-mentioned passages as referring to Jesus, and to take them instead as references to the necessity felt by the first Christian generation to explain the postponement of Jesus' Second Coming; indeed, it may well be that the last passages just above, referring to God (the Father) as being the sole repository of the knowledge as to when the Great Day was coming, is a reflection of this later uncertainty. In that case, of course, we should be left in complete ignorance of Jesus' own belief concerning the time of the Kingdom's arrival, and be compelled to assume no more than that he thought it very close at hand, contenting ourselves with the urgency of his central message – 'Repent' – throughout the Gospels. In any case, the initial transposition, the replacement of the expectation of the Kingdom by the expectation of the Second Coming of Christ, does not change the structure of these successive postponements.

Thus, even if we admit that the appearance of successive stages of postponement recorded in the Gospels is deceptive if associated with Jesus himself, we are left in any case with the assurance that he believed, at the very least, that the Kingdom was imminent if only in the sense that *this world* was nearing its end.

As for where the Kingdom was to take its point of departure, there is little doubt allowed by the Gospels. In accordance with well-established Jewish belief, it was to have its seat in Jerusalem. This is indicated not merely by the above-mentioned reference to *Luke*, where the disciples are filled with expectation at the immediate appearance of the Kingdom, but by the very fact of the silence of the Gospels on the point. It must have been too much a matter of course to warrant discussion, and it is obviously the point of Jesus' going up to Jerusalem for the denouement of the drama.

There is no mention in the Gospels of one aspect of the Jewish dream that had to do with the millennium, that is, the Messianic reign lasting a thousand years. This was to play a part in Christian speculation after Jesus, but he himself seems to have been content with preparing his people for the Kingdom of God without going into any transitional details. The Gospels give us an image simply of the *glorification* of this world through the installation in it of the Kingdom, in which men will live like angels in God's peace and justice. Perhaps Jesus simply thought of it (insofar as his thoughts have come down to us unaltered by subsequent bias) as the Feast mentioned in *Matthew* (22:2–14) and *Luke* (14:16–24).

To sum up:

Jesus is put forth in the Gospels as the Herald of the Kingdom of God, and whether or not he went into any details concerning the Kingdom or its advent it is clear that his conception of it was basically in harmony with ideas prevalent among the Jews of his time.

These ideas were as follows:

The expected Kingdom was a material transformation of the world effected by the will of God.

While Jesus did not think his own preaching would establish the Kingdom, he might have thought it would prepare people for it.

Such, at least, is the general picture presented by the Gospels.

7

JESUS' AUDIENCE

THE fact that Jesus' conception of the Kingdom of God was essentially in harmony with current Jewish thought brings us to a crucial point.

Whom was his message intended for? Who was supposed to benefit by it?

Put in another way, did he intend his message for the whole of mankind? Was he as universalistic as Christian theology, in pursuit of its own interests, has maintained to this day?

This is of course a cardinal riddle for religious thought; let us try to clarify it here only within the framework of history.

We have seen above that the very insistence with which he preached the advent of the Kingdom of God, and the plain fact that according to the Gospels themselves this was his basic message, in and for itself places him squarely within the Jewish tradition. Not only is the Kingdom of God itself prayed for every day in the Jewish *Shemoneh Esreh*, but nearly all of Jesus' *explicit* statements are uncompromisingly, even extravagantly, particularistic.

This is the more amazing since, as indicated above, the Gospels took shape in the perspective of the religion that arose after Jesus, over his dead body, so to speak, and moreover betray a consistent strain of hostility to the Jews, running directly counter to Jesus' own statements and to the situation as it must have been in Palestine during his lifetime.

This contradictoriness, enmeshed in the very fabric of the Gospels, is one more indication of the extreme complexity of the traditions that were embodied in successive layers of the documents ultimately sanctified by canonization. Though undoubtedly a problem for traditional belief, for the student of history they constitute a problem only in the sense of a puzzle.

It is true, oddly enough, that the Gospels, and especially *Matthew*, may actually exaggerate, if not Jesus' Jewishness as such, at least his biblicism, that is, his habit of referring authority to the Old Testament. This point has been made even by conservative Catholic critics; if so it would simply mean that the *very earliest* community, doubtless in a Jewish milieu and more than likely before the final triumph of the Pauline form of de-Judaized Christianity, was aware of being intimately involved with historic Jewish religion as it was to be consummated by the arrival of a Messiah heralding the Kingdom of God.

In any case, what Jesus himself is reported as saying seems unmistakable. Not only does he proclaim the unique validity of the Jewish Law, by quoting the focal prayer of Judaism:

And one of the scribes came up and heard them disputing with one another, and ... asked him, 'Which commandment is the first of all?' Jesus answered, 'The first is, "Hear, O Israel; the Lord our God, the Lord is one; and you shall love the Lord your God with all your heart, and with all your soul, and with all your mind, and with all your strength." The second is this, "You shall love your neighbour as yourself." There is no other commandment greater than these.' And the scribe said to him, 'You are right, Teacher; you have truly said that he is one, and there is no other but he; and to love him with all the heart, and with all the understanding, and with all the strength, and to love one's neighbour as oneself, is much more than all whole burnt offerings and sacrifices.' And when Jesus saw that he answered wisely, he said to him, 'You are not far from the kingdom of God' [Mk 12:28–34].

Not only does he indicate his belief in the absolute, eternal immutability of the Jewish law:

It is easier for heaven and earth to pass away, than for one dot of the law to become void [Lk 16:17].

Think not that I have come to abolish the law and the prophets; I have come not to abolish them but to fulfil them. For truly, I say to you, till heaven and earth pass away, not an iota, not a dot, will pass from the law until all is accomplished. Whoever then relaxes one of the least of these commandments and teaches men so, shall be called least in the kingdom of heaven; but he who does them and teaches them shall be called great in the kingdom of heaven [Mt 5:17–19].

But he seems to make a point of his mission's being meant for the Jews alone:

He answered, 'I was sent only to the lost sheep of the house of Israel' [Mt 15:24].

He actually goes so far as to maintain that his mission was meant for no one *but* the Jews:

Now the woman was a Greek, a Syrophoenician by birth. And she begged him to cast the demon out of her daughter. And he said to her, 'Let the children first be fed, for it is not right to take the children's bread and throw it to the dogs' [Mk 7:26–27].

This is paralleled by:

But she came and knelt before him, saying, 'Lord, help me.' And he answered, 'It is not fair to take the children's bread and throw it to the dogs.' She said, 'Yes, Lord, yet even the dogs eat the crumbs that fall from their master's table' [Mt 15:25–27].

In the Orient the word 'dogs' as applied to pagans had a particularly contemptuous ring. It may be echoed with even greater force in *Matthew*, where it is coupled with swine: 'Do not give dogs what is holy; and do not throw your pearls before swine' [Mt 7:6]. Though this is in a different context, we are bound to be struck by the similarity of the phraseology, surely rather crass.

In any case, the main point in these references to pagans is clearly not the question of Jesus' compassion, but the framework of his thought. Simply put, he extends his personal compassion to a non-Jew by way of exception, since, as he says, his mission is exclusively for those who accept the Torah as the centre of life and who are the only ones for whom the very idea of the Kingdom of God would have any meaning. These are the only ones whose repentance would be significant, since they would be expressing it within a structure of thought, faith, and hope that would link their repentance to its reward.

For the pagans of Jesus' day, that is, the conception of a Kingdom to be materialized by the Jewish God and heralded by the Jewish Messiah would be altogether incomprehensible or irrelevant, actually even meaningless. This point is made very vividly by what must be a very ancient passage in *Matthew* (19:28), in which the chronicler, by reporting Jesus' reassurances to the twelve Apostles that they would all be sitting on twelve thrones judging the twelve tribes of Israel, manifestly implies that the Kingdom of God was only for the Jews. The same theme is unmistakable in a saying put in the resurrected Jesus' mouth: 'So when they had come together, they asked him, "Lord, will you at this time restore the kingdom to Israel?"' (Acts 1:6), which in its matter-of-fact assumption that the Kingdom of God was for Israel alone must be very ancient too.

To be sure, by the time the Jews had developed a God who was not merely one god among others, but was the sole all-powerful God of the universe, there was nothing that stood in the way of conversion. Once the Jewish God had expanded beyond a purely local setting, as the god of a particular people (such as Baal for the Canaanites or Dagon for the Philistines, whom the ancient Hebrews had considered perfectly *valid* though inferior gods), and become not merely superior to other gods but God uniquely, anyone in the world might become a Jew, since it meant only accepting this simple belief and the burden of the rituals inherited from history as the One God's cult.

But in any given historical setting that would mean finding one's way to this unique God through the vestibule, so to speak, of Judaism, and however universalistic the implications of Judaism, hence ultimately of Jesus' Judaism too, it was the Jewish Torah alone that guided the way.

Even Jesus' miracles, which would have seemed to redound to his personal credit as at least a sign of his status, were merely ascribed in the normal way to his being favoured by the divine power:

And great crowds came to him, bringing with them the lame, the maimed, the blind, the dumb, and many others, and they put them at his feet, and he healed them, so that the throng wondered, when they saw the dumb speaking, the maimed whole, the lame walking, and the blind seeing; and they glorified the God of Israel

[Mt 15:30–31].

It is not Jesus who is 'glorified' by his ability to heal, but the God of Israel.

Nor is it only a question of specific statements attributed to Jesus: traces of the original religious harmony between his followers and other Jews are unmistakably recorded. We shall see later (Chapter 11) that Jesus' immediate followers, led by his brother, were proud of being pious Jews, 'held in high honour' by 'the people'; they actually worship in the Temple (*Acts* 2:47, 5:13, and so on). This statement in itself, which was recorded at a moment when it lay in the interests of the new religion to *disavow* the particularistic Jewish connexion, insofar as the target of conversion was now the pagan masses of the Greco-Roman world, would be enough to indicate the thoroughly Jewish content of Jesus' own message.

Yet throughout the Gospels he seems to be engaged in a perpetual debate with the 'Jews'. If Jesus was in fact a devout Jew himself, what could they have been at loggerheads about?

The whole question has been deeply obscured by the singular role ascribed in the Gospels to the 'Pharisees', who seem to be Jesus' principal adversaries. Indeed, the New Testament has congealed the word itself into a synonym for pedantic hypocrisy.

This represents an extraordinary perversion of the circumstances of Jesus' lifetime.

The Pharisees and Sadducees were the two dominant tendencies in Jewish life for the two centuries before and after Jesus. They differed in their attitudes towards the Jewish Torah.

Ever since Ezra (444 B.C.) the Torah had been the unchallenged religious source of religious authority for the whole of the Jewish people. Since it had been fixed in writing, however, it was obviously incapable of dealing with every specific problem that might arise in the course of time.

The Sadducees, as the aristocratic, priestly group, held the view that the Torah as written had to be supplemented by priestly decisions as the occasion arose. Thus the scope of the Torah tended to contract gradually with time.

The Pharisees, on the other hand, believed that the Torah was binding not merely by virtue of the collective oath taken by the representatives of the people in the time of Ezra but also because it was the direct expression of God's will. They enlarged the scope of the Torah, and made this socially feasible by evolving the concept of an Oral Law. This was as ancient as the words of the written Torah itself, and just as binding.

The Sadducees were conservative guardians of an ancient text; they considered the Pharisees innovators who acted as disturbers of the public order and as gadflies generally. The Sadducees were not an organized group, but were simply aristocrats, high priests, men of affairs and so on – in short, the vested interests – who had an old-fashioned, literalistic view of religion that enabled them to carry on affairs of state and business generally without being bothered too much by problems of doctrine.

For the Pharisees the Oral Law, the living, ever-changing heart of the religion, was absolutely vital. The Sadducees denied its existence altogether.

The Sadducees were intimately associated with the government and especially with the Temple, which they ran until its destruction in A.D. 70. After the Temple was destroyed, in fact, the Sadducees as a group vanished altogether, though their views survived them for some time and found an echo or two in Jewish life later on.

Though the Pharisees were not very numerous they were accepted as the representatives of the masses, even by those who did not submit to their discipline entirely. They developed both the synagogue and the schooling system into a powerful channel for the inculcation of religion in the lives of the people. They were never a political party as such, though events naturally made them take appropriate action in the pursuit of their aims. It was they who enabled Judaism to survive the fall of Jerusalem in A.D. 70 and even the total disruption of the Jewish people in A.D. 135. They are the fathers of Judaism as it has been practised in the Jewish Diaspora down to our own days.

In the time of Jesus the Pharisees, without being political, were essentially oppositionists; they found many sympathizers among those irked by the rule of the Sadducees.

In short, the historic role of the Pharisees in Jewish life was completely different from the impression given in the Gospels. Not only do we not see any general reason why Jesus should have been hostile to the Pharisees or they to him, but the very texts that labour this point reveal, in spite of themselves, a wholly different relationship. The impression is inescapable that the various Gospel accounts of disputes and controversies of one sort or another somehow do not ring true, or rather they ring true only in terms of the situation we know developed in the environment of the Gospel writers themselves after Jesus' death. The problems faced by the early Church in its debates with the Jewish rabbis were translated into the circumstances of Jesus' life as transformed by the evolving tradition. They do not concern Jesus.

It is true that, since disputation about the Torah must have been a favourite occupation in the Palestine of Jesus' time, he was very probably in the thick of it. He may have changed the emphasis on many points of doctrine and law.

In some respects, for instance, he seems to have insisted on a more severe interpretation of the Torah, as in the case of marriage, where in contradistinction to Moses he seems to have regarded marriage as indissoluble (Mk 10: 2–9). In other respects he seems to have been more lenient, as in his observance of the Sabbath. In still other respects, and more generally, he seems to have extended current Jewish precepts in such a way as to emphasize the *ideal point* involved, as when he seems to relax the Law of 'an eye for an eye' by saying: 'Do not resist one who is evil. But if any one strikes you on the right cheek, turn to him the other also' (Mt 5 :39), and so on.

The oddity is not that the early tradition refers to differences with the Pharisees. This simply reflects the later historical picture. What is curious is that the tradition shows us Jesus carrying on his discussions with the Pharisees in a purely *Pharisaic way*. He sees things in the perspective of the Pharisees, bolsters his interpretations by references to the Torah, interpreted to suit different occasions, and is preoccupied by the same problems. He differs with them, in short, on their own ground.

For instance, in defending his disciples for picking some grain on the Sabbath he refers to David and his famished soldiers eating the 'show-bread' on the Sabbath (Mk 2 :23): here the same authority is invoked by both the Pharisees and Jesus.

In insisting on the rigorousness of the marriage bond (Mk 10 :9) he does so in the name of the divine spirit as revealed in the Torah, and excuses Moses for having been lax in the matter because of the hardness of the people's hearts. When he disregards davidic descent as being indispensable for the Messiah (Mk 12:35-37), he buttresses his case by a reference to David himself.

Even Jesus' attitude towards the burdensome dietary laws of the Jews, which we might legitimately expect him to have proposed a milder interpretation of, must have been conventional. Here is a celebrated passage generally taken to mean the opposite:

[Jesus said], 'Hear me ... and understand: there is nothing outside a man which by going into him can defile him; but the things which come out of a man are what defile him' [Mk 7:14-15].

This follows a passage that sounds as though Jesus were against many of the Jewish ritual acts, such as purifying oneself before eating, and so on, as well as the washing of 'cups and pots and vessels of bronze', and so on (Mk 7:4).

Now, if these instances were really to be interpreted as a systematic form of opposition to Jewish ceremonial, it would be inconceivable why the tradition in the early Church, which eventually swept away the entire Jewish ritual, did not refer this back to Jesus. For the contrary is the case: in Paul's struggle against the 'Judaizers' in the early Church he could not base his relaxation of the Jewish ritual, including the cardinal Jewish rite of circumcision, on anything Jesus was reported to have said. Therefore, the above must be understood as having a specific reference that escapes us, or perhaps as being part of his general understanding of the Jewish ritual in terms of its spiritual content rather than its letter, an attitude he shared with many rabbis.

He was not actually opposed, as far as we can judge from the Gospels, to any of the ritual of contemporary Judaism, nor did he institute any ritual reforms: the rite of circumcision is never mentioned, nor are any ritual innovations. He did not even baptize, as John did; even when dispatching the apostles on their mission he gave them no instructions concerning baptism.

He never said anything against the veneration of the Temple.

Though the Gospels are taciturn on this point, the few references they make seem unquivocal: the fourth Gospel mentions several visits to Jerusalem on the great holidays (2:13, 5:1, 7:2), and *Mark*, after reporting his healing of a leper (1:42), mentions his telling him to take his sacrifice to the Temple as prescribed by the Law (that is, *Leviticus* 14). *Matthew* also refers to the necessity to making proper sacrifices at the Temple after making one's peace with one's brother, implying that it is at least a legitimate thing to do (*Matthew* 5:23).

These few passages indicate that whatever else Jesus may have preached, he did not attack the Temple cult as such; in this respect he does not seem to have shared the views of the Essenes (to whom attempts have been made to link him) who while revering the Law did not approve of the Temple cult as such, the writers and editors of the Gospels, writing at a time when the universalism of Christianity and its split with Judaism had become articles of faith, could scarcely have ignored such a tempting opportunity to trace this view back to Jesus, especially since he did take action against some current Temple practices (Chapter 8). Thus, even though we have no idea of what Jesus himself actually *thought* of Temple worship, it is impossible to explain these passages, as well as the passage in *Acts* mentioning the assiduity of the first disciples in the Temple, without assuming that the early tradition felt no contradiction between such actions and the recommendations of Jesus.

He even explicitly approved of the authority of the Pharisees:

Then said Jesus to the crowds and to his disciples, 'The scribes and the Pharisees sit on Moses' seat; so practise and observe whatever they tell you' [Mt 23:1–3].

This amounts to saying that he endorsed the religious authority of the Pharisees completely; in contradistinction to the Sadducean priesthood. He acknowledged, that is, the exclusive right of the Pharisees to interpret the sacred Law. It is true he goes on to rebuke them for their hypocrisy, but here again the point is that Jesus takes the authority of the Pharisees as his standpoint. He acts like a Pharisee himself, calling upon his fellow Pharisees to live up to their own standards.

Even in Jesus' daily practice (almost non-existent though its description is) there are so many instances of his Pharisaic habits left in the Gospels that once again we see him as framed in the general Jewish tradition. He broke bread, and carefully blessed the bread and the wine; he celebrated the Passover, and said the 'Great *Hallel*'. His celebrated remark that 'the Sabbath was made for man, not man for the Sabbath' (Mk 2:27), was evidently a Pharisaic turn of argument to justify a specific action, or category of actions in terms of the Law. The very wording of Jesus' remark is almost a duplicate of Rabbi Simon ben Menassiah's 'the Sabbath was given to you; you were not given to the Sabbath.' The same idea is expressed more pithily by Rabbi Jonathan, in the Babylonian Talmud: 'Profane a Sabbath in order to be able to observe many.' Moreover, the Pharisees themselves are recorded in the Talmud as using the same *a fortiori* argument as Jesus had used about the Temple and David's eating of the show-bread, in order to prove the general point that the needs of life outweigh ritual punctiliousness.

Consequently we can see that what Jesus both said and did was substantially at one with the Pharisaic tradition; for that matter he taught in the synagogues and was invited to feasts, and when we recall once again that the *tendency* of the Gospels is to castigate the Pharisees, the general designation for the Jewish leadership at the time the Gospels were edited, we can only be overwhelmed by this unequivocal identification of Jesus with the stream of Jewish life during his lifetime.

Thus, without going into the nuances of the legal disputes current in the Jewish community so long ago, and quite apart from the fact that the existence of good scribes as well as bad scribes is mentioned in the Gospels themselves, Jesus' emphasis on the spirit rather than on the letter of the Law in itself would have been entirely in accord with a well-established Jewish tradition, most noteworthy of course in the Prophets. This prophetic tradition, indeed, is just as old or older than the legalistic tradition itself, and may be regarded as an organic parallel to it.

Consequently all those instances in which Jesus seems to be going further than the normal observances of his time – concerning marriage, the Sabbath, love of one's neighbour, and so on – can scarcely be said to constitute a new doctrine: they are simply extensions, within the framework of the accepted Law, of basic principles to specific cases.

Indeed, one of the most vivid illustrations of the profound, anachronistic bias of the Gospel writers is just this harping on the Pharisees' hostility to Jesus. The moment the alienation between the Jewish parent community and its proto-Christian offshoot progressed to the point of blaming the Jews for Jesus' death everything in his life, too, was looked at from this standpoint. It was the cross itself, in fact, that constituted the dominant perspective for all events. Not only were the early Christians bent on making converts among the pagan masses of the Roman Empire, but it became increasingly difficult to make converts among the Jews. The interaction of these two factors removed any inhibitions that might have been felt with respect either to the sensibilities of the Jews or to historical likelihood.

One of the consequences of this progressive alienation was the lumping together of all Jews as enemies of Jesus. As the theological bias of the early Christians developed this in its turn entailed the addition of an element of timelessness: Jews had not only been hostile to Jesus historically, but were so *inherently*.

Soon after Jesus's death materials derived from actual events began being collected, but they were in the nature of things only understood as part of a theology. Both history and pseudo-history were fused indiscriminately; indeed, it would never have occurred to anyone to make a distinction. No conscious, conspiratorial decision was needed; it was simply that history was only understood theologically.

Within this general attitude plausibility was naturally looked for. Hence the basic hostility of the Jews had to be buttressed by the arguments between Jesus and the 'Jews' that play such a role in the Gospels. Controversies were contrived or exaggerated, a characteristic instance being the dispute in *Mark* concerning divorce: no Jew of the time could have contested the dissolubility of marriage.

It is true that the Gospel writers had enemies, but they were their own enemies. If there had really been any record of specific enemies of Jesus in his own time they would presumably have been singled out in the Gospels with some precision. But this is just what is lacking; there is actually very little evidence even in the most biased portions of the Gospels of any authentic hostility to Jesus on the part of the Jewish community as a whole. The fundamental indifference of the Gospel writers to the real circumstances of Jesus' life is indicated by just this vagueness in referring to his adversaries. The division of the whole Jewish community into the handful of Jesus' disciples and the rest of the Jews, implacably – and incomprehensibly – determined to undo him is manifestly artificial.

When specific instances of hostility are mentioned they have an air of historical plausibility. In *Mark* we read: 'The chief priests and the scribes were seeking how to arrest (Jesus) by stealth, and kill him' (Mk 14:1). In view of the general likelihood of the Temple aristocracy having been opposed to Jesus, and in view of the specificity of the phrase 'chief priests', it may well be that such words represent a hangover of the very earliest tradition, in which the Pharisees were not even mentioned.

It is just this likelihood of the Temple aristocracy having been opponents of Jesus that makes another element in the Gospel account highly significant. For the Temple aristocracy was composed of Sadducees; what could be more probable than that some, perhaps all, Sadducee elements were in close contact with the Romans, and hence collaborated in opposing Jesus? Yet scarcely a word is said against the Sadducees throughout the New Testament!

The explanation is simple: in Jesus' own lifetime it was the Sadducees who dominated the Jewish community, but while the Gospels were being composed it was the Pharisees. The Gospel writers merely transposed their own preoccupations to Jesus' day. This omission of the Sadducees is one of the most striking illustrations of their anachronistic bias.

The concentration of the Gospel writers' polemical intentions on the Pharisees and the followers of John the Baptist is equally understandable: they were the only groups close enough to be susceptible to the apocalyptic appeals of the new sect.

For that matter, despite the *general* atmosphere of conflict between Jesus and the Pharisees, the Gospels themselves, when examined in detail, give a very confused picture of this hostility. *Mark*, for instance, gives clear indications of the initial adherence to Jesus of the Pharisees as well as the scribes, while in *Luke* various degrees of friendliness are shown (Lk 7:36, 11:37, 13:31–33, 14:1, 17:20). Obviously, then, even though the basic mould of the Gospels was hostile to *official* Jewry, they already contained these contradictory elements, which must have come from the earliest tradition.

The striking fact recorded in *Luke* (13:31–33), for instance, where the Pharisees actually give Jesus a friendly warning to escape from Herod, is enough to illustrate this dramatically. It is so contrary to the entire structure of the Gospel tradition that it must be authentic.

There are a number of passages, to be sure, that seem to clash with this view of Jesus as wholly enclosed by Judaism. On closer examination, however, we shall see that these are due to the patchwork composition of the Gospels, in which episodes have come down to us either out of context or overlaid by theological intrusions subsequent to the early tradition.

One of the most famous of Jesus' sayings, for instance, is sometimes claimed as a proof of his determination to burst the bonds of particularistic Judaism:

No one sews a piece of unshrunk cloth on an old garment; if he does, the patch tears away from it, the new from the old, and a worse tear is made. And no one puts new wine into old wineskins; if he does, the wine will burst the skins, and the wine is lost, and so are the skins; but new wine is for fresh skins [Mk 2:21–22].

But a moment's reflection will indicate that this, like Jesus' remarks on the Sabbath and the dietary laws, must be an example of some reference to a specific incident long since lost: for if the *broad* interpretation of this were possible, that is, if Jesus meant that the 'old bottles' of Judaism were to be discarded, the situation would be irremediably enigmatic. It would be the only place where Jesus puts himself forth as a schismatic within Judaism, and quite impossible to reconcile with the earliest tradition, which must surely be embodied in such expressions of his total identification with Israel as we have seen in the gross passages about the 'children's bread' being 'thrown to the dogs', and so on.

The greater likelihood is that since the passage concerns fasting, where Jesus is defending his disciples for not fasting in the manner of the Pharisees, what he is concerned with is not the practice of fasting itself, but with what he may have regarded as an excess of pietistic vanity. The Law proper did not insist on any fast except that of the Day of Atonement (after sending the scapegoat out into the desert on the tenth day of the seventh month: *Leviticus* 16:29, 23:27). Everything else observed by pious Jews to deprive themselves of food according to a few recommendations made in the Prophets and in the historical Scriptures (such as II *Samuel* 12:16, *Isaiah* 58, *Jeremiah* 14:2, and so on) was no more than custom by Jesus' time. Thus he might have differed with other Jews in respect of fasting and still have said nothing against the Law. This is why the above-mentioned passage must be seen in some larger context before its implications can be understood; and since it is just this larger context that is missing we are bound to see it as a specific debating point, wrenched out of context. In any case *Mark* gives us neither the specific occasion on which Jesus uttered the phrase, nor the general framework in which it is to be understood; consequently we must interpret it, on the one hand, in terms of its specific content (that is, the assessment of fasting); and on the other, as a complement of Jesus' other sayings, which are unquestionably framed by his acceptance of the Torah.

Here is another passage, recording what Jesus is supposed to have said to some Pharisees, that at first sight seems to imply a revolutionary attitude towards Judaism: 'I tell you something greater than the Temple is here' (Mt 12:6).

If this 'something' actually refers to Jesus, and not to God, it must be ignored: it would be inconceivable for Jesus actually to have said this without being instantly accused of blasphemy. The statement is actually made only in *Matthew*; the passage as a whole, about the breaking of the Sabbath, which is paralleled in *Mark* (2:25-28) contradicts the point in the Marcan passage, which scholars agree was taken from the same primitive source (that is, the *Logia*, or 'Sayings' of Jesus). The particular point about the Temple must be part of the subsequent christological magnification of Jesus.

There is also Jesus' prediction of the destruction of the Temple (Mk 13: 1–2, 14:58), but this clearly does not imply contempt for the Temple as such; it merely resumes a familiar prophetic theme, as in *Micah* 3:12, *Jeremiah* 26:18, and the Apocryphal *Enoch* 40:28.

There is still another passage that definitely sounds like an act of schism with respect to the Jewish Law:

Jesus said to her, 'Woman, believe me, the hour is coming when neither on this mountain nor in Jerusalem will you worship the Father. You worship what you do not know; we worship what we know, for salvation is from the Jews. But the hour is coming, and now is, when the true worshippers will worship the Father in spirit, and truth, for such the Father seeks to worship him. God is spirit, and those who worship him must worship him in spirit and truth' [Jn 4:21–24].

Here, though Jesus says salvation comes from the Jews, he also definitely indicates that the Jewish Law as such is obsolete. But all independent critics agree that this passage is a manifest echo of Pauline Christianity (formulated *after* Jesus) and that it could not have been Jesus who expressed this thought but the editor or writer of the Gospel as it has come down to us.

In view, therefore, of the complete absence of any trustworthy source material that can be linked to Jesus, we are thrust back into accepting the above-mentioned passages from *Matthew* (5:17 ff.) about Jesus' having come, not to abolish, but to fulfil the Law and the Prophets.

Summing up once again, Jesus had the same attitude towards practices, rites, and the Holy Temple as he had towards the Law. He did not condemn, *in principle*, any of the things accepted by contemporary Judaism, though his general tendency was to emphasize the spiritual content rather than the letter of the Law, following in this too a well-defined strand of Jewish thought.

It should be recalled, parenthetically, that however divided the Jews of Jesus' day were, there was never any question of 'forbidding' one school of thought or another. The very idea that a belief was pernicious or wrong, in the sense of placing its holder outside the community, stems from a much later period, that of Greco-Roman Christianity. The isolated instances in *Acts* (Stephen, Jesus' brother Jacob, and so on) that sound like exceptions are all political in nature; they reflect the strain between the apocalyptic Jewish sects and the authorities (Chapter 11).

I think this restores the proper historical perspective for viewing Jesus' activities within the general framework of Judaism. But another question remains.

Hebrew prophets before Jesus had spoken of effecting a new alliance with God, which the prophets gave a certain flexibility to by conceiving it as a sort of indefinitely renewable covenant. *Genesis* 9:17, for instance, refers to the rainbow as an alliance between Yahweh and 'all flesh on earth', concluded with Noah and his descendants; in *Genesis* 17:11 the rite of circumcision demonstrates the alliance between Yahweh and Abraham's descendants; in *Exodus* (24:8 ff.) an alliance is renewed by blood between Yahweh and the people led by Moses after the handing down of the tablets of the Law on Mount Sinai.

In the prophetic tradition itself (*Jeremiah* 31:31 ff.) a new alliance is referred to as being about to be concluded between God and the houses of Israel and Judah, which is to last much longer than the covenants made with the Hebrews upon their exodus from Egypt, since God will inscribe his Law in the hearts of his people and God and his people will be one. In the same vein *Malachi* (3:1) announces the imminent arrival of the 'messenger of the covenant in whom you delight'.

Thus there was a long tradition of covenant-making between the Jews and God; the covenants did not cancel one another out, but in some sense fortified one another along the established lines; they reinvigorated and consolidated a basic covenant between God and the Jewish people.

Hence there was no reason even from within the Jewish tradition why Jesus might not have regarded himself as authorized to conclude a new covenant with God.

But did he?

The most obvious support for an affirmative answer to this is to be found in the words ascribed to him in *Mark*:

And he said to them, 'This is my blood of the covenant which is poured out for many' [Mk 14:24].

However, even if we can believe that Jesus actually uttered these words, they could scarcely have referred to the abolition of the Law – at most they would have been a rite similar to the ancient one recorded of Moses, of renewing in blood the covenant with God. This is surely demonstrated by the above-mentioned passage in *Acts* (2:46, 47) where Jesus' disciples pray assiduously in the Temple. If anything, the disciples seem to have prided themselves on their legalistic correctness towards the Torah; therefore there can be no question of their having understood Jesus' words as meaning its abrogation.

There are a couple of other passages that call for comment:

From the days of John the Baptist until now the kingdom of heaven has suffered violence, and men of violence take it by force. For all the prophets and the law prophesied until John [Mt 11:12–13].

This is echoed in *Luke*:

The law and the prophets were until John; since then the good news of the Kingdom of God is preached, and every one enters it violently
[Lk 16:16].

These two passages seem puzzling, since, whatever the point they are making, it seems to refer to John, not Jesus; if the Law stops at John, it is not Jesus who is the innovator but John. In any case the mission of Jesus does not seem to be involved.

However, apart from the curious phraseology, what is at issue here is, in all probability, not the abolition of the Law at all, but a mere qualification intended to pinpoint the actual announcement of the Kingdom. This may be part of the explanation of the unusual inverted order of words in the passage from *Matthew*, in which the Prophets precede the Law. The meaning of both passages – insofar as they relate to the purely doctrinal aspects of the mission of both John and Jesus – may be quite simply that the Kingdom had previously been announced by the Prophets and by the Law until John, followed by Jesus, came to perform the same task. Thus the Law is considered here simply from the point of view of its specific application to the announcement of the Kingdom; there is no question of abolishing it. It should also be noted that the formula 'since the days of John' seems better fitted to some later editor of the text than to Jesus himself, who could scarcely have referred to a contemporary by such a remote-sounding phrase.

Our information about the details of his belief is so scarce that it is, of course, perfectly legitimate to suggest that while Jesus had no intention of abolishing the Law he might have wished to extend it, by laying the emphasis on the subjective emotions of the individual and so on, again in accordance with the well-established prophetic tradition mentioned above. His own personal interest might have centred on the depth of personal emotion rather than on external appearances. He clearly considered that the cardinal aspect of religion was that of the heart, as indicated by his quoting the Supreme Commandment (Mk 12: 28–34; see also page 101) based on *Deuteronomy* and *Leviticus*, though even here he was in a close accord with a strong tradition within Pharisaism: after the destruction of the Temple in A.D. 70, Rabbi Yohanan, a disciple of the celebrated Rabbi Hillel, emphasized that works of loving-kindness were worth more than sacrifices and the Temple.

Any supposition that goes beyond Jesus' emphasis on the religion of the heart is unfounded speculation: if there is a contrast between the two types of religion it is not one that could have seemed relevant to Jesus and his generation, for whom the traditional structure of Judaism was quite capacious enough to encompass a variety of such differences of emphasis.

I think this confirms our general conclusion: however prophetic or non-legalistic Jesus might have been, it is impossible to consider him, from the point of view of his general religious outlook, as anything but a devout Jew.

The whole classical debate among liberal scholars about whether or not Jesus was 'universalistic' or 'particularistic' is entirely irrelevant. He never had any *occasion* for a choice between these two types of Judaism: as far as the permanent validity of the Jewish Law was concerned Jesus remained entirely within the Jewish enclosure, regardless of the emphasis he may have laid on one attitude or another within his matter-of-fact acceptance of the Law.

It is, indeed, his wholehearted identification with the Jewish Law that gives us the only possible perspective for his innovations or reforms within the Law. The very manner in which he expresses his criticisms of contemporary practice is really meaningful only if the framework of the Law as such is taken for granted. His so-called innovations actually demonstrate more cogently than anything else the unquestioning steadfastness with which he clung to Jewish tradition and preached to Jews alone. The exceptions in his behaviour are evidently reported either just because they are exceptions intended to illustrate Jesus' compassion, as in the case of the Syrophoenician woman and the Roman centurion, whose servant Jesus heals while marvelling at the centurion's faith, which Jesus has not found 'even in Israel' (Mt 8:10), or else because they embody later editorial amendments interpolated at a time when the newly evolving religion, rejected by most of the Jews, had already struck root in pagan soil. An endearingly naïve example of this bow in the direction of the pagan world is the episode of another centurion, who as witness to Jesus' crucifixion is summoned by the Gospel writer to endorse Jesus' status as 'son of God', and duly exclaims, 'Truly this man was a son of God!' (Mk 15:39).

This sort of thing is clearly *post facto* propaganda: the real point is that Jewish Messianism as such would have been quite simply unintelligible to non-Jews: the question of 'saving' the pagans could only arise at all if the pagans were to become Jews and participate in the great Promise made to the Chosen People. As long as they remained outside Judaism, the question of bringing them a message was simply nonsense.

In short, Jesus came for Israel alone; nor, in his own day, could it have been otherwise.

We shall, accordingly, abandon any discussion of the meaning of Jesus' 'message' from the point of view of later generations, and simply deal with it in terms of his own day and his own people. Taking as a starting point his unquestioning attachment to his religion, let us see what his attitude might have meant to the turbulent, oppressed, divided society of his time.

In speaking of his attitude in this broader sense, it is possible to establish a contrast between him and the Jewish authorities on what we could call today a social, or socio-economic basis. As a man of the people he was probably not particularly interested in either the exegesis of the sacred texts or the observance of the 613 written commandments of the Law and its numerous unwritten recommendations, which was the sort of thing that absorbed the attention of professional religionists. The bureaucratic encrustations of the religious schools might have seemed in some sense repugnant to him, especially since they were doubtless associated with the arrogance characteristic of any vested interest, the belief that the vested interest has in some sense a *monopoly* of authority, based on something inaccessible to the simple-minded.

There may be an echo of this in a sentence from *Matthew* already referred to:

For I tell you, unless your righteousness exceeds that of the scribes and Pharisees, you will never enter the kingdom of heaven [Mt 5:20].

The word translated here is righteousness (*dikaiosyne*) is used in the Greek of the New Testament in contrast to a word for sin (*hamartia*) and another implying ignorance of or contempt for the Law (*anomia*), as well as impurity (*akatharsia*). The Gospel writer is telling us that Jesus did not consider the pedantry of the religious experts either a necessary or a sufficient guarantee of an entry into the Kingdom of God. It is in a way an echo of John the Baptist, who seems to have thought that the Messiah could not come until the Jews had fulfilled the Law in every detail, and modified this in his own fashion to allow the New Elect, the New Israel, re-baptized in purity, to inherit the Kingdom.

Jesus' celebrated words 'Come to me, all who labour and are heavy-laden, and I will give you rest. . . . For my yoke is easy, and my burden is light' (Mt 11:28, 30) can be understood when we remember that he intended to fulfil, to the last jot and tittle, the Law *and the Prophets* too. This is another way of referring to the spirit of the Law that underlay its numerous legal specifications, and constitutes the distinction between himself and his contemporaries *within* the framework of Judaism: it seemed to him that the complex exposition and analysis that went into the contemplation of the Law was a very tortuous pathway towards virtue as he understood it.

This insight leads us still further. For while Jesus plainly had an aversion for the Bad Scribe, arrogant in his knowledge of legalistic punctilio while indifferent to the spirit of the Law, an attentive reading of the Gospels seems to indicate that Jesus was in some sense opposed to the Good Scribe as well. If he identified himself with the so-called *am ha-ares*, that is, the 'people of the earth', the common people of Israel who would have been too absorbed in their daily tasks to devote the attention to the Law the religious doctors thought appropriate, he might in effect have been against the learned classes generally.

On this question of observance, for instance, even the Good Scribe, as represented, say, by Hillel, celebrated for his indulgence, was hostile on principle to the inherent laxity of the working population. Hillel said: 'No *am ha-ares* can be pious,' which sounds like an echo of 'This crowd, who do not know the Law, are accursed' (Jn 7:49), put in the mouth of the anonymous 'Pharisees'.

Indeed, it was part of a pietistic convention to contrast these 'people of the earth' with the children of God, that is, the scholars of the Law.

Thus even in the Gospels we perceive that while Jesus Jewishly speaking, was essentially at one with the Pharisees, he may have been, *socially* speaking, against the institutional authority of contemporary society. Thus it may be possible to classify Jesus in the Jewish social spectrum of his day, using our own terminology, as being on the side of the simple people as against the 'upper classes' – the wealthy, the educated, the conventional, and so on.

This may be the ultimate significance of the remark in *Matthew*:

Those who are well have no need of a physician, but those who are sick.... For I came not to call the righteous, but sinners

[Mt 9:12-13].

And in *Luke*:

For the Son of man came to seek and to save the lost [Lk 19:10].

It may also, of course, be the ultimate, though distorted, significance of the celebrated phrase that has come down to us in the Sermon on the Mount:

Blessed are the poor in spirit, for theirs is the kingdom of heaven [Mt 5:3],

when we recall that this sentence is even simpler in *Luke*:

Blessed are you poor, for yours is the kingdom of God [Lk 6:20].

This may give us an insight of profound importance into the nature of the enterprise that led to Jesus' undoing; we may be able to discern the glimmerings of the social turmoil that will make his career intelligible.

Everything we have said about the essentially Jewish nature of Jesus' message and the audience it was intended for plants Jesus squarely within the Judaism of his time. Judaism was, to be sure, far less monolithic than has often been thought: it had far more tendencies, varying emphases, and differences of individual aims. It was also the intellectual world of a people harshly oppressed by an alien and odious power, which as we have seen was in the last analysis instrumental in Jesus' undoing.

It is this last point that must retain our attention. The Romans are well known to have taken pains to avoid meddling in the religious affairs of their subjects, and while they disliked the Jews for a variety of reasons – perhaps chiefly because of their stubborn devotion to an incomprehensible, disembodied deity – there is no reason to think they would have been disturbed by a purely religious movement within the Jewish community.

In the Gospel account, on the other hand, Jesus *seems* to have been preoccupied exclusively with abstract ethics and religion. His celebrated overt reference to the state power, 'Render to Caesar the things that are Caesar's, and to God the things that are God's' (Mk 12:17), clearly sounds as though it were designed to endorse the *status quo*.

Thus, while the Romans might have disliked Jesus' outlook, as they did all forms of Judaism, and despised his otherworldliness, it is difficult, in terms of the Gospel tradition, to grasp their role in Jesus' execution. Yet their executive role is unmistakable.

The same may be said about the Temple authorities. Though there are indications that Jesus might have been opposed, in some sense, to the Jewish upper classes generally, it is just this sense that eludes us. His sayings seem well within the bounds of Judaism, and, if his message is really summed up by what has come down to us in the Gospels, we cannot see why the Temple authorities, or the Jewish aristocracy generally, should have bothered implicating themselves in a plot to kill him. The Temple authorities might also have despised the visionary effusions of some provincial ragamuffin, but we do not see why he should have fallen foul of them with such violence as to warrant their malevolent intervention.

There must, after all, have been other Jews in those turbulent times roving about with their own interpretations of the Jewish Law; the Temple authorities could hardly have reacted with the malice reported in the Gospels to the presence of a mere chatter-box calling upon the Jews to do no more than improve themselves morally so as to be ready for the Kingdom of God whenever it suited the good Lord to establish it.

Now, the Gospels, despite their failure to report motivation, do allow us clearly to perceive a turning point in Jesus' career that, however inexplicable, is unmistakable. After he dispatches his disciples on their mission (Mt 10:5 ff.), giving them instructions that seem to radiate optimism and the hope of the Kingdom's imminence, there is an abrupt break in the narrative. Jesus' wanderings back and forth in Galilee, which in any case have no discernible rationale, are suddenly cut short : he brings his whole career to a sharp focus by a decision to go to Jerusalem.

The entry into the Holy City is obviously heavy with meaning. Jesus' reasons for going there have exercised the ingenuity of countless students of the Gospels: the account of what he does there is so arid and obscure that a great deal of latitude has been left for a variety of hypotheses.

There is no need to discuss them here. The Gospels are fundamentally indifferent to Jesus' real, that is, historic, motives: from their point of view it is obvious that his entry into Jerusalem introduces the drama of the Crucifixion, Resurrection, and Glorification. It is this vantage point, as we have seen, that dominates the whole of the New Testament. We are forced by the Gospels to look at the story of Jesus' entry into Jerusalem through the telescope of the point of view of the later Church, founded not on Jesus' life but on his glorious role as the Resurrected Saviour.

Here is a brief outline of the general role played in the theological Gospel plan by Jesus' entry into Jerusalem:

In *Mark*, our earliest account, the entry into Jerusalem is not only the climax of Jesus' career: it is its crux. The abrupt change of mind leading up to it is summed up in the following passage:

And Jesus went on with his disciples, to the villages of Caesarea Philippi; and on the way he asked his disciples, 'Who do men say that I am?' And they told him, 'John the Baptist; and others say, Elijah; and others, one of the prophets.' And he asked them, 'But who do you say that I am?' Peter answered him, 'You are the Christ.' And he charged them to tell no one about him. And he began to teach them that the Son of man must suffer many things, and be rejected by the elders and the chief priests and the scribes, and be killed, and after three days rise again. And he said this plainly. And Peter took him, and began to rebuke him. But turning and seeing his disciples, he rebuked Peter, and said, 'Get behind me, Satan! For you are not on the side of God, but of men' [Mk 8 : 27-33].

In this passage everything seems to be a prologue to the confession of Peter. Before this, Jesus' Messiahship was presumably hidden; afterward, in the plan of the Gospel writer, he is portrayed as the suffering Messiah moving on to glory by way of his crucifixion.

It is just this *plan* of the Gospel writer that belongs most evidently to later Church doctrine. A later generation, which *knew* the transcendental purpose of the Crucifixion and Glorification, and *knew* Jesus to be the Messiah, was bound to interpret the whole final act of the tragedy, as well as the Saviour's whole life, in such a way as to make it possible to swallow what Paul called the 'stumbling-block of the cross'. Without some esoteric interpretation this could only impress the Jews of Jesus' own time as peculiarly ignominious and repellent.

The fact that this exalted interpretation of the crucifixion is a subsequent, doctrinal rectification of the events, so to speak, can be demonstrated by these otherwise inexplicable passages:

He was near to Jerusalem, and ... they supposed that the kingdom of God was to appear immediately [Lk 19:11].

and:

Jesus said to them, 'Truly, I say to you, in the new world, when the Son of man shall sit on his glorious throne, you who have followed me will also sit on twelve thrones, judging the twelve tribes of Israel [Mt 19:28].

These clearly indicate that the group was filled with enthusiasm and anticipation of the longed-for event as they drew near Jerusalem, and, consequently that Jesus' predictions to his disciples of his suffering and death must have been put in later on (Mk 8:31, 9:31, 10:33 ff.) (See page 153.)

The same theme is given, in reverse, by a bald statement recording the plain fact that Jesus' followers were so disconcerted by the frustration of the hopes just mentioned that they took to their heels:

And they all forsook him, and fled [Mk 14:50].

Considering the piety of the time this was written, it is a masterpiece of reserve. The Gospels attempt to mitigate the behaviour of the disciples in various obviously apologetic ways, all implying that since Jesus had in any case foreseen everything they were bound to bow to the inevitablity of the whole event, but the *fact* of the disarray and abandonment remains. Historically speaking, it contradicts the serene, composed prediction of Jesus' end that is put into his mouth by the Gospel writers.

It is clear that the theological plan of the Gospels is incapable of explaining the climax of Jesus' career. Precisely while explaining the great redemptive significance of the crucifixion, the Gospel account gives us no explanation of the events that brought it about.

Disregarding for a moment the later interpretation of the *meaning* of the crucifixion, what might have been Jesus' practical object in coming to Jerusalem?

We must suppose that he decided to seek a decision in Jerusalem as a result of his failure in Galilee; despite some Gospel references to Jesus' popularity there, the overriding impression remains that he did not meet with sufficient popular acclaim. Indeed, there is a peculiarly savage indictment of the cities of Chorazin, Bethsaida, and Capernaum that must surely be a recollection of his disappointment, if it is not simply another editorial flourish.

Now, if we look on the showdown in Jerusalem from a purely spiritual point of view, what success could Jesus have hoped to have with the sophisticated, institutional, governmental milieu of Jerusalem, if he had not made enough of an impression on the simple folk of Galilee to make it worth his while to stay on there? The Jerusalem aristocracy – to say nothing of the Romans! – would presumably have considered him an overweening provincial upstart, and ignored or rejected him entirely.

On the basis of everything reported in the Gospels – Jesus' spiritual teaching, his proclamation of an other-worldly Kingdom of God, his limited popular success – we cannot see either why Jesus decided to make a solemn entry into Jerusalem or why once he did so he came to such a cruel and ignominious end.

Yet there is no doubt that this was what happened.

8

RECONSTRUCTION:
ACTION AND DISASTER

WE have now managed to penetrate to some basic facts, or at any rate probabilities, beneath the numerous wrappings of the Gospel narrative. But they do not, somehow, hang together. Our jigsaw puzzle seems only partially assembled.

On the basis of what we have, is it possible to piece the rest of the jigsaw puzzle together with the help of other elements hinted at in the Gospels, or legitimately to be deduced?

It will be seen that even in the present version of Jesus' activity, distorted though it is, there are enough elements to serve as building blocks for an alternative explanation of the events. In the Gospel narrative as it now stands, it is only the core that is missing: the surviving scraps and snippets of historical likelihood can be extrapolated in order to outline the missing centre-piece.

Let us resume our account of the climax of Jesus' career.

What are the bare bones of his activity in Jerusalem? What is the lowest common denominator of the various versions that have come down to us?

The core of the Gospel narrative is this: Jesus entered Jerusalem at the head of a group of men; he occupied the Temple for a while; he was betrayed; he was then tried, condemned, and executed on a charge of sedition.

Now, if once again we take Jesus' crucifixion as our starting point, our attention is bound to be arrested by one other element in this skeleton summing up of Jesus' downfall that is far more startling in its implications than even the crucifixion.

It is the simple fact that he occupied the Temple.

How could this have been possible?

The Jewish Temple, celebrated in antiquity as the most splendid shrine in the world, was a vast edifice. Destroyed by Nebuchadnezzar in 586 B.C., it had been rebuilt in 518–516 B.C. *upon* the return of the Jews from their first exile. When Pompey conquered Judea in 63 B.C., the Temple had been a formidable obstacle to him and his Roman legions.

It was restored on a still more magnificent scale by Herod the Great; more than 200 yards wide and 450 yards long, its rebuilding began in 20–19 B.C. The work was so extensive that by the time of Jesus – forty-six years later, according to *John* (2:20) – it was not yet completed. Actually, the work on the outbuildings and the courts was to go on for eighty years altogether; it was not finished until A.D. 62–64; it was burned to the ground in A.D. 70 during the siege of Jerusalem.

The Temple was not merely a house of worship. The building referred to as the 'Temple' so reverentially in the Gospels in reality comprised the sanctuary and all its precincts on the Temple hill (*Har hab-Bayith*), which constituted a huge complex of all sorts of administrative buildings, houses for attendants, offices, stables and a number of great courtyards. The Temple was not only enormous in extent; it also had a gigantic staff of attendants, supposed to number as many as 20,000, for a great variety of functions.

In addition to being the nerve centre of Jewish life, the Temple was a public market-place. It was also a great public treasury; like other shrines in the Oriental world of the time, and even more so, it amounted to a national bank. There was immense wealth in the form of wrought precious metal, as well as great sums of coins and vast deposits made by individual creditors, not only by widows and orphans, but also by the rich. These deposits were not allowed to remain idle: the Temple was not a hoard; the money was continuously being worked. The Jews, together with the rest of the Hellenistic world, had inherited from Babylon the whole system of bills of exchange, bonds, and personal cheques invented there long before, and the vast wealth of the Temple was constantly being deployed in money transfers all over the world. Though it is true that Jews were prevented from taking any interest in transactions between

A reconstruction of the Temple at the time of Jesus, showing the immense courtyards and complex of buildings. The temple was more than 200 yards wide and 450 yards long. It was staffed by as many as 20,000 functionaries, and protected by a Roman cohort of 500 to 600 men.

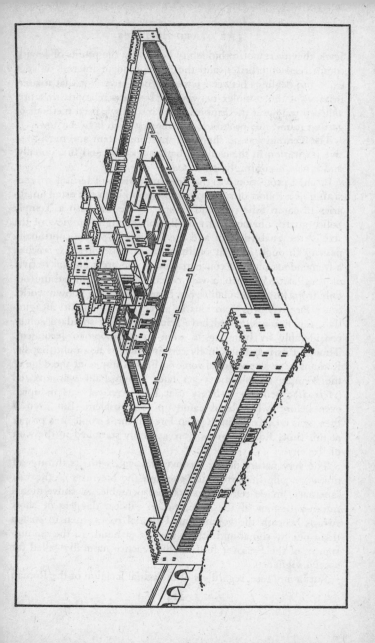

Jews, they were not forbidden to benefit by the profits of Jewish commercial enterprises, and the prohibition of interest did not extend to dealings between Jews and non-Jews. For that matter, in view of the complex network of business relations that prevailed throughout the Empire, there must have been methods of getting round this prohibition of interest even between Jews.

The Temple was, in short, the most important and most massive institution in the country, both physically and functionally, and it was, accordingly, *protected*.

Its chief protection was the Roman garrison of Jerusalem, consisting of a cohort of some 500 to 600 men, with the usual auxiliaries in camp followers and troops. There was also a Temple police guard, obviously of considerable strength, in view of the size of the establishment and the throngs of people continually passing through even at ordinary times. The pressure reached a tremendous pitch of concentration at the great annual festival of the Passover, when a vast concourse of pilgrims came not only from Judea and Galilee but from all over the known world. Since Passover was notorious as an occasion for political agitation, the Romans would have reinforced their standard cohort considerably by bringing in even more troops to Jerusalem. Though this is not absolutely certain, there is no doubt that the Romans kept a substantial force in Fort Antonia, at the edge of the Temple area, some years later, when Paul was arrested (*Acts* 21); hence it is likely that Fort Antonia was occupied even before, when Jesus came up to Jerusalem. But even if there was no substantial Roman force in the Temple area proper at this time, Roman troops were certainly stationed in the west of the city.

The very nature of the Passover festival, with its throngs of unknown pilgrims streaming through the precincts of the vast sanctuary, made reinforcements indispensable. A conventional military custom of the time was to conceal daggers or short swords beneath the voluminous Oriental robes, then to snatch them out by signal and attack anyone at hand. In the circumstances of the Passover festival this practice naturally called for special vigilance.

But in any case, regardless of the actual location of the Roman encampments, or the details of the Roman security measures, it is obvious that the seizure of the Temple could have been accomplished only by an act of violence, *by armed force*.

Jesus could hardly have dropped in at the Temple, bandied a few sour remarks with the Temple police and priests – to say nothing of the Roman soldiers on duty or the infuriated money-changers! – and purely as a result of his personal, *spiritual* authority, actually held the Temple for any length of time whatever.

Most dogmatic or theological interpretations of this episode accept the account of Jesus' occupation of the Temple as a fact (which is natural, since orthodox students regard the whole Gospel account as literally true), but they make the event spiritual or symbolical.

Liberal students of the New Testament, on the other hand, generally doubt the historicity of the event, but their reasons are essentially naïve; they all agree that it would have been a major enterprise requiring force, and say that *therefore* it never took place.

But the relationship of Jesus to the Temple is so central a theme in the Gospel story, it is so obviously the springboard for his arrest and trial, that its historicity must be taken for granted.

Let us weigh its full implications. There is a passage in the fourth Gospel that gives us a material hint:

In the Temple [Jesus] found those who were selling oxen and sheep and pigeons, and the money-changers at their business. And making a whip of cords, he drove them all, with the sheep and oxen, out of the Temple; and he poured out the coins of the money-changers and overturned their tables [Jn 2:14–15].

Here the words 'whip of cords', though they unmistakably imply violence, equally unmistakably represent a sort of minimal toning down of what actually must have been a massive undertaking. If we simply imagine the size of the Temple, the tens of thousands of pilgrims thronging into and through it, the numerous attendants, the police force, the Roman soldiers, as well as the normal reactions of the ox drivers themselves, to say nothing of the moneychangers, to such high-handedness, we see that it must have taken much more than mere peremptoriness to accomplish it at all. The scene behind this fragmentary recollection in the fourth Gospel *must* have been vastly different; the chronicler has softened it by 'spiritualizing' it out of all reality.

This spiritualizing tendency has gone even further in the other Gospels; in *Matthew* it simply says:

And Jesus ... drove out all who sold and bought in the Temple, and he overturned the tables of the money-changers and the seats of those who sold pigeons [Mt 21:12].

In *Mark* the chronicler reports a seemingly innocuous visit by Jesus to the Temple:

[Jesus] entered Jerusalem, and went into the Temple; and when he had looked round at everything, as it was already late, he went out to Bethany with the twelve [Mk 11:11].

This sounds as though the final remnant of incriminatory evidence had been removed; it is followed by the equally colourless '[Jesus] began to drive out,' and so on, though the sentence immediately after this phrase, usually translated as 'he would not allow any one to carry anything through the Temple' (Mk 11:16) is thought by some to require 'armour' instead of 'anything'. If so, this would be another indication of the martial element cloaked by our present text.

In short, Jesus must have had an armed force powerful enough for him to seize this vast edifice and hold it for some time, judging by his reference to the 'day after day' he had spent 'teaching' in the Temple in his response to his captors, when he questions their coming out to seize him by arms (Mk 14:19, and parallels).

In addition he must have had a force large enough to withstand the opposition not only of the Roman soldiery or the Temple police alone but presumably also of the many thousands of other Jews who were doubtless out of sympathy with the Galilean upstart (if we are to take seriously the reported hostility of the Jewish mob after Jesus' condemnation).

In a word, to overcome armed force Jesus' followers must have been armed.

And so they were. The evidence for it seems to me very convincing. In addition to attenuated but unmistakable references to arms scattered through the Gospels, ancient authorities refer to the martial character of Jesus' enterprise in the most matter-of-fact way. Here are a few samples taken from outside sources:

Tacitus, for instance, the Roman historian, simply takes it for granted that from the Roman point of view Jesus was an enemy; in discussing the attempt made by Nero to blame the burning of Rome, which slanderous rumours had attributed to him, on 'those whom the common people called Christians', he adds that this name came from one Christ, 'who was executed by Procurator Pontius Pilate under Tiberius'.

The notorious persecutor of Christians, Sossianus Hierocles (quoted by the Church Father Lactantius), who was Governor of Phoenicia, Arabia Libanitis, and Bithynia, and a Prefect of Egypt under Diocletian, and so in a way a successor of Pontius Pilate, says off-handedly that Jesus was the leader of a band of highway robbers numbering more than 900 men. A medieval Hebrew copy of a lost version of a work of Josephus also reports that Jesus had more than 2,000 armed followers with him on the Mount of Olives.

It should be noted that in the quotation from Lactantius the word used for highway robber, which sounds contemptuous in translation, was simply a current word for the bands of insurgents who were active against Rome both before and after Jesus.

It was in fact the equivalent in modern terminology of rebel; it recurs even in the Gospels, where it is used concerning the 'companions' crucified together with Jesus. The conventional translation in all editions of the Gospels obscures the historic significance of this basic word, which, for that matter, was applied to Jesus also:

One of the criminals who were hanged railed at him, saying, 'Are you not the Christ? Save yourself and us.' But the other rebuked him, saying, 'Do you not fear God, since you are under the same sentence of condemnation? And we indeed justly; for we are receiving the due reward of our deeds; but this man has done nothing wrong.'

And he said, 'Jesus, remember me when you come into your kingly power' [Lk 23:39-42].

Here the notion of their 'companionship' is expressed in unmistakably concrete terms: the 'same condemnation' is simply reported. It is all that makes sense of the 'criminal' exhorting Jesus to save him because he is the Messiah: why should the Messiah as such save a random criminal?

The phrase, 'This man has done nothing wrong', is clearly incomprehensible in this context, since Jesus, according to the same Gospel, had acknowledged the charge of being King of the Jews; it can only be understood as an interpolation by some later scribe or editor with a notion of piety different from that of Jesus.

But there is also direct evidence in the Gospels of actual arms being carried by Jesus' followers. Here is the Synoptic account of their arrest:

But one of those who stood by drew his sword, and struck the slave of the high priest and cut off his ear. And Jesus said to them, 'Have you come out as against a robber, with swords and clubs to capture me?' [Mk 14:47-48].

And when those who were about him saw what would follow they said, 'Lord, shall we strike with the sword?' And one of them struck the slave of the high priest and cut off his right ear
[Lk 22:49-50].

Then Jesus said to the chief priests and captains of the temple and elders who had come out against him, 'Have you come out as against a robber, with swords and clubs?' [Lk 22:52].

One of those who were with Jesus stretched out his hand and drew his sword, and struck the slave of the high priest, and cut off his ear. Then Jesus said to him, 'Put your sword back into its place; for all who take the sword will perish by the sword' [Mt 26:51-52].

At that hour Jesus said to the crowds, 'Have you come out as against a robber, with swords and clubs to capture me?' [Mt 26:55].

In the previous passage, it is true, *Matthew* has Jesus say, 'Put your sword back into its place,' and so on. This is clearly a later addition; not only is it contradicted by the logic of the situation involved, but in still another of Jesus' sayings that survived the 'pacifying' attempts of later editors and scribes, a background of violence is clearly implied:

[Jesus] said to them, 'But now, let him who has purse take it, and likewise a bag. And let him who has no sword sell his mantle and buy one. For I tell you that this scripture must be fulfilled in me, "And he was reckoned with transgressors," for what is written about me has its fulfilment.' And they said, 'Look, Lord, here are two swords. And he said to them, 'It is enough' [Lk 22:36-38].

Attempts to explain this 'symbolically' or 'allegorically' crumble in the face of the textual evidence, combined with the actual course of events as dimly perceived beyond the texts.

In point of fact the 'fire and sword' passages in *Matthew* and *Luke*, though not so specific as the above-mentioned references to actual weapons being held by Jesus' band, are clearly genuine: like the others they too have survived all conciliationist attempts to smooth them over:

I came to cast fire upon the earth; and would that it were already kindled! ... Do you think that I have come to give peace on earth? No, I tell you, but rather division; for henceforth in one house there will be five divided, three against two and two against three; they will be divided, father against son and son against father, mother against daughter and daughter against her mother, mother-in-law against her daughter-in-law and daughter-in-law against her mother-in-law [Lk 12:49-53].

Do not think that I have come to bring peace on earth; I have not come to bring peace, but a sword. For I have come to set a man against his father, and a daughter against her mother, and a daughter-in-law against her mother-in-law; and a man's foes will be those of his own household [Mt 10:34-37].

There is a further curious reference, in *Luke* (13:4), about eighteen people killed by a fall of the tower of Siloam; this tower of Siloam is considered to have been one of the towers of the city wall of Jerusalem. It was rediscovered during the course of excavations carried on in Jerusalem during 1913-14 under the guidance of the director of the Edmond de Rothschild excavations, Major Ramond Weill, a French officer of engineers and

Professor of Egyptology at the Ecole Pratique des Hautes Etudes of the University of Paris. This conclusion had already been reached by other scholars merely as a result of the examination and comparison of various statements made in Josephus concerning the city wall in the neighbourhood of the pool of Siloam.

Now, it is unlikely that in these fortifications, which had only recently been restored by Herod the Great after the storming of the city by Pompey, a tower would simply have fallen by itself. An earthquake, on the other hand, would surely have been mentioned if only as a profoundly significant portent. Also, there is a rabbinic tradition that no building had ever fallen in Jerusalem, one of the 'ten wonders granted to our fathers in the sacred place', doubtless to be understood more prosaically as a result of the whole of Jerusalem being constructed on solid rock. This curious phrase about the 'eighteen killed by a fall of the tower of Siloam' may be an echo of the siege operation that must have been executed by the Romans in order to recover control of the Temple hill after it had been taken by Jesus and his insurgents. It would have been a siege carried out by the conventional battering ram and *testudo* of the Romans. Why would they have done something like it against their own garrison town unless they had been forced to ?

This suggestion of a siege is paralleled by the 'Galileans' mentioned in the same passage (Lk 13:1) as having had their blood mingled by Pilate with their sacrifices. They may very well have been the group who took and held the Temple, in conjunction with the other operation directed against the Tower of Siloam; the two 'criminals' crucified together with Jesus may have been the insurgents in command of these two points: this not only explains the plea of Jesus' fellow rebel to him to save himself and them, but also provides an understandable background for the other 'criminal' who accepts the will of God: he is prepared to 'share the cup' with Jesus, his leader and king, and thus is given Jesus' promise to be with him in paradise.

Even if this phrase has been embellished by *Luke* with the moralizing tendency that has produced the pious legend of the 'good' and the 'bad' thief, it seems likely that here again there is a murky recollection of deeds of violence.

There is another passage that is even more persuasive in its utter – and inexplicable – simplicity: the casual way this whole operation is simply referred to, without explanation, in *Mark*:

And among the rebels in prison, who had committed murder *in the insurrection*, there was a man called Barabbas [Mk 15:7],

where the words 'in the insurrection' are left without comment. No commentator has ventured to explain as yet this simple phrase in an intelligible, 'non-political' way. It recurs in a parallel passage in *Luke*, where Barabbas is said to have been thrown into prison 'for an insurrection started in the city' (Lk 23:19). This is evidently an attempt to slur over in a plausible way some mutilation or omission in an earlier account that must have been nearer the authentic events.

It should be noted that the above quotation from *Mark* (15:7) does not explicitly say that Barabbas was a rebel himself, but was simply 'among' them. This reticence may contain a hint for us, since the name implies the possibility that Barabbas, which is the Greek spelling of 'Bar Abba', son of the father, or possibly Bar Rabba, son of the Rabbi, may have been arrested by the Romans in error, and in fact was one of the Temple hierarchy. It may of course convey the further hint that some of the Temple hierarchy (the younger men?) were sympathetic to Jesus' enterprise and collaborated with him. In any case, if Barabbas, whose other name, by what sounds like a *very* strange and perplexing coincidence, was *Jesus* Barabbas, was actually one of the Temple hierarchy, we have here an insight into the origin of the inexplicable Roman *custom* of releasing a prisoner on the mob's request. If it was merely a single instance grounded in the mistaken arrest of some Temple dignitary, or his son, who was liberated 'for the feast' – or rather in time to participate in the holiday – this may have been the germ of the custom that was then gradually built up in the literary way mentioned above (page 33). If this is so, then Pilate's question in *Mark* 15:9, asking whether he should release the King of the Jews, may be based on a mere mistake in names: hearing some people

– those Jews opposed to the insurrection, or probably the Temple coterie itself – call for 'Jesus Barabbas', he at first thinks they mean Jesus, and is ruffled by their presumption. Then, on learning that they mean Barabbas, a member of the ostensibly pro-Roman party who had been arrested by mistake, he releases him. Unfortunately, the Gospels contain nothing more substantial to justify this speculation, intriguing as it is.

Once we accustom ourselves to the idea of the violence that must have been involved in the culmination of Jesus' career, we shall be better prepared to cope with further hints at the real nature of his entire enterprise.

Of these hints there is an abundance.

First, let us consider the whole point of Jesus' having disciples at all. Once again this is an element so rooted in Christian tradition that it seems grotesque to question it, but their practical function has actually never attracted nonscholarly attention.

What were Jesus' disciples supposed to do, as a matter of fact?

His purpose in selecting them is never intelligibly explained: the only things he calls on them to do are to cast out devils (that is, heal the sick), and to understand his parables and, presumably, spread them. But it is expressly stated that the parables were incomprehensible to them; when they ask for an explanation they are told that the parables are *meant* to be baffling to the multitudes, though an explanation has been accorded to *them*:

To you has been given the secret of the kingdom of God, but for those outside everything is in parables; so that they may indeed see but not perceive, and may indeed hear but not understand; lest they should turn again, and be forgiven' [Mk 4:11, 12].

Unfortunately, however (disregarding this curiously sadistic explanation of the Jewish failure to accept Jesus, or rather to accept the Church claims concerning him), it is not only those 'outside' who fail to understand the parables; the disciples themselves are evidently baffled:

And he said to them, 'Do you not understand this parable? How then will you understand all the parables?' [Mk 4:13].

These mystical allegories are the sole explanation offered of the Kingdom of God in the Gospels; devised according to Jesus' words to elude the understanding of the masses, they also puzzle the disciples who are supposed to enlighten the masses.

The disciples are a curiously ineffective band altogether: full of vacillation, with no understanding for their leader or his mission (Mk 9:6, 10; 10:13-16, 28-31, 32), who lack his power (Mk 9:18) and quarrel about precedence (Mk 9:34; 10:35-45); one of them, Judas, actually betrays him, and after his arrest they all desert him and flee (Mk 14:50). Even Peter, who seems to be Jesus' favourite, is treated rather cavalierly by the chronicler; though acknowledged as being the first to understand that Jesus was the Messiah, he is reported as failing to see the necessity of the Passion (Mk 8:27-34); he caps his short-comings by actually denying Jesus through fear (Mk 14:66-72).

It is easy to say that the disciples were all too human: so they were, but this curiously denigratory, yet evasive, treatment of them in the earliest tradition suggests precisely their humanity, the reality that existed before the institutional, 'official' myth about them had taken shape. There is something clearly incoherent in the very conception of the 'discipleship' in terms of the Gospel narrative: the institution itself seems to hang in the air, lacking any understandable function. Indeed, the fact that the word 'apostles', a synonym for 'disciples', is used so rarely in the Gospels casts great doubt on the historicity of Jesus' institution of the apostolate, especially since, as we have seen, it is so difficult to grasp its point. It is possible, of course, that the specific number of 'twelve' apostles came about somewhat later as a way of symbolically encompassing Jewry, by means of the twelve Tribes; it is also possible that Jesus merely happened to be left with twelve principal followers at his death.

But even if Jesus did not institute the apostolate himself, it is clearly ancient, since the passage in *Matthew* (19:28) about the twelve Apostles judging the twelve Tribes of Israel obviously belongs to the very earliest stage of the tradition, implying as it does the existence of Jews alone in the Kingdom of God.

But once again that is only in terms of the *present* account: if we imagine that the disciples were not mere preachers of a word that was as incomprehensible to them as it was to the people they were preaching to, but were in fact Jesus' *lieutenants*, the picture is restored to its proper perspective. This may mean lieutenants not only in a military sense but also through being in charge of an organized enterprise that as we have seen also contained a military factor.

It was only later, after the worldly aspects of Jesus' enterprise had to be excised from a tradition that could not tolerate a fiasco, that the authentic function of his disciples was subtracted from the traditional accounts, leaving an unintelligible void.

It is, in fact, only within the framework of this insight into the organized-cum-military character of Jesus' movement that we can understand what might have been the point of his proto-disciples. This perspective will also enable us to understand the sole intelligible reason for Judas' betrayal. If we try to explain his treachery either psychologically or functionally on the basis of the present Gospel account, it remains altogether enigmatic, while if we take as our starting point the existence of an armed contest between an insurrectionary force and the powerful institutions it was assaulting we can begin to see its point.

Judas *did* have something to betray – the hiding-place, not merely of a popular preacher lecturing to multitudes in a vast public square, but of the leader of an armed revolt. If the story of Jesus' coming to Jerusalem only during the day and spending his nights in Bethany (about a mile and a half away from Jerusalem, on the road to Jericho) conserves an element of historic actuality, then perhaps this is to be taken as a somewhat denatured remnant of another recollection – that after the collapse of the insurrection, after the Roman cohort and the Temple police had broken the back of the revolt and restored order, Jesus took refuge there, and it was this hiding-place that Judas betrayed to the authorities.

To be sure, this leads us no further into the psychological tangle; nothing could, since in the total absence of information there is no limit to the number of psychological explanations that can be devised *ad hoc*, but it does provide us with a point of view from which the betrayal is at any rate functionally meaning-ful.

But Judas is not the only eccentric follower of Jesus: even to the unaided eye there is something odd about the number of others. These oddities not only conform with the impression that the seizure of the Temple must have been accomplished through an armed coup; they also hint at the social background of Jesus' movement.

This is the account of their selection:

[Jesus] called his disciples, and chose from them twelve, whom he named apostles; Simon, whom he named Peter, and Andrew, his brother, and James and John, and Philip, and Bartholomew, and Matthew, and Thomas, and James the son of Alphaeus, and Simon who was called the Zealot, and Judas the son of James, and Judas Iscariot, who became a traitor [Lk 6:13-16].

He appointed twelve, to be with him, and to be sent out to preach and have authority to cast out demons: Simon whom he surnamed Peter; James the son of Zebedee and John the brother of James, whom he surnamed Boanerges, that is, sons of thunder; Andrew, and Philip, and Bartholomew, and Matthew, and Thomas, and James the son of Alphaeus, and Thaddeus; and Simon the Cananaean, and Judas Iscariot, who betrayed him [Mk 3:14-19].

The word 'Zealot' has been changed in *Luke* to make it sound as though Simon simply came from Canaan: in the Greek trans-literation there is a slight phonetic similarity between the two words. We are reminded of the case of 'the Nazarene' explained above (page 62).

Now let us consider the implications of this sobriquet – the 'Zealot' (mentioned again in *Acts* 1:13).

Today the Zealots would be called diehards or irreconcilables. They were extremists who refused to accept the rule of Rome or her vassals. The word 'Zealot' itself applies to one who was zealous for the Law; it was taken from a celebrated passage in one of the Old Testament Apocrypha, *1 Maccabees* 2:27-31:

And Matthew cried out in the city with a loud voice, saying 'Whoso-ever is zealous for the Law and maintains the covenant, let him come forth after me.' And he and his sons fled into the mountains and forsook all they had in the city. Then many that sought after justice and judgement went down into the wilderness to dwell there, they and their sons and their wives and their cattle ... they went down into the secret places in the wilderness.

Their inspiration was essentially religious: from their point of view submission to Rome meant lapsing from Jewish monotheism; it was, in fact, a form of apostasy. Their attitude was ultimately based on the celebrated 'royalty law' of *Deuteronomy* (17:14–15), which forbade Jews to submit to the domination of foreigners (pagans).

Because of their intransigence – compounded, of course, by their ultimate bloodstained defeat – they have gone down into history, at least most history, with a bad name. They are generally referred to in writings concerning this period as 'robbers', 'highwaymen', 'criminals', and so on, words that, as indicated above, almost invariably mean militant insurgents against the foreign power of Rome and her vassals.

At the extreme limit of the spectrum of Jewish political life, they came to the surface after the conquest of Judea by Pompey in 63 B.C. For a long time they undoubtedly had the sympathy of the bulk of the Jewish population, including the popular religious party of the Pharisees; they were, in fact, Pharisees themselves – what might be called their extremist wing.

After the Roman conquest it was the Pharisee elders who had gone to the Romans and said that, in view of the Mosaic injunction not to be ruled by anyone but the priests of their God, Jews ought not to be ruled by a king. It is easy to imagine what the Roman reaction to this was; in any case no attention was paid to this request put forth by the Jewish 'moderates'; the extremist opposition was inevitably strengthened.

But it was the half-Jewish satrap of Rome, Herod the Great (reigned 37–4 B.C.), who fanned the smouldering resentment of the Jews into a flame that ultimately fused the intransigent elements of the country into an actual organized group. This group remained the most dynamic and unruly element in Jewish national life until its disintegration.

These diehards had already been inflamed by the Romans' importing into Judea all the characteristic Hellenistic institutions – the gymnasium, the arena, and, most outrageous of all, the trophies (images to be worshipped), which were an abomination to pious Jews. Herod's idolatry and bloodshed merely brought their public opposition to a head.

The Zealot movement was a movement even before its members became known as Zealots; they were also known as 'daggermen' (*Sicarii*) because of their custom of carrying daggers beneath their cloaks. One of their first public acts, when the movement began to assume an organized form, was an attempt to assassinate Herod. Ten citizens of Jerusalem tried to use these daggers, only to have their plot betrayed and to be tortured to death themselves.

Another significant incident occurred towards the end of Herod's life, when he ordered a large golden eagle to be set up over the great gate of the Temple in such a way that it would gleam resplendently in the rays of the sun. This was violently opposed by two masters of the Law, Judas ben Sarifai and Matthew ben Margaloth, who exhorted their followers to put a stop to it. Together with forty young men they pulled the eagle down: they were all burned to death.

The chief initial inspirer of this dissident wing in Jewish life is generally taken to have been a certain Judas the Galilean, or Gaulanite, whose whole family was celebrated for its intransigence. His father Hezekiah, with a group of these 'bandits', had been executed by Herod, and Judas and his sons and grandsons spent their lives in fanatical opposition to the idolatrous Roman power. Judas first took up arms against the Romans in the footsteps of his father in A.D. 5; by this time a whole system of organized assassination and violence had been instituted in pursuit of these politico-religious aims.

It was the political element in their activity that earned them their unfavourable reputation: most of what we know about them has percolated down to us in the writings of Josephus, who as a professional client of the Romans takes every possible opportunity to sneer at them. Nevertheless, in one of his more neutral remarks he gives us the summary of their philosophy: 'Others again [the Zealots] call no one Lord except God, even though one should torture or kill them.'

Herod died in 4 B.C. to be succeeded by his son Archelaus

(reigned 4 B.C.–A.D. 6), under whom Judea began to swarm with these 'robber bands'. The Passover of Archelaus's succession was celebrated in Jerusalem by a vast slaughter of pilgrims; when Quirinius, Governor of Syria (A.D. 6–7) introduced the census (A.D. 5 or 6: mentioned in *Luke* 2:1–2), which, as a device for increasing the burden of alien taxation, incensed the Jews still further, Judas the Galilean began harassing the Roman power itself.

He was not the only prominent rebel: in Peraea a man called Simon, a former slave of Herod's renowned for his good looks and physical strength, came to the fore, as well as a shepherd with the odd name of Athrongas, also celebrated for his gigantic stature and extraordinary physical strength.

Both these men put forth their claims to the rule of Judea. They were both executed, but Judas the Galilean held out 'on the outside' – in the mountains and deserts, even after the revolt of 4 B.C. was crushed by the Roman general Varus and thousands of the insurgents were crucified.

When Quirinius introduced his census, Judas the Galilean reappeared; his end is obscure, but his work was carried on by his sons and by the Zealots; the latter growing more and more desperate, especially during the period from A.D. 49 to 64. Matters finally came to a head in A.D. 66, with the next to the last of the Jewish wars against Rome, under Tiberius Alexander, which led to the extinction of the Jewish state in A.D. 70. The final revolt was led by a son of Judas the Galilean's, Menahem, who was killed by rivals in his own camp on his way to Jerusalem to be crowned King of the Jews. The Galilean's other two sons, Simon and Jacob, were crucified by the Romans in A.D. 67.

As Roman oppression increased, one diehard after another presented himself to his tormented people as the promised Messiah. The Zealots, essentially Pharisees themselves who had begun with the support, either explicit or tacit, of the main current of Pharisee opinion, as mentioned above, were ultimately, as they grew more and more fanatical, outlawed by the Pharisees as well as by everyone else.

In short, the presence of an avowed Zealot among the disciples of Jesus is illuminating. There must have been something about

Jesus' movement that was attractive to this extremist wing of the opposition to Rome.

It is not a case of a random, former Zealot turning up among the disciples of Jesus. There were others.

Even if one disregards the temptation to look upon the otherwise mysterious nickname applied to James and John the sons of Zebedee, 'surnamed Boanerges, that is, sons of thunder', as an obvious reference to their violent natures, the extraordinary name given to Peter himself, precisely at a moment when Jesus on the eve of the decisive action in Jerusalem, is making him in effect his deputy, is intriguing.

In a celebrated passage (claimed by the Roman Catholic Church as its divine sanction) Jesus says this to Simon Peter, when the latter, for the first time, acknowledges him as the Messiah:

Blessed are you, Simon Bar Jona! ... I will give you the keys of the kingdom of heaven, and whatever you bind on earth shall be bound in heaven, and whatever you loose on earth shall be loosed in heaven [Mt 16:17, 19].

Aside from Jesus' plain meaning that in this ancient metaphor he was assigning the deputyship of his status, however conceived, to Simon Peter, what is arresting is the curious name 'Bar-Jona', usually translated as 'Simon son of John'.

Now, the famous proto-Zealot referred to above, Judas the Galilean, is occasionally referred to as a 'man living on the outside'. This curious phrase is clarified by another remark, in the Talmud, about a nephew of the famous Rabbi Yohanan ben Zakkai who was called the 'dagger-man', and was the head of the *baryonim* of Jerusalem.

The word *baryonim* comes from an Aramaic word meaning open country; they were those people living in the open country outside the towns, that is, the outcasts, outlaws, and extremists that the country was full of. Paul himself was mistaken for such a daggerman by a Roman captain of a cohort:

Are you not the Egyptian ... who recently stirred up a revolt and led the four thousand daggermen [or assassins] out into the wilderness? [*Acts* 21:38].

It is plain from the context that these *baryonim* were similar in all respects to the Zealots; they are doubtless to be thought of as a faction of the same opposition to Rome. Both Zealots and *baryonim* would thus be cognate with the so-called 'fourth school of philosophy' euphemistically referred to by Josephus in addition to the Pharisees, Sadducees, and Essenes.

In the celebrated passage in *Matthew,* the word *bar* is not to be taken as the Aramaic for 'son of'; the name Bar-Yona is in all likelihood to be understood, not as Simon the *son* of John, but as an echo of Simon Peter's original calling, that is, Simon the *Baryon*, Simon the extremist, the daggerman, the outlaw, that is, an adherent, like Simon the Zealot, of the ideas expressed by Judas the Galilean or someone like him.

This question of living 'on the outside' is not a mere matter of geography. From a devout Jewish point of view 'leaving the towns' was profoundly significant as a method of avoiding the apostasy, or the sin, or at the very least the impurity, of living under idol-worshippers.

For in view of the power of Rome there were only two ways for such pious Jews to follow the Torah (the Deuteronomic 'royalty law'): defeat the Romans or flee.

Since the entire inhabited world was Roman and subject to the rule of the 'Prince of this world', the only way of eluding apostasy was to renounce all and go into the desert, to be purified there like the ancient Hebrews.

There was, to be sure, a third way – that of the quietists who were content to wait patiently until it suited God to liberate his people from the pagan yoke. This meant allowing oneself to be steeped in sin, with no excuse except that of weakness. This quietist course naturally had the advantage of not inflaming the authorities; individual quietists could be allowed to creep harmlessly about. From the Roman point of view they were ideal. Quietist Jews, though like other devout worshippers of Yahweh they too loathed the iniquity of their pagan overlordship, did not come to violent ends.

We are, accordingly, back once again at the stark fact of Jesus' violent death; the savagery of his sentence is finally explained.

We are forced to the conclusion that Jesus came to his cruel death for reasons that in Roman eyes were eminently compelling. Even the sketchiest attempt to fill in the social background against which Jesus was executed highlights the hollowness of the 'misunderstanding' that is conventionally put forth to explain the crucifixion – that is, the notion that blind, ignorant men were bent on destroying a paragon of abstract and timeless virtue because he had a message beyond their comprehension.

However timeless Jesus' ethical message might have been – however timeless, that is, the ethical code of Judaism – he involved himself and his followers in an organized enterprise that had its roots in the circumstances of his own specific society. He had placed himself squarely in the long line of Jewish religious insurgents against the power of the idolatrous Roman state.

We can now see the climax of Jesus' career in an unexpected light; by entering Jerusalem with a group of armed men large enough, or powerful enough, or with enough popular support to overcome the defences of its headquarters, he arrogated sovereign power to himself. Whatever his own interpretation of this, whatever his specific motivation, whatever his ultimate purpose, this act of armed and organized violence was obviously bound to bring down on his head the swift retaliation of the Roman authorities.

From the Roman point of view, his being described on the cross as 'King of the Jews' was a simple statement of fact; there was nothing otherworldly for them about it at all – it referred to a basic act of insurrection, which was punished as such.

Nor was it only the Roman power that was threatened by Jesus' enterprise: the seizure of the Temple was directed just as much or more at the actual priesthood in charge of it, and, in a larger sense, doubtless at the entire Jewish aristocracy, which however unwillingly, had become an outpost of the Roman state in Judea.

Thus, when Jesus' forces seized and held the Temple he fell foul of the Jewish aristocracy and of the priesthood. For while as indicated above he did not disapprove of the Temple cult *in principle*, and had no theory of reform, there was undoubtedly an element of social protest in his movement.

It would be rash to overemphasize the social teaching of some-one who thought this world due for liquidation from one day to the next, but there is an undeniable note of indignation through-out the Gospels at the condition of the poor. It seems evident that Jesus was a prophet of the people; he represented the 'humble of Israel' and the *ammei ha-ares*. Within the framework of Judaism he was on the side of the downtrodden.

Hence it is more than likely that his attack on the Temple had the additional motivation of protest against social unrighteous-ness, as well as of a prophetically inspired aversion to the element of idolatry in the images on the Roman and other coins kept in the Temple. There is a revealing passage in Josephus that gives a startling picture of the oppression of the poor of the time by the rich, *via* the Temple: he reports that the insurgents wanted 'to destroy the moneylenders' tallies and to prevent the exaction of debts, in order to win over a host of grateful debtors and to rouse the poor against the wealthy with impunity.'

Indeed, the passage in *Mark* (6:8) expressly, forbidding his disciples to carry money, and enjoining them to take nothing for their journey but a staff, with no bread, no bag, and no money in their belts, may even be a distorted recollection of Jesus' aver-sion to money *as such*.

In the Gospel account the genuine, compelling motives for the attack on the Temple have been blurred beyond recognition. The only things left are the banal slogans about the transformation of the 'universal house of prayer' into a 'den of burglars', as though it were a mere question of ethical theory divorced from the turbulence of the times. In the Synoptics generally, as a matter of fact, the chief motive underlying the resentment of the Temple authorities is given as Jesus' lack of a rabbinical educa-tion. The very simple-mindedness of this 'explanation' high-lights the suppression of the authentic background of the Temple occupation.

The violence involved in the seizure of the Temple implies that it was deeply rooted in the social conflicts of the time, ideo-logized by religion as of course they were. The squeezing of the poorest classes by the middlemen interposed between them and the Temple hierarchy must have contributed to the explosive character of a movement that was bound to involve Jesus in a clash not only with the Romans but also with the Jewish aristocracy. The populace was exploited in the Temple, for instance, not only by its various exactions, but doubtless by such devices as a sliding scale of payments, in which the beasts bought by the pilgrims were assessed at a maximum price, while those who were selling animals for Temple disposition would always be told their animals had all sorts of blemishes making them unfit for sacrificial use.

The Temple, the unassailable and impregnable seat of socio-religious authority, must have provided parasitic priests and middlemen with an effective shield against any nonviolent popular protest. It was Jesus' attempt to smash this shield, as part of his larger enterprise of presiding over the installation of the Kingdom of God in defiance of the Roman power, that set in motion the events leading to his downfall.

Moreover, as we have seen, Jesus was entirely in harmony with the prophetic tradition, still alive in Israel, that had already completely spiritualized the relations of the Jews with their God. The entire Temple traffic in wine, oil, incense, wood, and animals for sacrifice might have seemed odious to him, at least in its exaggerated forms, whatever his acceptance of the Temple cult in principle.

Thus, his enterprise was bound to collide with the Roman and the Jewish authorities simultaneously even though Jesus thought himself a faithful interpreter of Judaism. The moment he resorted to action, as distinct from prophecy, he defied all institutional life and was, in fact, on the highroad to adventure.

9

RECONSTRUCTION CONTINUED: JESUS AND JOHN

I have resisted the temptation of 'filling in' this shadowy picture with persuasive, imaginatively elaborated details. As indicated, there is actually no source material for a full biography of a living, breathing Jesus. Even his specific actions are hidden from us by the dearth of information, in which random fragments are disclosed to us only through the distorting mirror of the earliest Christian tradition. The nuggets of historic actuality, or at least probability, that might be recovered are completely silted over by layers of later tradition: they remain isolated oddments with few interconnexions.

Since a connected narrative is impossible, it seems best to be content with those salient points that in accordance with our cardinal criterion of authenticity are most plausible. We thus return to Jesus' death, as the one most unquestionable, most solid and most significant event of his otherwise obscure life; we can now retrace our steps once again to see whether our criterion can help assemble still other probabilities.

Let us take up the thread of our analysis. We have seen that the presence of at least two and more probably four Zealots, or Zealotically-minded men in the small group of Jesus' followers must have had profound meaning.

Now, in considering this question of violence as a factor in Jesus' movement, the violence that also ended John the Baptist's career cannot be overlooked; it leads us to the consideration of an important fact.

For the likelihood is that the Baptist was also a *baryon* – an extremist living 'on the outside'. This is probably the real significance of the passage:

And there *went out* to him all the country of Judea, etc. [Mk 1:5, also Mt 3:5].

This sounds innocuous, but it actually refers to a form of

sedition, perhaps echoed, as we shall see, in Jesus' own command to 'renounce all and follow' him.

For in view of the Baptist's violent end, it is inherently improbable that his message could have been construed at the time as a mere exhortation to personal virtue, an admonition to wait for a divine miracle. This would doubtless have been welcomed by the hated authorities as a form of pious quietism – 'pie in the sky'.

What is far more likely is that John was regarded as a dangerous agitator and that the end he came to was appropriate. This is perhaps demonstrated most clearly by the celebrated passage from *Matthew* and *Luke* already referred to on page 101 in another connexion:

Among those born of women there has risen no one greater than John the Baptist. . . . From the days of John the Baptist until now the kingdom of heaven has suffered violence, and men of violence take it by force. For all the prophets and the law prophesied until John [Mt 11:11–13].

The law and prophets were until John; since then the good news of the kingdom of God is preached, and every one enters it violently [Lk 16:16].

Once the idea is accepted that John the Baptist met his end for a very good reason – from the point of view of his executioners – it is possible to grasp the meaning of these otherwise cryptic words. The implication is clear that before the Baptist, people were satisfied with talk; he was the first to *do* something.

We can see now who the 'men of violence' are: Jesus is thinking of the persistent tumults that began to proliferate under Herod and reached a high pitch under his successor Archelaus and afterward; he is referring to the Zealots, the guerrilla fighters for Jewish independence. The Kingdom of God that they tried to 'take by force' was the attempt to re-establish a national kingdom by the grace of God – in other words, a Messianic theocracy.

Now we can appreciate the inwardness of Josephus' singularly reserved reference to the Baptist as being no more than a 'good man'. Josephus emphatically implies that the Baptist was perfectly innocuous politically; there is no suggestion in his account that John was animated by any nationalistic aims or in general by any political designs. What Josephus is saying, for the benefit of his Greco-Roman readers, who were doubtless aware to some extent of the prevalence of these Messianic Zealots in Judea, is that John the Baptist was not one of them. Since Josephus himself was violently opposed to all forms of Messianism, in which he foresaw the doom of his people – with some justice, it must be admitted restrospectively – he is systematically unreliable whenever he refers to them: he is famous for his apologetic, 'harmless' explanations of Jewish behaviour in such a way as not to arouse any suspicion of Jewish intransigence, rebelliousness, and so on, in the minds of his pagan readers. Consequently his portrait of John as an abstract moralist is inherently suspect, for in a milieu where everyone was expecting cataclysmic events, and the authorities were on the watch for anything that might seem to them seditious, it is scarcely conceivable that a purely abstract preacher, such as Josephus tries to present us with in his picture of the Baptist, could have arisen in the first place, or that if he had the authorities would not have been overjoyed by the addition of a soothing unguent to the turbulent brew they were trying to calm. If his abstractions had been as harmless as they sound he would doubtless have been welcomed.

But Josephus gives himself away: the phrase he uses about John is unintentionally revealing. He says John exhorted the Jews to apply themselves to the practice of virtue and justice between themselves and of piety towards God, and called upon them 'to be united by a baptism'. Now, the Greek original of this phrase is *baptismo synienai*; the verb unmistakably implies a ritual of intiation, which in its turn implies an association of some kind. In this case, since Josephus, despite his reluctance, is also compelled to report that Herod intervened, this association must obviously be considered a seditious group of some sort; it is John's influence over the people that is explained as having led Herod to jail and execute him (page 67).

The framework of the Baptist's activity must have been the wilderness, 'the outside'; the reason for his followers flocking to him there was the religious impulse referred to above – their desire to avoid pollution by idol worshippers, in accordance with the 'royalty law', and the adoption of a 'good life'. There is an ancient biography of the Baptist according to which he advised his followers to 'leave the towns', a programme that would of course have alarmed the authorities if it had assumed sizeable proportions. This would have been a 'popular secession'; they would naturally have intervened, and equally naturally with violence.

This circumstance, together with the fact that the apparently general exhortation to purity was in fact an intiation rite into a disaffected group, clarifies a celebrated passage in *Luke* :

[John] said therefore to the multitudes that came out to be baptized by him, 'You brood of vipers! Who warned you to flee from the wrath to come? Bear fruits that befit repentance, and do not begin to say to yourselves, "We have Abraham as our father"; for I tell you, God is able from these stones to raise up children to Abraham. Even now the axe is laid to the root of the trees; every tree therefore that does not bear good fruit is cut down and thrown into the fire.'
And the multitudes asked him, 'What then shall we do?' And he answered them, 'He who has two coats, let him share with him who has none; and he who has food, let him do likewise.' Tax collectors also came to be baptized, and said to him, 'Teacher, what shall we do?' And he said to them, 'Collect no more than is appointed you.' Soldiers also asked him, 'And we, what shall we do?' And he said to them, 'Rob no one by violence or by false accusation, and be content with your wages' [Lk 3:7-14].

The speech, which has always been interpreted conventionally as a mere homily of a general nature, an exhortation to the good life, is plainly rather watery and banal: but it has some point if we note that the word translated here as 'soldiers' (in Greek, *stratiotai*) in reality means 'combatants' (*strateuomenoi*). If we assume that John was not merely exhorting some anonymous multitudes to live better, but was actually giving specific instructions for the conduct of a guerrilla campaign being conducted on a national basis against a hated oppressor, we may perceive its point. The 'multitudes' reported as asking John for advice thus represent the swarms of adherents who had followed him to 'the outside', and were being given instructions by him how to repair their sins, that is, how to resist the idol-worshippers. This would also explain the curious inclusion of tax collectors, singled out as a category of those seeking advice: the word translated as 'tax collector' is to be understood as indicating approval of taxes in a worthy cause; only the Roman super-taxation for inherently impure purposes was execrated.

John's baptism, in short, was an instance of what has been referred to above: for the followers of the diehard anti-Roman movements among the Jews the baptism was intended to be the rite of initiation into a new Israel. This is why, when the 'multitudes' came to him for baptism and purification, claiming a special privilege as children of Abraham, he specifically discounted their old-fashioned Jewish status as giving them any priority whatever in the Kingdom of God. The sin of serving the Roman idol worshippers had reduced them to the level of the heathen; John's baptism was meant to purify them of this cardinal sin and establish them in the *new* Israel. This is the basic and particular – not general – meaning of the phrase baptism in 'the name of the Lord'. John called for recognition of God as the true and sole ruler of the world, and of the national king, the Messiah, while at the same time he called for the false gods of this world to be abjured. As John put it, according to Josephus, the Jews could be governed only by the Almighty who had sent him.

This is clearly the logical deduction from the Deuteronomic 'royalty law': it clarifies John's baptism as being in effect an oath of allegiance to the one true God and his Messiah, and it forms the 'way of the law' that was practised by John the Baptist and Judas the Galilean.

Thus, John's admonition to the 'soldiers' in *Luke* 3:14 must be the remnant of the sort of pep talk made by an army chaplain. The baptism in the new army of God was actually a soldier's oath. This was the origin of the use of the word 'sacrament' in the later Christian church: sacrament meant a soldier's oath of allegiance, and John's baptismal confession was the oath of the soldiers entering the army of the fighters for the Messiah.

Thus the new Israel, as foreshadowed by both John the Baptist and the Zealots, was to be regenerated by John's baptism into a 'new covenant' with the ancient national, now universal, God of the Jews: those 'children of Abraham' who did not take the oath and thus undergo the rite of lustration for the army of the Messiah were to be regarded as backsliders into heathenism.

Incidentally, the antiquity of this fragment about God being 'able from these stones to raise up children to Abraham,' is demonstrated by the Hebrew pun concealed in the Greek translation: 'stones' = *abanim* in Hebrew, 'children' = *banim*.

This is the significance of John's rite of baptism as an instance of the old Jewish baptism prescribed for all converts: since the unregenerate Jews still serving the Roman idol worshippers were considered apostates they had to be treated in the same way as pagans seeking conversion to Judaism.

In terms of the epoch this baptism was thus the first outward sign of the desire for 'liberty' that John was accused of inciting the people to seize for themselves. This 'liberty' was actually the Kingdom of God, as against the kingdom of this world, that is, heathenism, idolatry, and temporal power and wickedness.

To be sure, John, like his follower Jesus, also believed in the imminence of the Kingdom of God; doubtless he meant his baptism, by virtue of this reinitiation, to be a way of escape from the 'wrath to come' as well – the Last Judgement. It was a 'washing for salvation' – salvation as understood in the pre-Christian concrete sense of being saved from the destruction that was about to be visited on 'this world' of sin and violence.

Hence Jesus' celebrated eulogy of John the Baptist as the greatest man who ever lived is full of significance. John could hardly have been referred to so extravagantly simply for heralding the coming of someone else; it must mean that Jesus regarded him as the father of the movement exemplified by the Zealots – the first effective leader to arise in the campaign to restore the Jews to their ancient independence. In other words, looking back on this from our own vantage point, John is to be considered as having represented the same form of politico-religious dissidence as Judas the Galilean. He was doubtless a rival or a successor.

A different picture is beginning to emerge of the relationship between Jesus and John: both preachers of the imminent advent of the Kingdom of God, both at loggerheads with the powers that be, and – both executed by the authorities.

But their methods must have been different. Jesus, after following John or collaborating with him for some time after his baptism, must have fallen out with him later, presumably about strategy.

What could have been the point of difference?

Let us consider this curious question of baptism, of such cardinal significance to the Christian religion that was to develop after Jesus' death but that Jesus himself never seems to have used.

I have mentioned the odd discrepancy in the fourth Gospel concerning Jesus' attitude towards baptism; Jesus baptizes (Jn 3:22; 4:1) but doesn't (Jn 4:2).

It must be recalled that there is not a single instance throughout the first three Gospels that shows Jesus either baptizing or preaching baptism, with the exception of the famous passage:

Go therefore and make disciples of all nations, baptizing them in the name of the Father and of the Son and of the Holy Spirit [Mt 28:19].

This is put into the mouth of the Risen Christ; all independent critics agree it cannot be attributed to Jesus.

Consequently the passage in the fourth Gospel is decisive:

Now when the Lord knew that the Pharisees had heard that Jesus was making and baptizing more disciples than John (although Jesus himself did not baptize, but only his disciples), he left Judea and departed again to Galilee [Jn 4:1-3].

Here the immediate disclaimer of baptism – 'Jesus himself did not baptize, but only his disciples' – is bound to carry conviction. By the time this was written down, baptism had already become a basic rite of initiation into the Christian community, and both the original author of the fourth Gospel and its later editors could not have failed to attribute this cardinal institution to the Saviour unless the weight of the tradition they were being guided by could not be gainsaid.

The simple phrase is all the more significant since it appears in the form of a correction of a prior statement (Jn 3:22) that

Jesus *had* baptized, and in fact had baptized more disciples than John ever had (Jn 4:1).

It seems sensible to assume that by Jesus' having baptized more disciples than John the pious writer was symbollically referring to the *results* of Jesus' preaching, that is, the number of Christians in his own day; the moment he is recalled to a consideration of Jesus' personal practice he enters the correction directly into the text.

There can be little doubt that whatever may have been Jesus' practice when he was a disciple of the Baptist's, when he embarked on his own campaign he did not use baptism.

Now, there is a reference in the fourth Gospel to a dispute between John's followers and a 'Jew' (or 'Judean') over purifying:

... a discussion arose between John's disciples and a Jew over purifying. And they came to John, and said to him, 'Rabbi, he who was with you beyond the Jordan, to whom you bore witness, here he is, baptizing, and all are going to him.' John answered, 'No one can receive anything except what is given him from heaven. You yourselves bear me witness, that I said, I am not the Christ, but I have been sent before him. ... He must increase, but I must decrease'
[Jn 3:25–28, 30].

Scholars have long thought that the original of this curious passage must have read, not 'a Jew', but 'the followers of Jesus'. It is hardly likely that the change was made as the result of a mere copyist's error: the whole passage is clearly one of those designed to establish a hierarchical relationship between Jesus and John in favour of Jesus.

But the relationship between the two groups seems incoherently recorded, even if we were to disregard the singular disclaimer of Jesus' use of baptism in the passage about Jesus leaving Judea. It must be assumed that the unintelligible, unexplained, unmotivated, and obviously superfluous mention of the 'Pharisees' in the above quotation (Jn 4:1) is to give Jesus a plausible reason for leaving Judea without involving John's disciples.

Accordingly, the original must have read:

When the Lord learned that ... he left Judea.

Now, what Jesus learned could not have been the dispute itself, since he would have been a party to it; the passage must refer to his having learned that John himself had found out about it.

If Jesus and John were collaborators in a military-religious movement, and Jesus left Judea for competing with John, he must have done so as a consequence of a basic division of opinion.

Either Jesus wanted to avoid competing, or appearing to compete with John, or else John's original authentic declaration about Jesus must have been altogether different from what has come down to us. John could not have sponsored Jesus after their divergence, as the present text reads; he must have disavowed him. John did not say, 'He must increase, but I must decrease' (Jn 3:30): he said the opposite.

This is surely the significance of the dispute about purification, which in the traditional text sounds like a fine-spun debate about homiletics.

Jesus must have split with John, after their collaboration, because he no longer shared his views on baptism.

We have seen that baptism was a rite of initiation into a religious group organized to oppose the authorities through physical secession from their territorial jurisdiction. Therefore a dispute about baptism was not a fine point of doctrine alone; it must have stood for a certain type of military organization, as well as a conception of strategy with respect to the prime task of combating the hated oppressors. In our present text all that survives of what must have been a complex situation is the one point of baptism, which by the time the Gospels were written had lost its primitive significance and sounded like a mere question of ritual. Its presence in the text, however veiled, enables us to perceive that in the divergence of views epitomized in this mutilated reference to baptism, Jesus' departure had some basic significance. It could only have had that significance if it had been preceded by collaboration.

In short, the relationship between Jesus and John culminated in a rupture.

When Jesus preached and baptized in Peraea with John, he had done so as a disciple of John: it had not been his own baptism; he had not been launching his own movement. The baptism given by him as John's disciple had been the rite of initiation into the New Elect of Israel by way of secession from the sway of the idolaters.

When he left John he left John's movement and John's ritual, including baptism. Henceforth he baptized no more; baptism and all it stood for was left behind in Jesus' own career. He was launching a wholly independent enterprise, in which baptism as a sign of secession and reinitiation no longer had a role to play.

The purification at issue is no mere cleansing of the soul; it is a reference to a basic organizational and programmatic question that led to the split between Jesus and John. The Baptist stayed 'on the outside', in the wilderness, preaching his own type of seditious secession. Jesus went back to the towns, back to civilization, consorted with 'tax collectors and sinners' and 'stirred up the people' in the settled areas of Galilee and Judea.

John met his death for involving his followers in a massive secession from the state, while Jesus was crucified for storming the Kingdom of God in Jerusalem, the very citadel of his religion as well as the capital of the secular régime.

The rupture between Jesus and John so blurrily implied in the fourth Gospel is a historic fact of great importance. Its retention in the text of the Gospels, despite its conflict with the whole evolution of the official view of Christianity concerning the relations between the two men, vouches for its historicity.

Still other signs of divergence between the two movements have been preserved in our Gospels:

The Baptist is described as having been an ascetic, while the point is made repeatedly that Jesus' life was in complete contrast:

John came neither eating nor drinking, and they say, 'He has a demon'; the Son of man came eating and drinking, and they say, 'Behold, a glutton and a drunkard, a friend of tax-collectors and sinners!' [Mt 11:18, also Lk 7:33].

Here is another passage:

Now John's disciples and the Pharisees were fasting; and people came and said to [Jesus], 'Why do John's disciples and the disciples of the Pharisees fast, but your disciples do not fast?' [Mk 2:18].

This would seem to indicate a clear-cut awareness of the separateness of these three groups, or rather, the singling out of John's followers and Jesus' from the broad body of Pharisees, as well as an awareness of a basic difference of ritual in addition to the disagreement on baptism.

There is a point of added interest in the omission of John's name in this account; it seems to imply that John had already disappeared from the scene either after his death or his imprisonment. It was his followers who were carrying on his movement.

There is another revealing hint of this split between the two men preserved in *Matthew* (11:2–6), where John, while in prison, is supposed to send messengers to ask Jesus whether he is in fact the awaited Messiah: Jesus refers to his deeds, presumably as 'signs' of his status: the episode ends with his saying, 'Blessed is he who takes no offence at me.'

The chronicler's failure to report the reaction here either of John or of his disciples must be considered of paramount importance: it can only mean that the response to Jesus' claims, even if interpreted as a sort of code referring to Messianic status, was reserved if not downright negative. Otherwise the pious chronicler would surely have been delighted to reiterate this point, already made elsewhere, that John was merely Jesus' forerunner and acknowledged himself as such.

Probably the chief reason our present text is in such confusion is that one of the primitive documents had originated in a Baptist milieu (see page 68), and thus had to be docked and contorted in order to make it fit the aim of the Christian writer. The object of this conflation of sources, as indicated above, was to retain the advantage of John's authority over his still-existent movement while subordinating it to that of Jesus. Thus, in accordance with the interest of the later Christian community in harmonizing the claims of the two leaders in this way, pains are taken to indicate that John's mission was *also* divine:

The chief priests and the scribes and the elders ... said to [Jesus], 'By what authority are you doing these things, or who gave you this authority to do them?' Jesus said to them, 'I will ask you a question; answer me, and I will tell you by what authority I do these things.

Was the baptism of John from heaven or from men ? Answer me.'
And they argued with one another, 'If we say, "From heaven," he
will say, "Why then did you not believe him ?" But shall we say,
"From men ?"' – they were afraid of the people, for all held that John
was a real prophet. So they answered Jesus. 'We do not know.' And
Jesus said to them, 'Neither will I tell you by what authority I do
these things' [Mk 11 :27–33 ; also Mt 21 :23–27 and Lk 20 :1–7].

Aside from the engaging and characteristically wily casuistry
shown here by Jesus, perhaps the most important point is not
only that Jesus thought John had divine authority but also that
the chief priests themselves were compelled to adopt such a
defensive position because of the general popularity of the Baptist; it is an indication of the strength of his movement, and a
further hint that Jesus himself was in a strong current of popular
favour.

The link between the two, on the other hand, is kept under
careful control: while it is reported that Jesus is sometimes
thought to be John resuscitated, the point is made elsewhere that
John 'was not the light, but came to bear witness to the light'
(Jn 1 :8); because of its insistent tone we must assume this remark to have been a shaft aimed specifically at the surviving
disciples of the Baptist. We have here a hint, not perhaps about
the Baptist himself, but about the followers he left behind whom
the early Christians were intent on absorbing, naturally on their
own terms.

Perhaps another precision of their relationship is to be seen
in the curious remark Jesus makes about the Baptist, after eulo-
gizing him as the greatest man ever born : 'Yet he who is least in
the Kingdom of Heaven is greater than he' (Mt 11 :11).

This, which sounds like a rather peculiar way of compliment-
ing someone, may be more intelligible if it is translated, as some
scholars have suggested, as 'Yet his junior in heaven is greater than he.' It is assumed that this 'junior' is Jesus himself:
after having followed John in his attempt to install the Kingdom of God, Jesus now regarded himself as leader of the movement.

Thus we begin to discern the outline of two movements, both
characterized by opposition to the secular order of the time, the

idolatrous Roman Empire and its vassals, but differing in methods of approach. Since we can only get at the substance of Jesus' activity from the utterly different perspective of the chronicles set down after his divinization, it is naturally impossible to arrive at a view of details that were in consequence either falsified or forgotten.

If John the Baptist called on Jews to renounce life under a pagan overlord, and be baptized into the New Israel of those awaiting the Messiah, and if Jesus, after collaborating with him for some time, finally changed his mind and went to seek a decision in the sacred city that was the only place such a decision could manifest itself, we have here a comprehensible order of events, elusive though its details must be.

It seems likely that the contrast between Jesus' apparently quietist – 'meek and mild' – statements and his 'fire and sword' statements must somehow be linked with this, though the sequence is bound to remain obscure.

Jesus might simply have abandoned John's movement, for instance, and started one of his own, more dynamic and aimed directly at the centre of secular and religious power in Jerusalem. In that case we should have to ascribe his 'quietist' statements, as they are preserved in the Gospels, to the period when he may still have been gathering support for his new enterprise: this would also explain the curious ambiguity or secrecy about his intentions – his admonition to his disciples to say nothing about his special status, his speaking in parables, that is, innuendoes, and his going about the country as though in flight, all of which seems to relate to someone trying to avoid attention.

His attitude seems to have changed abruptly:

What I tell you in the dark, utter in the light; and what you hear whispered, proclaim upon the housetops. . . . whoever denies me before men, I also will deny before my Father who is in heaven
[Mt 10:27–33].

Is a lamp brought in to be put under a bushel, or under a bed? . . . For there is nothing hid, except to be made manifest
[Mk 4:21, 22; also Lk 8:16 *et seq.*; Mt 5:14 *et seq.*].

This sounds as though it meant that the whole project was out in the open and that Jesus was now a publicly proclaimed leader of a movement of disaffection. Having begun by preaching the 'better righteousness', at some point he changed his mind and moved on to Jerusalem and death.

A passage that seems to sum up the transition is the following:

[Jesus] said to [the disciples], 'When I sent you out with no purse or bag or sandals, did you lack anything?' They said, 'Nothing.' He said to them, '*But now*, let him ... who has no sword sell his mantle and buy one' [Lk 22:35–36].

The 'but now' seems pregnant with reversal.

The difficulty is that it is impossible to tell the sequence of stratification in the various layers that make up the Gospels; some of the elements in them, after all, come from the time Jesus was actually associated with the Baptist, and thus may be an echo of the Baptist's own summons, the basic slogan they had in common, 'Repent, for the kingdom of God is at hand.'

One of Jesus' most celebrated exhortations is the following:

Therefore I tell you, do not be anxious about your life, what you shall eat or what you shall drink, nor about your body, what you shall put on. Is not life more than food, and the body more than clothing? Look at the birds of the air: they neither sow nor reap nor gather into barns, and yet your heavenly Father feeds them. Are you not of more value than they? And which of you by being anxious can add one cubit to his span of life? And why are you anxious about clothing? Consider the lilies of the field, how they grow; they neither toil nor spin; yet I tell you, even Solomon in all his glory was not arrayed like one of these. But if God so clothes the grass of the field, which today is alive and tomorrow is thrown into the oven, will he not much more clothe you, O men of little faith? Therefore do not be anxious, saying, 'What shall we eat?' or 'What shall we drink?' or 'What shall we wear?' For the Gentiles seek all these things; and your heavenly Father knows that you need them all. But seek first his kingdom and his righteousness, and all these things shall be yours as well.

Therefore do not be anxious about tomorrow, for tomorrow will be anxious for itself. Let the day's own trouble be sufficient for the day [Mt 6:25–34].

This sounds like a clear echo of the renunciation of the temporal order that was also characteristic of John. Conceiving of it as a timeless rule of conduct, as is so often done by those with a denominational commitment, is to project an alien meaning into Jesus' activity. Since he thought the Kingdom of God was about to be installed, he may have thought this particular type of renunciation a means of heralding or, possibly, of accelerating the installation: he trusted in God in a specific context of space and time – as part of a movement necessarily bound up with a programme, which he changed upon realizing that his confidence was not being justified by God's decision.

In any case, however, whether Jesus was a quietist before joining the Baptist, or whether he became one after leaving the Baptist, and then abandoned that too in favour of his final onslaught on the citadels of the powers of this world, he made his fateful decision, and went on to Jerusalem not only like the Herald of the Kingdom but also like the Herald of the Kingdom bringing it about *in power*.

Jesus was, if not the Messiah himself, at least a Messianic Herald.

But was he the Messiah *too*?

10

JESUS THE JEWISH MESSIAH?

WE have seen why Jesus' entry into Jerusalem, culminating in his occupation of the Temple, was Messianic from the point of view of the Romans. Jesus came into the city in a Messianic demonstration; by seizing and holding sway within the Temple he actually exercised sovereignty, as 'King of the Jews'.

But could the Romans simply have misunderstood the nature of the demonstration? What did the Jews think of it?

Let us look at it from the Jewish point of view. Did Jesus come to Jerusalem as Messiah?

There is no doubt that the Gospel writers *intended* to describe a Messianic entry: the beginning of *Mark* 11 (1–11) is obviously meant as such. It uses terms taken from the Old Testament prophet Zechariah (9:9), who is also the prophet referred to in *Matthew*:

This took place to fulfil what was spoken by the prophet, saying, 'Tell the daughter of Zion, Behold, your king is coming to you, humble, and mounted on an ass, and on a colt, the foal of an ass' [Mt 21:4, 5].

There is also evidence, if the Gospels are acceptable on this point, that Jesus was actually acclaimed by the people as Messiah. The 'Hosanna' passages are illuminating:

And many spread their garments on the road, and others spread leafy branches which they had cut from the fields. And those who went before and those who followed cried out 'Hosanna! Blessed be he who comes in the name of the Lord! Blessed be the kingdom of our father David that is coming! Hosanna in the highest!'
[Mk 11:8-10].

And the crowds that went before him and that followed him shouted, 'Hosanna to the Son of David! Blessed be he who comes in the name of the Lord! Hosanna in the highest!' [Mt 21:9].

The whole multitude ... began to ... praise God ... saying, 'Blessed be the King who comes in the name of the Lord! Peace in heaven and glory in the highest!' [Lk 19:38].

Now, while the meaning of all this is clear and most revealing, the actual phrase that is repeated, '*Hosanna* in the highest', is nonsensical.

As a rule the word '*hosanna*' is taken to be a transliteration of a Hebrew word meaning 'save us', and is assumed to be a reference to Psalm 118:25 – 'Save us, Yahweh, save us!'

But it can also be taken to be a similar Aramaic word that appears in all Syriac versions as the equivalent of 'Free us!' in the current Aramaic speech of Jesus' time.

But no matter how it is translated, the idea of either being 'saved' or 'freed' in the heights, or in the highest, is clearly absurd: both notions have a value only on earth; they are a perfectly mundane outcry on the part of the 'multitude' that followed Jesus and went on before him. The absurdity of the above passage from *Luke* is highlighted by contrasting it with another sentence from the same Gospel, where the kink has been ironed out;

Glory to God in the highest, and on earth peace among men with whom he is pleased! [Lk 2:14].

In *Mark*, quoted above, the word 'in the highest' must be assumed to be some kind of insertion on the part of an editor or scribe to whitewash Jesus of the suspicion of Messianism: the intent was thus to dilute the passage by inserting 'in the highest' as follows:

Blessed – in the highest – be he who comes in the name of the Lord! Blessed – in the highest – be the Kingdom of our father David!

The sense is completely restored when we remove this apologetic intrusion, which was intended to convey the impression that some pious pilgrims were simply saying that the Messiah and his Kingdom were blessed in the heights above, and had nothing to do with anything the authorities might have found objectionable.

The same thing applies to the quotation from *Matthew* above: 'Hosanna to the Son of David!' is senseless: the expression 'to the Son of David' must have been taken from the preceding verse. When corrected the whole thing would read:

The crowds ... shouted to the Son of David, 'Free us!'

Here the intent of the copyist is even more obvious: he was trying to obscure the Messianic outcry of the mob, addressed to Jesus, by displacing the meaning 'Free us!' of Jesus' colloquial Aramaic to the 'Save us!' of the Hebrew *Psalm* 118:25; that is, he was trying to interpret it as an appeal by the crowd to God to 'Help the Son of David!' which would sound fairly harmless, or as harmless as possible.

In *Luke* 19:38 (above) the 'hosanna' vanished altogether; it was simply omitted, and in order to make the correction plausible the words 'the whole multitude ... began to praise God' were inserted in the preceding verse.

It is amusing to recall here that it is because of this artificial alteration of the colloquial Aramaic *osha'na* – 'Free us', into the Psalmist's Hebrew *hoshia'na* – 'Save us', that the fourth Gospel has brought down to us a record of 'palm branches' being carried in this Messianic procession. The festal bouquets of the Feast of Tabernacles were colloquially known as '*Hoshannas*': their principal item was a palm branch. As is indicated in *Mark* above, the pilgrims did not carry the 'palm branches' in their hands; they strewed the ground with the leafy branches cut from the fields. The notion of their carrying them in their hands is a revealing instance, since the only text we have of *John* was translated and edited in Greek, of later Greek ignorance of Jewish affairs.

As a result of this repeated apologetic manipulation, the words of the actual acclamation have been thrown into a confusion that passes unnoticed by most people, who have repeated them by rote since childhood. It is one of the numerous ways in which the events leading up to the tragic climax of Jesus' career were obliterated to such an extent that the climax itself has become grotesque and unintelligible.

Jesus did not address himself to a circle of mystics, but to a people longing for liberation from an alien yoke. Nor did this liberation mean what Paul later meant by 'liberation from bondages', that is, from sin and wicked spirits. Jesus' Jewish partisans simply meant, quite literally, liberation from worldly oppression in the name of a classic religious ideal.

In our own terms, Jesus was a national leader, one of the many who as we have seen sprang up among the Jews during their long-drawn-out subjugation by Rome.

None of the above tells us what Jesus himself thought of all this. Did *Jesus* think himself the Messiah? Or did he imagine himself to be no more than the Herald of the Kingdom, inspired by God and performing, perhaps, a Messianic function, but not actually the Messiah himself?

According to Jewish conceptions current in his time, the Messiah was indubitably a man like another; hence this question has no theological significance. Bar Kochba, for instance, the leader of the Second Jewish Revolt against Rome in A.D. 133, was acclaimed as Messiah by the celebrated Rabbi Aqiba. There was never any question of Bar Kochba's singularity in any other sense.

Unfortunately, however, the scanty information and the anachronistic perspective of the Gospels veil Jesus' thought on this point as on so many others.

It is obvious that since the Gospel writers took their certainty of Jesus' resurrection as their starting point, as indeed his earliest disciples did too (see Chapter 11), they necessarily retrojected this assumption into Jesus' lifetime. It was only natural for them to make the further assumption that he could scarcely have failed to be aware of his own mission.

But on this point the evidence of the Gospels as a whole is altogether baffling. The celebrated Messianic secret, Jesus' constant admonition to his disciples for at least part of his mission to remain silent concerning his status, cannot really be understood except as a makeshift device for reconciling the attitude of the Resurrected and Glorified Jesus' subsequent worshippers with the historic fact that Jesus never actually gave himself out as the Messiah. He is never actually reported to have said, 'I am the Messiah'.

There are some individual passages that buttress this impression substantially. Here is one from *Mark*, which I quoted on page 80 as one of the varying estimates of the imminence of the Kingdom:

[Jesus said], 'Truly, I say to you, I shall not drink again of the fruit of the vine until that day when I drink it new in the kingdom of God' [Mk 14:25].

In this announcement of the Messianic feast Jesus says nothing about a special place being reserved at it for himself; if there has been any recollection of such a portentous utterance among his followers the chronicler would surely have made a point of mentioning it.

There is a passage in this connexion that, though somewhat obscure, is most convincing. I have quoted it before (page 108) as an indication of the dramatic change of mind that deflected Jesus' career into a fatefully different direction, but it is also of great significance with respect to Jesus' view of his own person. It is almost certainly to be interpreted as a disclaimer of Messiahship:

Jesus went on with his disciples ... and ... asked [them], 'Who do men say that I am?' And they told him, 'John the Baptist; and others say, Elijah; and others one of the prophets.' And he asked them, 'But who do you say that I am?' Peter answered him, 'You are the Christ' and he charged them to tell no one about him.

And he began to teach them that the Son of man must suffer many things, and be rejected by the elders and the chief priests and the scribes, and be killed, and after three days rise again. And he said this plainly. And Peter took him, and began to rebuke him. But turning and seeing his disciples, he rebuked Peter, and said, 'Get behind me, Satan! For you are not on the side of God, but of men' [Mk 8:27–33].

Now, the *structure* of this passage indicates the desire of the chronicler to situate this incident, which in *Mark* is the crux of Jesus' whole career, in the light of the Divine Plan of early Christianity, in which Jesus foresees everything that is going to happen to him.

Historically, however, the fact that Jesus actually forbade Peter incomprehensibly, to disclose his Messiahship to anyone, and then sharply rebuked him afterward for having clung to his own opinion nevertheless, must mean that while some of Jesus' disciples may have believed he was the Messiah there was no firm recollection of his ever having admitted this himself.

In short, what the Gospel editors were trying to do was to reconcile their own conviction of Jesus' Messiahship with the facts of his career: since they could not believe he himself hadn't shared their own mystical certainty of this they had to invent the otherwise incomprehensible secrecy of his whole mission, and imagine that he intimated his status by means of *signs* that were meant to be misunderstood.

Yet the fact remains, despite the floods of argumentation produced by Jesus' failure to declare himself openly, that if he thought himself the Messiah there seems to be no good reason why he should not have said as much.

The traditional (or apologetic) explanation of this is that Jesus was unquestionably the Messiah and naturally knew it, but since his Messiahship was of a type that was completely novel in Israel it could not be given out as such for fear of arousing the contempt or opposition of his listeners.

This explanation seems incredible.

In the first place, there is no record in Jewish Messianic belief of a *suffering* Messiah. To circumvent this there has been speculation (chiefly among scholars who disbelieve in Jesus' historic existence altogether) on the possibility of certain Jewish sects whose Messianic conceptions had been distorted by the dying and rising gods of the pagan mystery cults (see Chapter 12). But the difficulty here is that there is absolutely no evidence of such sects: the mythological school who do not believe Jesus existed have been obliged to imagine a Jewish background for what they regard as the 'myth' of his agony, while apologetic Christian scholars, on the other hand, feel impelled to harmonize later Christian theology with the facts of Jesus' life in their own way.

The real point, however, is that if the originality of Jesus' Messianic conception could actually be considered historically possible, it would have to be explained at some length in the

Gospels themselves, which is never done. Jesus would have been obliged at least to try to explain to his audience just what his view of the Messiah was, precisely if it was a novel one.

How could his followers have understood him otherwise?

Just as with the Kingdom of God, no attempt is made in the Gospels to give a novel interpretation of Messiahship, and we must assume that in his own lifetime Jesus could only have made use of ideas that at least his most intimate followers would have understood.

Besides, as we have seen, Jesus *did* try to take the Kingdom of God by storm. Hence, even if he did not think himself the actual Messiah his role was certainly martial. It would have corresponded with the then current Jewish conception of the Warlike Messiah, and since there was no room in Jewish Messianic belief for a Pacific Messiah an apologia was eventually bound to be called for in the evolution of Christian belief as soon as it became necessary to tone down the political aspects of Jesus' career.

It is the extraction of this whole element of violence from the Gospel accounts that has left the so-called 'Messianic secret' hanging in the air, to provide one more hurdle for the apologists who later were obliged to retain a pacific version of Jesus' activity while simultaneously establishing his claims to Messiahship. This particular stage in the development of Christian theory was of course relatively brief. It was only meaningful while the belief in Jesus was confined to his immediate Jewish followers, who had already compensated for the failure of his enterprise by an ardent belief in the imminence of his Second Coming, which became synonymous with the installation of the Kingdom of God. Once the belief in Jesus' Messiahship was transposed to Hellenistic terrain, it was quickly overlaid by his rapidly evolving divinization, and thus lost its importance.

But there are other, even more unmistakable indications, in both *Acts* and *Luke*, that clearly imply that Jesus was not thought to be the Messiah during his own lifetime. They are all the more significant since *Luke* and *Acts* were written in fairly close connexion with the events of Jesus' career, and by someone entirely persuaded, of course, of Jesus' Messianic elevation *after* the Resurrection:

In *Luke*, for instance, we read:

And he said to them, 'What things?' And they said to him, 'Concerning Jesus of Nazareth, who was a prophet mighty in deed and word before God and all the people' [Lk 24:19].

While in *Acts* there is the following:

'Men of Israel, hear these words: Jesus of Nazareth, a man attested to you by God with mighty works and wonders and signs which God did through him in your midst, as you yourselves know ... This Jesus God raised up, and of that we all are witnesses. Being therefore exalted at the right hand of God, and having received from the Father the promise of the Holy Spirit, he has poured out this which you see and hear ... Let all the house of Israel therefore know assuredly that God has made him both Lord and Christ, this Jesus whom you crucified' [Acts 2:22, 32, 33, 36].

And also:

You know ... the word which was proclaimed throughout all Judea ... how God anointed Jesus of Nazareth with the Holy Spirit and with power; how he went about doing good and healing all that were oppressed by the devil, for God was with him [Acts 10:36–38].

All these passages, by omitting the mention of Jesus' Messiahship during his actual lifetime activity, give us the vivid impression that the chronicler did not extend this claim of Messiahship to Jesus' own life, and that Jesus had not, consequently, presented himself to Israel as the Messiah. In fact, these passages from *Luke* and *Acts* merely confirm the conclusion we have already come to, that Jesus had presented himself to his people basically as the Herald of the Kingdom,

saying 'The time is fulfilled, and the kingdom of God is at hand; repent, and believe in the gospel' [Mk 1:14].

We are back once again to the portrait of Jesus as recorded in the Gospels – it is that of an old-fashioned Prophet, inspired by God and exhorting his people to follow God's ways in order to accommodate themselves to the establishment of the Kingdom of God. He does not seem to have emerged in public life as a claimant to Messiahship, and it was not as Messiah that he launched his movement.

We have seen that this portrait has been piously retouched to smooth away those aspects of Jesus' enterprise that were to prove indigestible to later Christian theory – the violence that attended Jesus' movement, its anti-Roman political implications, and, above all, perhaps, its material failure – all were either forgotten or obliterated in the new perspective of Jesus' cultic magnification. This is why, as I have pointed out before, the nuggets of historic probability still embedded in the text are so valuable.

Even in the present text we can dimly perceive that something happened to make Jesus change his mind in mid-career, as we have seen, and embark on an effort to bring about the establishment of the Kingdom by means of a massive insurrection against the power of Rome and her local vassals, and that it was this that led to the agonizing climax of his life.

It is tempting to look for the occasion that led to his change of mind; we may find it in a situation that has been recorded outside the Gospels.

Josephus tells us that Pontius Pilate attempted to set up the standards of the Roman legions inside the Temple area. These standards bore medallions with exchangeable portrait heads of the emperors. The Roman forces were stationed principally in the city; there was only one cohort stationed in Fort Antonia, but since the Jews regarded this as part of the Temple area, which they took to embrace the whole Temple hill, they reacted violently to the setting up of these profane images. Josephus gives us an impressive account of their consternation and fury: they were determined to allow Pilate to slaughter them unless the standards bearing Caesar's image were removed.

Pilate, baffled by what he must have considered incomprehensible fanaticism, finally gave way.

The point is that the Jews regarded the setting up in the Temple area of images to be worshipped as the fulfilment of a prophecy to be found in *Daniel* (11:31), that of the 'abomination of desolation' (or the 'desolating sacrilege') being 'set up where it ought not to be' (Mk 13:14). In *Daniel* (12:11) this desecration of the sanctuary was to usher in 'the last times', calculated to extend over a period of about three and a half years, more than 1,290 days; at the end of this period the death of the Messiah was to be expected, as well as the devastation of the Holy City in the Messianic war. This would continue until the 'end of days' and terminate with the annihilation of the Prince of this world, the adversary of God, and of the godless in general, by means of another flood like the one that had wiped out the human race at the time of Noah.

Many Jews interpreted Pilate's action as the defilement of the sanctuary foreseen in *Daniel*; this is Jesus' apocalyptic speech:

But when you see the desolating sacrilege set up where it ought not to be ... then let those who are in Judea flee to the mountains; let him who is on the housetop not go down, nor enter his house, to take anything away; and let him who is in the field not turn back to take his mantle. And alas for those who are with child and for those who give suck in those days! [Mk 13:14–17; also Mt 24:15].

Jesus and many of his contemporaries seem to have expected the destructive flood to follow this desecration, in accordance with the prophecy in *Daniel*.

This is very suggestive; it may actually give us the specific occasion that set Jesus off on his career, and by pin-pointing his change of mind within the framework of his general opposition to the contemporary social order shed some light on his reasons for taking the road of violence in quest of his 'otherworldly' aims.

We have seen the curious insubstantiality of the Gospel accounts of Jesus' trials, both Jewish and Roman, though at the same time they disclose a hard core of truth – the Roman charge of sedition and the Roman punishment of crucifixion. I say 'hard core': it would be better to call it an oasis in a desert, for the entire Synoptic narrative of Jesus' entry into Jerusalem gives us an overriding impression of emptiness. The verbosity and repetitions in the discourses do not lessen the effect of this emptiness; if anything they heighten it. Events that must have caused a vast commotion, that led to an agonizing death for Jesus and to the bitter frustration of his followers, have come down to us as glimpses of shadows.

After all, the devotion of Jesus' followers to him was enough to generate their faith in his Resurrection and Messiahship; it is inconceivable that they failed to retain a vivid though naturally painful memory of the crucial week in his tragic career. It is just this gap in recollection that is the most dramatic proof of the process we have referred to so often, that of the transformation of the entire view of Jesus' career by the perspective of his triumphant Glorification, which led to the obliteration of essential facts relating to his activity in Jerusalem, including his reasons for going there. It is also surely the reason for the curious effect of anti-climax in the Gospel accounts of Jesus' entry into the city. Though unmistakably a Messianic demonstration in all four Gospels, there is an inexplicable gap, both chronological and causal, between the entry itself, with its open defiance of the Romans, and Jesus' punishment. The chronological dislocation involved is evidently the handiwork of a later doctrinal transposition. Subsequent theological apologetics drained our documents of whatever facts their original versions might have contained, leaving the void we must cope with.

In fact, as we have seen, the inscription on Jesus' cross gives us as succinctly as possible the explanation of his death. Not only was the charge of setting himself up as 'King of the Jews' an entirely adequate reason for executing him from the Roman point of view; it was perfectly intelligible and cogent from the Jewish point of view too, considering the secular as well as the religious content of the status that would automatically have been assumed by anyone doing what Jesus tried to do, even without claiming to be the Messiah.

The national significance of this title is revealingly emphasized in a little by-play between Pilate and the 'chief priests of the Jews' reported in the fourth Gospel:

Pilate also wrote a title and put it on the cross; it read 'Jesus of Nazareth, the King of the Jews.' ... The chief priests of the Jews then said to Pilate, 'Do not write, "The King of the Jews," but, "This man said, 'I am King of the Jews.' " ' Pilate answered, 'What I have written I have written' [Jn 19:19, 21, 22].

Pilate's point is clear: when the Temple authorities tried to exculpate the Jews of disaffection toward the Romans by putting the blame for the insurrection on Jesus alone, Pilate reminded them that from his point of view Jesus' seizure of power had not merely been an outburst of individual fanaticism but had also had a collective character. Jesus had been *acclaimed* King, and for a time had, in fact, exercised sovereignty with the consent of a sizeable portion of the community. The brevity of his reign was a matter of legal indifference to the Roman procurator: the mere notion of the Jews having a self-appointed King was reason enough for Roman intervention.

The above passage from the fourth Gospel sounds like an echo of some other deliberations between the 'chief priests', in another curious passage, where Jesus' attraction for a substantial part of the population is confirmed in an inverted way:

So the chief priests and the Pharisees gathered the council, and said, 'What are we to do? For this man performs many sins. If we let him go on thus, every one will believe in him, and the Romans will come and destroy both our holy place and our nation.' But one of them, Caiaphas, who was high priest that year, said to them. 'You know nothing at all; you do not understand that it is expedient for you that one man should die for the people, and that the whole nation should not perish' [Jn 11:47–50].

This has a genuine ring to it. Of course, it is difficult to see just how the discussion taking place in this privy council could have been transmitted to a follower of Jesus, but historically it is at least a sensible attitude to imagine the Temple party as having taken. Indeed, in spite of the chronicler's manifest intention of exploiting the incident as another way of inculpating the Jews, it may not even imply real hostility to Jesus. Caiaphas's plea is the choice of a lesser evil; it sounds like a man of the world's attempt to save the nation from the consequences of its own hot-headedness.

Jesus' role as a national Jewish prophet is poignantly conveyed in *Luke*:

And there followed him a great multitude of the people, and of women who bewailed and lamented him. But Jesus turning to them said, 'Daughters of Jerusalem, do not weep for me, but weep for yourselves and for your children. For behold, the days are coming when they will say, "Blessed are the barren, and the wombs that never bore, and the breasts that never gave suck!" Then they will begin to say to the mountains, "Fall on us"; and to the hills, "Cover us" ' [Lk 23:27–30].

And all the multitudes who assembled to see the sight, when they saw what had taken place, returned home beating their breasts [Lk 23:48].

The Romans appear here as the enemies both of Jesus and of the Jewish people simultaneously, which of course they were. The solidarity of Jesus and the Jews is here confirmed, in contrast with the later, fancifully tendentious tradition that has the Jewish mob incomprehensibly calling out for Jesus' blood when he is about to be crucified on Pilate's orders. Jesus is actually speaking here, as it were *ex cathedra*, as a national leader. In addition, this passage provides us with some positive evidence that despite the indications of Jesus' failure to carry the whole Jewish people with him in his assault on Rome, he nevertheless had a substantial popular following.

For the above-mentioned passage is scarcely likely to be an invention of the author of *Luke*, which, like the other three Gospels, reports a Jewish mob forcing Pilate's hand; consequently the retention of this fragment seems to favour its historicity. Indeed, though if it were an invention it might be thought to be a sentimental adornment, it is probably no invention at all. The whole point of early Christianity was that the Christ had been despised and rejected of all; hence this is not a mere edifying literary detail; it must be authentic.

There are other instances of the deep and entirely mundane gloom that must have been recalled by the earliest witnesses to the catastrophe of the cross:

And taking with him Peter and the two sons of Zebedee, [Jesus] began to be sorrowful and troubled. Then he said to them, 'My soul is very sorrowful, even unto death.' . . . Going a little farther he fell on his face and prayed, 'My Father, if it be possible, let this cup pass from me . . .' [Mt 26:37–39].

And being in an agony he prayed more earnestly; and his sweat became like great drops of blood falling down upon the ground [Lk 22:44].

There is a melancholy in these and parallel passages that must embody a lingering recollection of the state of mind of Jesus' company at the time of the tragic climax. The details, to be sure, cannot claim to be well attested, for who could have overheard Jesus? Nevertheless this somewhat embroidered form must conceal something substantial.

The same applies to a curious incident recorded in *Luke*. Jesus after his Resurrection, approaches two of the apostles, who are going to Emmaus, some seven miles from Jerusalem, and chatting on the way:

[Jesus] said to them, 'What is this conversation which you are holding with each other as you walk?' And they stood still, looking sad. Then one of them ... answered him, 'Are you the only visitor to Jerusalem who does not know the things that have happened here in these days?' And he said to them, 'What things?' And they said to him, 'Concerning Jesus of Nazareth, who was a prophet mighty in deed and word before God and all the people, and how our chief priests and rulers delivered him up to be condemned to death, and crucified him. But we had hoped that he was the one to redeem Israel' [Lk 24:17–21].

This incident, seemingly so trivial, is striking because it contains a recollection of the disheartenment of his immediate followers after the crucifixion, and gives us further confirmation of what it was that they had been hoping for, namely, the redemption of Israel. Also it indicates that their faith in Jesus as the one to effect it had been shaken.

It is likely to be a very ancient fragment, and would then go back to the period *immediately* following the crucifixion, before his scattered band of followers had had time to become firmly anchored to their faith in his Resurrection:

Jesus said to them: 'You will all fall away, for it is written, "I will strike the shepherd, and the sheep will be scattered"'

[Mk 14:27 and parallels].

As we have seen before, that such a detail has survived the homogenizing process of the whole early tradition, which was bent on emphasizing Jesus' masterful serenity, implies that it was unshakably rooted in some early tradition too well attested to be tampered with.

But of course the tragic climax of Jesus' career could not be summed up more poignantly than in the first two Gospels, where sheer despair is put directly and unequivocally into Jesus' own mouth:

My God, my God, why hast thou forsaken me? [Mk 15:34, Mt 27:46].

This cry of despair must be historical; it is given in both Gospels in Jesus' native Aramaic speech, which is the earliest layer of the Palestinian tradition and is presumably used whenever for some reason actual words or fragments of speeches had become hallowed enough to be recalled in their original form. It is in flagrant and irremediable contradiction with the systematic tendency of the Gospel writers to present Jesus as invariably in untroubled communion with the divine will and serene at all times in the face of suffering.

Nor is it conceivable that the first generations of Christians could have devised this despairing outcry as an edifying detail in the process of enveloping their Saviour with a variety of legends: hence its mention in *Mark* and *Matthew* testifies to an absolutely undeniable tradition that withstood all apologia. If anything, it is further strengthened by the obvious fact that the oldest tradition does not stress the actual physical torments of Jesus on the cross; therefore its recollection of his moral agony is all the more significant, considering the supposedly perfect communion with God naturally attributed to him.

It may be legitimate to doubt the historic authenticity of these words as coming from Jesus' own mouth; who could the witnesses have been? But as a personalized reflection of the despair of Jesus' immediate followers, they seem incontestable.

The wording of the outcry, to be sure, comes from *Psalm 22*, which goes on to conclude on a more reassuring note. This has made some students attempt to explain the note of despair in the phrase itself, which sounds so heart-rending, as in reality a mere hint to the wise, designed to raise their spirits. This explanation is extraordinarily farfetched. It gives the outcry the character of a textbook reference; if conceivable at all the explanation would make it impossible to understand why the compilers of *Luke* and *John*, who were, after all, closer to the original situation than ourselves, should have failed to disclose its meaning. The outcry's originating in a Psalm tells us nothing: both Jesus and his earliest chroniclers were imbued with the Old Testament in general and doubtless with the Psalms in particular.

We are obliged to regard Jesus' cry of despair on the cross as essentially authentic.

Luke and *John*, of course, are already well away from the stark and human simplicity of Jesus' end. *Luke* sentimentalizes the final scene by putting in Jesus' mouth an appropriately phrased statement of trusting communion:

Father, into thy hands I commit my spirit! [Lk 23:46].

By the time of the fourth Gospel the christological process has gone to such an extreme that the cross has become a sort of throne, from which Jesus sets the seal on the consummation of the Divine Plan:

[Jesus] said, 'It is finished,' and he bowed his head and gave up his spirit [Jn 19:30].

It is just these otherworldly, theological preoccupations of *Luke* and *John* that confirm all the more graphically the genuineness of the bitter cry borne witness to by the other two Gospels.

Let us sum up the results of the preceding chapters.

Jesus was the Herald of the Kingdom of God, and he tried to take it by storm. In the strangely blurred and mutilated recollections of his career we can dimly discern the outlines of a visionary who was also a man of action and who attempted to set in motion the machinery of God's will.

He was squarely in the tradition of the Jewish religious patriots, tortured by the crushing weight of the Roman Empire, who arose in Palestine and assaulted the Roman power and its vassals.

We see his enterprise frustrated and himself undone; his

followers scattered and his movement, doubtless, drowned in blood. He ended like many others in Israel – in agony and death, a prey to the powers of this world.

But that was not the end of it; his memory was to kindle a new religion, and his name to become enshrined as the focus of a completely different movement among nations he had never given a thought to. The idea of this new religion, with himself as its deity, was something he could never have had the slightest inkling of. As Charles Guignebert put it, 'It never even crossed his mind.'

How did this happen?

How did it come about that Jesus' entire enterprise, enclosed by Judaism and Jewish national life, diverged completely from its origins and became increasingly hostile to it?

How was the gulf bridged between Jesus' life and the religion that sprang up in his name?

If Jesus died a Jew, why are his followers not Jews?

II

JESUS TRANSPOSED

This question of the bridge between Jesus and Christianity is really the most involved of all. It is independent of Jesus' life.

The birth of the new religion is, in detail, very obscure; the period immediately following Jesus' death is almost unknown. The murkiness through which we have peered at his career and personality becomes altogether impenetrable after his death. The very vague ending of *Luke* gives us a vision of Jesus ressurected and blessing his disciples:

While he blessed them, he parted from them. And they returned to Jerusalem with great joy [Lk 25:51, 52].

This is all we know of how the disciples went back to Jerusalem and there presumably established the little community of those who believed Jesus to be the Messiah and who remained in the Holy City awaiting his return. To them, it is clear, this would have inaugurated the establishment of the Kingdom of God.

The bridge between these events is completely missing: when we read in *Acts*, to our amazement, that one of Jesus' brothers, the Saddiq Jacob, that is, James the Just, one of the same brothers who according to *John* (7:5) 'did not believe in him', was head of the Jerusalem community of believers in Jesus, we have no idea of how one situation led to the other.

In general the events enveloping the arrest, trial, and execution of Jesus are deeply mysterious. What is particularly puzzling is the fate of the disciples; the account of their activities as Jesus' lieutenants, curiously inane to begin with, is worthless as far as their finish is concerned. Whether or not this emptiness of function points to the tendentious suppression of their military role, their conduct at Jesus' execution and afterward is never mentioned anywhere at all. Their actual behaviour during the crisis was altogether forgotten by the earliest tradition. Not only do they 'all forsake' Jesus and flee; they do not – even more surprisingly – reappear during Jesus' trial nor are they present at his execution, nor are they the ones who bury him.

Where could they have been? More particularly – how is it they were not directly involved in the final denouement? Why were they not arrested? Is there some special significance to be attached to Peter's denial of his Lord? Some doubt has been cast on the historicity of this episode; if it is a later invention, or perhaps a symbolic fiction of some kind, it of course becomes all the more revealing as a development of the later tradition, and possibly of the factional disputes that played a role in the postapostolic community.

It is clear that a veil has been drawn over the conclusion of Jesus' career; perhaps the only way to explain Peter's denial at cockcrow is to assume that it symbolizes a recollection of the manner in which Jesus' followers escaped the punishment meted out to him. By disavowing complicity, perhaps, or simply by fleeing, they managed to slip through the net of Roman justice.

We are faced by a gap: we next see the little band of Jesus' followers peacefully worshipping at the Jewish Temple (*Acts*, Lk 24:53). They seem to have come back to Jerusalem from Galilee fairly soon.

Let us try, not to ascertain the actual course of events – which our scanty information forbids – but to see how the disciples recovered from the bitter discouragement that must have befallen them after Jesus' crucifixion and that made still more poignant the failure of the Kingdom of God to appear.

The question boils down to how the belief in Jesus' Resurrection was generated and how this belief evolved into Christianity. This subject is of course one of boundless complexity and obscurity: I shall give only the broadest outline of some salient points. These will depend on the extraction of the most primitive data possible from documents written down many years after Jesus' death, and above all edited and compiled more than a hundred and fifty years later as the manual of belief of an already constituted Christian community, preoccupied by questions of its cult and not of its history.

The contradictions in the four Gospel accounts of the discovery of Jesus' empty tomb, and the extreme barrenness of the one common statement they do make: that the tomb Jesus was placed in on the evening of his death was found empty a few days after, indicate that the earliest tradition knew of no witnesses to the physical resurrection of Jesus from the tomb. Not only that, but it is perfectly evident that during the first few centuries after Jesus' death the whereabouts of his tomb remained unknown; it was only 'located' in A.D. 326 under the Emperor Constantine, as the result of 'divine inspiration'.

The most primitive tradition relies on the appearance of Jesus to some of his disciples in a *vision,* first to Peter, then presumably to others. The mere discovery of an empty tomb could never have launched the faith in Jesus' Resurrection. He would have had to be seen somewhere else first; the empty tomb alone would mean nothing. The *proof* of its significance ultimately rested on the interpretation of the visions of Jesus resurrected.

Thus, in the logic of the situation, it must have been the conviction of Jesus' *reappearance* that started the stories about his having been laid in a tomb later found empty. This logic is simply confirmed by the incoherence of all the details of the tomb story.

It must be emphasized that we have no actual record of the Resurrection in the form of any eyewitness accounts, trustworthy or not. The Gospel account does not pretend to describe the earliest visions as seen by Jesus' followers; on the contrary, we have nothing but a ritually stylized account of how the earliest Church, some fifty years and more after the events, expressed its view of the Resurrection of the Christ.

The very oldest record we have of Jesus' appearances after death is that of Paul; this was at least twenty-five years after Jesus' death, and could not very well be put in a vaguer form:

[What] I delivered to you as of first importance ... I also received, that Christ died for our sins in accordance with the scriptures, that he was buried, that he was raised on the third day in accordance with the scriptures, and that he appeared to Cephas [Peter], then to the twelve. Then he appeared to more than five hundred brethren at one time, most of whom are still alive, though some have fallen asleep. Then he appeared to James [Jacob] then to all the apostles. Last of all, as to one untimely born, he appeared also to me

[I Cor. 15:3–8].

In this passage Paul is thus giving us the basic outline of what the earliest belief must have been. It has practically no details of any kind, such as appear in the Gospels themselves, and it seems apparent that Paul had no knowledge of such details. The words 'he appeared' are too simple to sustain any elaboration, and the fact that he uses the same phrases about himself, while indicating elsewhere that he never actually saw Jesus in the flesh, is itself highly significant. It is the same word as that used to refer to the vision that 'appeared' first to Peter, and it pinpoints it as just that – a vision.

The starkly simple quality of these visions is attested by the very bareness of the word used to describe it. The notion of 'he appeared to', or 'was seen by', which is the meaning of the Greek word used (*ophthe*), implies a complete independence of any of the legendary scenes recorded in the secondary or tertiary layer of the Gospels. These represent a later attempt to buttress Jesus' reappearance by circumstantial details, such as his having dinner with his disciples, and so on, as in *Luke* and *John*. Since Paul used this same word in describing his own vision of Jesus, and since in Paul's case there is no question of his having actually seen Jesus in person, we must conclude that Peter and the rest of Jesus' followers simply had an overpowering sensation of the presence of their leader. The very simplicity of the account is, of course, an excellent summing up of the most characteristic single feature of hallucination, or at any rate of the emotional interpretation given to a visual phenomenon of a certain vagueness.

An ampler, and far more stylized account of the visions of Jesus that underlay the early tradition is given in *Matthew*:

Now the eleven disciples went to Galilee, to the mountain to which Jesus had directed them. And when they saw him they worshipped him: but some doubted. And Jesus came and said to them. 'All authority in heaven and on earth has been given to me. Go therefore and make disciples of all nations, baptizing them in the name of the Father and of the Son and of the Holy Spirit, teaching them to observe all that I have commanded you; and, lo, I am with you always, to the close of the age' [Mt 28:16–20].

Here the final sentence (a magnificent summing up of the Church's fundamental theme) gives us the point of view that establishes the purpose of the entire account. It has all been designed to lead up to this profound reaffirmation of the Christian faith as it took shape generations after the death of Jesus. The *details* in it are interesting, however, because of the admission, presumably ineluctable, that some of the disciples had had doubts. Historically this leads to the presumption that the faith in Jesus' Resurrection, guaranteed by the visions, spread only gradually, doubtless beginning with Peter, and, according to Paul's catalogue of these visions, spread first to the twelve Disciples, then to the remaining circle of Jesus' followers, including his brother the Saddiq Jacob. This last mention of Jacob may indicate how he overcame the family scepticism concerning his brother that is reported in the Gospels several times.

These doubts of Jesus' resurrection must have been very solidly established in the earliest tradition; they are attested by a celebrated passage in the fourth Gospel:

Now Thomas, one of the twelve, called the Twin, was not with them when Jesus came. So the other disciples told him, 'We have seen the Lord.' But he said to them, 'Unless I see in his hands the print of the nails, and place my finger in the mark of the nails, and place my hand in his side, I will not believe.' Eight days later, his disciples were again in the house, and Thomas was with them. The doors were shut, but Jesus came and stood among them, and said, 'Peace be with you.' Then he said to Thomas, 'Put your finger here, and see my hands; and put out your hand, and place it in my side; do not be faithless, but believing.' Thomas answered him, 'My Lord and my God!' Jesus said to him, 'Have you believed because you have seen me? Blessed are those who have not seen and yet believe' [Jn 20:24–29].

There is no need to emphasize the profound significance for the Church of the final sentence. It has, of course, been its cornerstone since it was founded. Since Christian doctrine was to serve generations that could never have known Jesus, this terse equation between faith and non-experience is evidently vital for the functioning of the Church. Its mere indispensability for the creed indicates its remoteness from any conceivable historical scene, even if the phrase ascribed to Thomas – 'My Lord and *my God!*' – was not wholly inconceivable in the mouth of any Jew of Jesus' own milieu.

There is an incident that may give us the key to the mechanism, so to speak, by which the faith in the Resurrection was launched. It is reported in the curious passage at the end of the fourth Gospel:

After this Jesus revealed himself again to the disciples by the Sea of Tiberias; and he revealed himself in this way. Simon Peter, Thomas called the Twin, Nathanael of Cana in Galilee, the sons of Zebedee, and two others of his disciples were together. Simon Peter said to them, 'I am going fishing.' They said to him, 'We will go with you.' They went out and got into the boat; but that night they caught nothing.

Just as day was breaking, Jesus stood on the beach; yet the disciples did not know it was Jesus. Jesus said to them, 'Children, have you any fish?' They answered him, 'No.' He said to them, 'Cast the net on the right side of the boat, and you will find some.' So they cast it, and now they were not able to haul it in, for the quantity of fish. That disciple whom Jesus loved said to Peter, 'It is the Lord!' When Simon Peter heard that it was the Lord, he put on his clothes, for he was stripped for work, and sprang into the sea. But the other disciples came in the boat, dragging the net full of fish, for they were not far from the land, but about a hundred yards off. When they got out on land, they saw a charcoal fire there, with fish lying on it, and bread. Jesus said to them, 'Bring some of the fish that you have just caught.' So Simon Peter went aboard and hauled the net ashore, full of large fish, a hundred and fifty-three of them; and although there were so many, the net was not torn. Jesus said to them, 'Come and have breakfast.' Now none of the disciples dared ask him, 'Who are you?' They knew it was the Lord. Jesus came and took the bread and gave it to them, and so with the fish. This was now the third time that Jesus was revealed to the disciples after he was raised from the dead [Jn 21:1-14].

This passage is particularly interesting because it entirely contradicts the preceding chapter, which refers to the appearances of the resuscitated Jesus in Jerusalem and is unmistakably the natural ending of the fourth Gospel. The final chapter in our present fourth Gospel abruptly moves the locale of Jesus' appearances back to Galilee, and by doing so changes the perspective as well. It is no longer a question of the glorious apostles consecrated by the spirit of Christ as his vicars on earth, but of poor fishermen, discouraged by the frustration of their campaign against Jerusalem, who have gone back to their native soil and resumed their former occupations.

This switch in perspective is abrupt, and so out of harmony with the glorifying tendency of the Gospels that in accordance with our criterion of authenticity it is at bottom bound to carry conviction, regardless of how it too has been stylized to confirm with the general tendency.

There is one traditional strand in the Gospels that fixes Jerusalem as the locale for Jesus' reappearance after death. It is illustrated by two passages in *Luke* (24: 13-53), by Chapter 20 in the fourth Gospel (the excerpt given above, page 170), and by the conclusion to the extant version of *Mark*. On study, however, these passages may be seen to be secondary – both in the framework of the text as well as for logical considerations – to the earlier tradition that situates them in Galilee, where presumably Jesus' followers fled after the Jerusalem fiasco.

There is also some confusion with respect to the number of times Jesus was supposed to have 'appeared' to his followers, and in what order these appearances took place; it seems most likely that it was Peter who had the very first vision, followed doubtless by the other disciples (summarily referred to as 'The Twelve').

The vacillation in the very earliest tradition about these primordial details may be seen by comparing the above-mentioned passage from Paul's *First Letter to the Corinthians* with the record of appearances given in the Gospels. On the one hand Paul's list is too long, since he includes five hundred disciples, then Jesus' brother Jacob, then all the apostles, who are not mentioned in the Gospels. On the other hand, it is too short, since he omits the incident given in *Luke* of the disciples on the road to Emmaus (page 162). In addition Paul seems quite ignorant of the secondary legends concerning Jesus' tomb; he knows nothing of Jesus' body's being placed in it or of its disappearance.

The manner in which everything else is arranged in the Gospels gives one the unmistakable impression that the kernel of the entire tradition is the belief of Peter and the other immediate companions in the resuscitation of Jesus after their seeing him in a vision. This has been densely overlaid, in accordance with the very nature of the Gospels and New Testament as a whole, by subsequent details of an edifying nature, designed to base the authority of the primitive Church on the 'apostolic tradition', and thus to justify the very existence of the Church itself, though this, as we have seen, was the last thing Jesus could have been thinking of.

The stubborn mention of early doubts is the exception to this. The account of these doubts, especially the curious episode of Doubting Thomas, preserves a scrap of knowledge in the informational vacuum of the first generation after Jesus, and vouches for the gradualness of the growing faith in the Resurrection itself.

There is no need to argue about whether or not the appearances of Jesus *require* an explanation, that is, an explanation of something considered to be supernatural. For our purposes it is quite enough to establish the formation of the belief that they had taken place. There may be a difference in whether Peter actually saw a vision or merely thought he saw one: but since we can perceive the event only through documents that record the beliefs of individuals, it is obvious that from our point of view it is a matter of indifference whether Peter was right or wrong. Indeed, it really is the same thing, after all – seeing a vision or thinking so. A vision is just that – something thought to be seen. As for the so-called objective basis of this subjective impression, there is nothing, of course, in the Gospels or the New Testament as a whole that would enable such a discussion even to be begun, especially since in the minds of the people living in those times there was no line of demarcation whatever between such things. There was not, that is to say, any body of opinion that would have been able *a priori* to deny the possibility of resuscitation, and *a fortiori* the possibility of seeing someone resuscitated. It is superfluous to emphasize the obvious fact that the belief in miracles, still common today, was even more so then.

The point that should be made here is that the resuscitation of Jesus was not considered to be a mere renewal of life in a terrestrial body : it was not a duplication of Jesus' own miracles in raising Lazarus and Jairus's daughter from the dead. In their cases the presumption was that they had in effect died prematurely, and in due time would die normally. Jesus' Resurrection, on the other hand, was a miracle of an altogether different order ; it made him invulnerable to death for all eternity.

Jesus' Resurrection, that is, was understood as the equivalent of his Glorification at the right hand of God ; it is this that gives the miracles of his 'appearing' to his disciples and others their essential meaning, and also demonstrates its nonphysical nature.

In any case, it is clear that the disciples were not prepared for Jesus' Resurrection : as we have seen, when Jesus explained to them how it was all going to take place, as recorded in *Mark* (8 :31, 9 :10, 31–32 ; see page 153) they were completely obtuse. The only assumption we can make is that Jesus never said anything of the sort but that after the faith had been established it must have been repugnant to the earliest chroniclers that their Lord had not foreseen everything. The appropriate corrections were duly retrojected as the faith evolved.

For that matter the whole insistence, in the Gospels as well as in Paul's Epistles, that everything had been accomplished in fulfilment of the Scriptures seems puzzling. No such belief – in the death and resurrection of the Messiah – is recorded among the Jews at all, and certainly not in the Hebrew Scriptures.

Now, the oldest portions of the Gospels indicate that the disciples made their way back to Galilee at first : this is demonstrated most succinctly by a phrase put in Jesus' mouth (in *Mark*): 'But after I am raised up, I will go before you to Galilee' (Mk 14 :28).

As indicated above, we must take this as our starting point : we find Peter and a band of other disciples, shattered by the collapse of their movement and by their leader's dreadful death on the cross, going back to Galilee heartbroken. Jesus' pseudo-prediction, in *Mark*, 'You will all fall away; for it is written, "I will strike the shepherd and the sheep will be scattered"' (Mk 14:27), actually sums up what must have happened; as a fictional device to humiliate the presumed inspirers of the apostolic tradition it seems pointless.

Consequently, we must imagine that after leaving the scene of disaster full of grief, doubtless in the mood revealed by the passage in *Luke*, 'But we had hoped that he was the one to redeem Israel, (Lk 24:21), they *nevertheless* could not believe that things had come to an end. Despite the clear record of their incomprehension and flight, substantially soft-pedalled as it no doubt must be, they must have been so identified with their leader that they could not resign themselves to acquiescing in the apparent verdict of the events.

Peter seems to have been the first to have seen Jesus resuscitated, or rather had a vision of him *resurrected in glory*. As we have seen, there is a vital distinction between seeing a corpse revived and seeing someone glorified, not in the flesh, but at the right hand of God.

Peter's primacy is based on the authority of Paul and on the story of the miraculous catch of fish in the fourth Gospel (Chapter 21), as well as on one phrase in *Luke* and on another in the fourth Gospel (20:6).

Once the fact of Peter's having had a vision of Jesus is accepted, the doctrine of the Resurrection, the cornerstone of the incipient religion, may be conceived of as having been established. For after the first vision the mere multiplication of visions afterward is still easier to imagine, considering the well-known contagiousness of collective visions, hallucinations, and so on.

Let us sum up the conditions that gave rise to this initial spark of hope, which was to kindle the outburst of the new faith :

Jesus' followers, shattered by defeat, return to Galilee; but they are too attached to his memory to give up entirely the hopes that had been focused on him. Some of them refuse to acquiesce in his permanent absence; they cannot accept his death.

Consquently, to explain the very first impulse that was later to be elaborated with such theological complexity, we need only imagine a state of extreme emotional tension on the part of Jesus' followers, surely temperamental by nature. Peter, perhaps the closest to Jesus of all his followers, and thus subject to the greatest despair, was the first to experience the vision. He was followed by some of the others and ultimately by most of the group.

For our purposes this is sufficient, especially since there is nothing more to be hoped for from the complete void in our information for this period. We are at a loss to explain just how the group of Jesus' followers that had first gone to Galilee later retraced their steps and established themselves in Jerusalem, where the 'Mother Church' was to come into being. And we are almost equally in the dark for the actual inception of the missionary movement that spread the new faith elsewhere.

A word of caution repeated:

The basic source of confusion in the study of this extraordinary development – why Jesus' followers are not Jews – is that the later Church took as its starting point a belief (in the Kingdom of God) that had failed *in fact*. This belief had been part of the movement begun by Jesus; it had been held by him and by his first followers. With the undoing of the movement by the Romans, no elements were left over to serve as the background for a new faith that might have continued Jesus' apocalyptic and/or insurrectionary activity. The very Glorification of Jesus that launched the new religion was inherently alien to everything that had concerned Jesus himself. By springing up over his crucified body and taking the Resurrection and Glorification of the martyr as the central theme of the new cult, the early Church became fundamentally indifferent to the actual events of Jesus' life and his own aims.

Jesus' Gospel, as we have seen, was the proclamation of the imminence of the Kingdom of God, accessible to those who had repented; this was transformed by the Church into the *Gospel of Christ,* which was the doctrine of salvation through Jesus' death and Resurrection. The oldest *doctrinal* message made individual salvation dependent on the person of Christ, while the oldest historical message we can disentangle from the complexities of the Gospels, contained in *Matthew* 10 (Jesus' instructions to the disciples), is silent about Jesus himself. In Jesus' instructions he says nothing at all about the necessity of a period of trials and tribulations before the coming of the Kingdom, nor is there any suggestion that his own death would be in any sense at all prerequisite for the advent of the Kingdom.

As I have indicated before, it is the cross itself that marks the line of demarcation between Christianity as a religion and its origins in Jesus' life and activity: between the prehistory of the religion and the religion itself.

Without the death of Jesus, there would have been no Christianity at all. In the epigram of Alfred Loisy, 'What Jesus proclaimed was the Kingdom of God, and what arrived was the Church.'

Or, as Paul put it,

If Christ has not been raised, then our preaching is in vain and your faith is in vain [I Cor. 15:14].

For Hellenic Christianity the cross was the central symbol of the entire mechanism of salavation: it was the very repulsiveness of the cross that led Paul to say,

Jews demand signs and Greeks seek wisdom, but we preach Christ crucified, a stumbling-block to Jews and folly to Gentiles

[I Cor. 1:22–23].

It was the dynamism inherent in this contradiction that led Paul to transform the catastrophe into the archsymbol of hope.

But for the Jews proper the cross remained a bafflement, since not only was the very notion of a failed Messiah a logical contradiction for them, but crucifixion was considered to be a punishment of someone accursed by God, according to *Deuteronomy* 21:23, recalled by Paul:

'For it is written, "Cursed be every one who hangs on a tree"'
[Gal 3:13].

Consequently, among Jesus' Jewish followers in Palestine the crucifixion remained what it was to remain for Jews generally, a stumbling-block that in essence could only be apologized for and played down, and at best had to be compensated or overcompensated for by the Resurrection, which both cancelled out the disgrace of Jesus' death and explained it away.

Because of this basic and above all unavowed transformation of perspective, the transition between Jesus' activity and the belief in the Christ, that is, the belief in individual salvation through the Saviour's crucifixion and Glorification, is profoundly obscure.

For the most striking thing about the *earliest* origins of the nascent sect is its thoroughgoing identity with Judaism.

Whatever the impulses that led the initial band of disciples, or certain individuals among them, to come to Jerusalem, we have only the *Acts of the Apostles* and Paul's *Epistles* as a source of information concerning their activities. There are profound disagreements between them.

Let us clarify a small chronological detail: the Gospels, though written a generation *later* than Paul's *Epistles*, describe events that took place substantially *before* Paul's *Epistles* were written: *Acts*, also written much later (at least forty years) than Paul's *Epistles*, partially overlap them as a description of events. In a still larger sense, since Paul's interpretation of the newly evolving religion was ultimately successful, everything in both the Gospels and *Acts* probably came under Pauline influence in one form or another.

This is of course a vast field of inquiry for any detailed investigation. For our purposes let us continue to use our cardinal criterion – we shall retain whatever goes *against* the universalizing, harmonizing tendency of the religion, and *against* the current of the homogenizing of its canonized texts.

We have already referred (page 89) to the fact that Jesus' followers, headed by his brother Jacob, were assiduous worshippers at the Temple in Jerusalem. This, oddly enough, is the keynote on which *Luke* comes to an end, when, after reporting the resurrected Jesus' final words to his followers (page 166), the chronicler goes on:

And they returned to Jerusalem with great joy, and were continually in the Temple blessing God [Lk 24:52–53].

This simple sentence is surely the leitmotif of the description of the little community that seems to have formed in Jerusalem around a common devotion to Jesus; it is reported often:

Many wonders and signs were done through the apostles. And all who believed were together and had all things in common; and they sold their possessions and goods and distributed them to all, as any had need. And day by day, attending the Temple together and breaking bread in their homes, they partook of food with glad and generous hearts, praising God and having favour with all the people [Acts 2:43–47].

And [the apostles] were all together in Solomon's Portico.... The people held them in high honour [Acts 5:12, 13].

And every day in the Temple and at home they did not cease teaching and preaching Jesus as the Christ [Acts 5:42].

Nor was it a mere question of attendance; the point is both emphasized and unintentionally allowed to slip in that they were even punctilious with respect to the laws of ritual purity:

But Peter said, 'No Lord; for I have never eaten anything that is common or unclean' [Acts 10:14].

So when Peter went up to Jerusalem, the circumcision party criticized him, saying 'Why did you go to uncircumcised men and eat with them?' [Acts 11:2, 3].

But some men came down from Judea and were teaching the brethren, 'Unless you are circumcised according to the custom of Moses, you cannot be saved' [Acts 15:1].

The unequivocal statement is also made that not only were many Pharisees members of the little group,

But some believers who belonged to the party of the Pharisees rose up, and said, 'It is necessary to circumcise them, and to charge them to keep the law of Moses' [Acts 15:5],

but that even priests had joined them:

And the word of God increased; and the number of disciples multiplied greatly in Jerusalem, and a great many of the priests were obedient to the faith [Acts 6:7].

And taken as a whole, the group congratulates itself on being 'zealous for the Law':

And when they heard it, they glorified God. And they said to him, 'You see, brother, how many thousands there are among the Jews of those who have believed; they are all zealous for the Law'

[Acts 21:20].

The above passages are astonishing; they indicate that for a whole generation after Jesus' death his followers were pious Jews and proud of it, had attracted into their fold members of the *professional* religious classes, and did not deviate *even* from the burdensome ceremonial laws.

Moreover, not only did they attend the Temple; they actually preached that *Jesus was the Messiah* (Christ). We have already seen that the mere belief in the Messiahship of a human being was not blasphemous in terms of the Jewish Law, as it was not blasphemous to say as much about oneself. It might be considered a quirk, blunder, mania, obsession, or delusion, and so on, but it involved no question of piety as such; consequently there was no reason why a Jew should not have followed Jesus' own prescriptions regarding obedience to the Jewish Law in its entirety, while at the same time cherishing a belief about the mission of one human being. Since in this Jewish milieu there could be no question of *worshipping* Jesus, such a belief was essentially a private matter.

It is true that the corollary of this belief, in the minds of the very first Jerusalem community, was that Jesus, selected by God as his Messiah, was going to come again. This was the first displacement, so to speak, or the first transformation of the original hope of Jesus and his followers: they were now awaiting the return of the Messiah in glory instead of the Kingdom of God alone. Or rather, this glorious return was to herald the installation of the Kingdom; thus, while for all practical purposes they were still concentrating on the same thing, a profound difference had taken place nevertheless. From the point of view of potentialities, Jesus' followers now understood the divine economy through the prism of their attitude towards Jesus *personally*. This fact alone laid the foundations for the future magnification of Jesus, for his progressive elevation from the Jewish Messiah, to the Vice-God, ruler of the cosmos, and to God himself, at least in one of its aspects.

But all this took place later. On the terrain of Jerusalem, in the early community of those of his followers who were still awaiting his return, we are still dealing with a group of pious Jews who had no thought of starting a new religion at all, but who considered themselves wholehearted members of a pious Jewish milieu, sharing a pious hope that could have meaning for no one but Jews.

Consequently, in *Acts,* we have scattered evidence of a situation that managed to survive the process of dogmatization involved in the Hellenistic christology exemplified by the apologetic tendency of the New Testament as a whole. It is a situation in which belief in Jesus as the Messiah not only did not prevent its holders from attending the Temple, the stronghold of the Jewish religion; it did not even prevent them from trying to persuade other devout Jews of its correctness.

Jesus' brother lived until A.D. 62. His death seems to have been caused, not by anything to do with his presumed belief in his brother's Messiahship, but by a matter of personal rivalry between himself and the High Priest, a Sadducee. He was stoned to death, in circumstances that remain mysterious, after the High Priest had convened the Sanhedrin on his own authority. This action aroused the violent resentment of the major Jewish party, the Pharisees, and on their insistent complaint, the Jewish King of the time (Agrippa II) deposed the High Priest for malfeasance. It is clear that the accusation laid against Jacob of infraction of the Law must have been a pretext; he was famous for his rigorous legalism. Also, he was condemned together with 'others', according to Josephus, who were not followers of Jesus at all. If they had been, the earliest tradition would surely have made a point of remembering them as early martyrs, of which the Jerusalem community had scarcely any. If his belief in Jesus' Messiahship had played any role in his execution it would simply show that Jacob and the little community of Jesus' followers enjoyed the sympathy of the Pharisees, judging by their resentment of his execution. In that case the implication would be that the new group was opposed only by the Sadducees. Indeed, it would not be at all paradoxical to maintain that Jacob's entanglement in Temple politics to the point of falling foul of a politically influential rival is, if anything, another indication of the identity of the Jerusalem community with Judaism and for that matter with Pharisaism. The expulsion from Judea of the Greek-speaking Jews (see below) might have reinforced this unquestioned identity once the friction they caused had died down.

In any case the little community went on living in Jerusalem until around 70, when the Romans finally crushed the Jewish state and levelled the Temple. Throughout this period, ever since its constitution some time after Jesus' death, the little community had only three losses by violence: Stephen through stoning, the execution of Jacob (James), son of Zebedee (one of the 'Sons of Thunder'), and Jacob, Jesus' brother.

The various mentions in *Acts* of the Jewishness of Jesus' followers are not isolated: they are confirmed by the evidence of Paul's *Epistles* written more than a generation beforehand. These indicate the contest that must have taken place between the faith of the Jerusalem community and Paul's view of the doctrine, or rather Paul's doctrine, since the evidence of both *Acts* and Paul's *Epistles* does not show the slightest trace of any *doctrine* at all in the 'Mother Church' in Jerusalem. It indicates, in fact, as we have seen by the above quotations from *Acts,* that the 'Mother Church' was not a Church at all: it was no more than a group operating within, and accepting, the Jewish Law in all its details. Had the new religion been confined to the Jerusalem Jewish community, probably nothing would ever have been heard of it. With the Second Coming indefinitely postponed, and with no mutational possibilities within the structure of Jewish monotheism, the faith in the singularity of Jesus the man would have been reabsorbed by the main current of the religion his immediate followers in any case felt themselves part of.

But the tiny shoot of the belief in Jesus' person, barely distinguishable from the massive trunk it had sprung from, was snapped off and transplanted to the lush terrain of Greco-Roman civilization.

It is this transplantation that marks the beginning of Christianity proper.

12

JESUS ABROAD

THE branching out of the faith in Jesus as Messiah from the original community of Jesus' followers in Jerusalem, the gradual transformation of that faith into a proto-Christian doctrine revolving around Jesus' divinity, the religion of salvation based on his Resurrection, and the manner in which all this happened are attested by Paul's *Epistles* and *Acts*.

The contradictions between them are numerous; more particularly, the character of each source is quite different. *Acts* represents a much later attempt to record in a soft, conciliatory light the beginnings of what came to be the Christian Church. Broadly, the point of view is friendly to Paul's notions, but it smooths over all the differences that are nevertheless unmistakably, though blurrily, indicated. Paul's *Epistles*, on the other hand, are far nearer the violent controversies that must have upset the scattered little community; they are more like impromptu reactions to current events. Paul was engaged in a struggle: he naturally presents it to his readers in such a way as to advance his own cause.

The struggle, which Paul seems ultimately to have won, since Christianity became 'Pauline', revolved essentially around the simple problem referred to above: How could pagans be admitted into the fold of a Jewish sect without accepting the rules of Judaism? This meant all the various commandments and rites, such as circumcision, the ceremonial apparatus (ritual cleanliness, dietary laws), and everything else meant by the 'yoke of Torah'.

Both *Acts* and Paul's *Epistles* indicate unmistakably that as pious Jews the 'pillars' of the Jerusalem community (Jesus' brother Jacob, Peter, and John) took it as a matter of course that conversion to the newly forming, but as yet not consciously differentiated sect, involved conversion to Judaism *ipso facto*: they insisted on the 'yoke of the Torah'. As 'Apostle to the Gentiles', Paul fundamentally believed, contrariwise, in flinging off this Jewish yoke in favour of the new doctrine that was beginning to coagulate on an entirely different basis. Here is Paul's basic position epitomized:

If justification were through the [Jewish] law, then Christ died to no purpose [Gal. 2:21].

This contains in germ the whole of the new faith, for it implies as a matter of elementary logic that the agony of Christ was in fact the new criterion of faith; the Jewish Law was obsolete by definition.

The evidence of the struggle is unmistakable: Paul himself constantly refers to those who preach a different Christ and a different Gospel, and whom he evidently regards as his bitterest opponents. He is continually justifying his own version of the Gospel to his readers, pleading with them to accept it and to disregard his pernicious rivals. The fact that he was not entirely aware of the implications of this himself, and often wrote as though being a Jew, rather than a Gentile sinner, somehow gave one an inherently privileged position, is of greater interest with respect to Paul's psychology than to the implications of his activity. For aside from his volatile emotional nature, it was this basic tendency in his preaching that led to the success of his mission to the Gentiles; it contained the seeds of the ultimate schism and hostility between the new faith and Judaism.

The problem here, of course, is what the word 'Gospel' could have meant before the success of Paul's version of it. It is impossible to say in detail. When we read Paul's words,

It has been reported to me ... that there is quarrelling among you, my brethren. ... Each one of you says, 'I belong to Paul,' or 'I belong to Apollos,' or 'I belong to Cephas,' or 'I belong to Christ' [I Cor. 1:11–12],

we are baffled. All we can legitimately conclude is that in the dim world of the newly forming sect, however hard we peer into it through the haze of our ignorance, there were different points of view that were only 'reconciled' by the victory of *one* point of view. We read in *Acts* that a certain Apollos, a Jew from Alexandria, mentioned in the above quotation from Paul,

was an eloquent man, well versed in the Scriptures. He had been instructed in the way of the Lord; and being fervent in spirit, he spoke and taught accurately the things concerning Jesus, though he knew only the baptism of John [Acts 18:24-25].

This baffles us still more. The statement that someone who 'knew only the baptism of John' could teach 'accurately the things concerning Jesus' shows us, by virtue of its inexplicability, how little we understand the activities of the first generation after Jesus. The inchoate early community lost its original character in the very process of acquiring self-consciousness. Before the formation of its doctrine it must have been highly plastic, but the details are beyond our reach.

For our purposes it is enough to show that the Hellentistic world, throbbing with variety, was to exercise the dominant influence on the formation of Christianity. Its overwhelming role was reinforced by the loss of a counterweight – the early community of Jesus' Jewish followers. As long as the Jerusalem community had existed, until the destruction of A.D. 70, these Jewish followers had had to contend with Hellenistic influences streaming in from the Greco-Roman world, influences that were deeply corrosive of the simple, primitive Jewish belief in Jesus' glorious Messianic return. When the Jerusalem community vanished as an organized factor, there was nothing to withstand them.

The channel that brought Hellenism into play at first was, naturally enough, the Jewish 'Diaspora' (dispersion) – the Jews living outside Palestine. These more or less Hellenized Jews played a fateful role in the genesis of the new faith.

For many centuries, ever since the Assyrian and Babylonian captivities, Jews had been living in communities that were scattered far and wide over the known world; during Jesus' generation and afterward there were flourishing Jewish communities throughout the Roman Empire. Josephus quotes the Greek geographer Strabo as saying, about 85 B.C., that the Jews 'have already gotten into all cities; and it is hard to find a place on the habitable earth that has not admitted this tribe of men,' and adds on his own account that 'there is no people upon the habitable earth that have not some portion of us [the Jews] among them.'

There were roughly about 3,500,000 Jews scattered throughout the Roman Empire, apart from another 1,000,000 in Babylonia; there were 1,000,000 Jews in Egypt, 1,500,000 in Syria and Asia Minor, and another 1,000,000 in North Africa, Greece, Gaul, Spain, and elsewhere in Europe. This was, according to authoritative estimates, roughly the number of Jews in Palestine proper, where they were concentrated and consequently of much greater specific weight, since they substantially outnumbered the 500,000 Syro-Canaanites, Greeks, Arabs, and Romans. It seems likely that a substantial portion of the 3,500,000 Jews in the Roman Empire were converts to Judaism; it is hard to imagine their all having originated in little Palestine.

The Jews enjoyed a special constitutional position under the Roman Empire; they were allowed to carry on their own religious observances unmolested. They were more or less autonomous with regard to their own affairs; they were quite strict in all their religious observances, keeping the Sabbath, celebrating the feasts, practising circumcision, and by and large keeping the dietary laws. They were also strongly attached to the Temple in Jerusalem; not only would they make generous contributions to the Temple treasury, but many would undertake the pilgrimage to Jerusalem once a year.

By the first century, on the other hand, though instances of deliberate assimilation into Hellenistic life seem to have been rare, Jews living outside Palestine, except for scholars, had lost the knowledge of Hebrew or Aramaic as a spoken language, and spoke only the vernacular of their own country. In the overwhelming majority of cases this was Greek, the *lingua franca* of the entire eastern Mediterranean and beyond.

More importantly, perhaps, in purely intellectual circles many Jewish thinkers were deeply impressed by Greek philosophy, and attempted to make a harmonious accommodation between the Torah and Greek thought: Philo of Alexandria may be said to have devoted his life to this.

Considering the destiny of the small Jerusalem community in the generation after Jesus' death, the most important thing to note is that the faith in his Messiahship had a particular success with the Greek-speaking Jews who had come to Jerusalem for the annual pilgrimage and who seem to have stayed on. It is impossible to say how many of them there were, but in any case there were enough to form a separate wing of the original community. They seem to have set up synagogues of their own, on a geographical basis: we hear of '. . . those who belonged to the synagogue of the Freedmen . . . and of the Cyrenians, and of the Alexandrians, and of those from Cilicia and Asia' (Acts 6:9).

It is obvious, though detail eludes us, that some Greek-speaking Jews came in contact with the small band of Jesus' followers, and were ultimately attracted to their view of Jesus. It seems likely that this was facilitated by the presence among these Greek-speaking Jews of pagans who had become thorough-going converts to Judaism but still retained a Hellenistic outlook. Such pagans and the Greek-speaking Jews themselves, doubtless to a lesser degree, were in all probability disposed by their very natures to *amplify the conception of Jesus*, that is, to emphasize the practices and mannerisms of the Palestinian Jewish followers of Jesus in such a way as to accentuate the differentation of this potential sect from the rest of Judaism. The fact that this did not happen without friction is indicated quite clearly in *Acts* (though the explanation given, to be sure, leaves something to be desired):

Now in these days when the disciples were increasing in number, the Hellenists murmured against the Hebrews [Acts 6:1].

The cause of complaint is given as the irritation of the Greek-speaking Jews and proselytes at their widows' being 'neglected in the daily distribution'. Accordingly, the 'twelve' suggest that 'seven' be selected to handle the distribution of food, while the 'twelve' go on preaching and praying.

This episode seems obscure, but its obscurity is surely to be traced to a split in the little community. The author of *Acts*, eager as always to play down differences and emphasize the basic unity of the right-minded, has blurred the entire account. What is important for us is that it enables us to detect the glimmerings of a schism in the actual organization of the very earliest community: the 'twelve' in charge of the Judaizing followers of Jesus, and the 'seven' in charge of the Hellenizers.

Acts gives a further hint, in the martyrdom of Stephen and the dispersion of the Greek-speaking community, that it was these Hellenized Jews who first began carrying on propaganda of a kind that ultimately implicated the authorities. The person of Stephen must be taken to represent the Greek-speaking followers of the new movement; his vigorous debate with his Greek-speaking fellow Jews, belonging to the synagogues mentioned above, is doubtless an attenuated and smoothed-out account of how the Hellenists collided with the Jewish authorities and were in fact dispersed. The point is that the Judaizing segment stayed on in Jerusalem, as is indicated in a shadowy way by *Acts* when it says:

On that day [the day Stephen died] a great persecution arose against the church in Jerusalem; and they were all scattered throughout the region of Judea and Samaria, except the apostles [Acts 8:1].

The phrase 'except the apostles' must be a reference to the Jewish branch of the early community, those governed by the 'twelve' in contrast with the 'seven'.

The demure retention of the phrase 'except the apostles' – except, that is, the heads of the Church the persecution was presumably aimed at! – highlights both the editorial manipulation of diverse composite and ambiguous sources in the service of an overriding apologetic tendency, and the clumsiness of the manipulation.

This impression of the one-sidedness of the repressive action is further reinforced by the following assurance in *Acts* that the 'Hebrew' followers of Jesus were not persecuted after the expulsion of the Hellenists:

So the church throughout all Judea and Galilee and Samaria had peace and was built up; and walking in the fear of the Lord and in the comfort of the Holy Spirit it was multiplied [Acts 9:31].

It was, accordingly, the Greek ferment, operating in the minds of the Greek-speaking Jews, converted to a faith in Jesus as the Messiah, doubtless *understood in their own manner*, that was the specific agent in transporting what was not yet an actual faith, but only its seeds, on to Hellenistic terrain.

We shall see that this was the reason for the importance of the schism so obscurely hinted at in *Acts*, since the Jewish community was doomed to extinction in any case as a result of its fatal war against Rome in A.D. 66–70. Because of this, the Jewish influence on the very earliest stirrings of the new faith, undoubtedly represented by the Greek-speaking Jews in Jerusalem, was totally checkmated, and the new faith was flung abroad into the Hellenistic maelstrom.

The early split in the Jerusalem community indicates in embryo the basically inhibitory effect of Judaism on the new faith, and the stimulating influence of Hellenism in the person of Jews reared in the Greek language and culture.

This whole process is epitomized in this passage, which in capsule form recapitulates the very germination of Christianity:

Now those who were scattered because of the persecution that arose over Stephen travelled as far as Phonicia and Cyprus and Antioch, speaking the word to none except Jews. But there were some of them, men of Cyprus and Cyrene, who on coming to Antioch spoke to the Greeks also, preaching the Lord Jesus. And the hand of the Lord was with them, and a great number that believed turned to the Lord [Acts 11 : 19–21].

This passage is unusual in *Acts* for its trustworthiness; since Chapter 10, which precedes it, is obviously much later, abstractly symbolizing as it does the conversion of the Greeks in bulk by means of the story of the conversion of Cornelius, the retention of the fragment just quoted argues for its authenticity. The motif, running through both Chapters 10 and 11, of Peter's hesitation and his need to *justify* the conversion of Cornelius, can also only be understood against the background of a general feeling, doubtless traceable to Jesus (Chapter 7), that Jesus' original message concerned the Jews alone.

In a contradictory way the importance of this step is indicated by the first sentence, 'speaking the word to none except

Jews.' It is this that lends full force to the succeeding and contrasting phrase, 'spoke to the Greeks also'. This simple phrase
contains the essence of the development that was to engender
the new faith.

According to this key passage, which sounds as though it
came from the very earliest stratum of information used by the
chronicler of *Acts*, the Hellenized Jews, dispersed from Judea,
began broadcasting their version of the faith in Jesus at first in
the Synagogues, as they had doubtless been doing in Jerusalem;
it was only later that they ventured abroad to carry it to the
Gentiles.

But these Gentiles could scarcely have been pure pagans. Let
us turn back to the Jewish Diaspora for a moment. Throughout the Diaspora there were, in addition to the substantial
number of pagan converts to Judaism proper, very large numbers of what were called 'God-fearers' clustering round the
synagogues. These were pagans who had been sufficiently impressed by Judaism to adopt the worship of the Jewish God
without being able to make up their minds to assume the 'yoke
of the Torah'. These 'God-fearers', though not Jews at all from
any orthodox point of view, were nevertheless quite at home
in the neighbourhood of a synagogue. Paul mentions them
often, for instance, in the synagogue at Antioch of Pisidia:
'Men of Israel, and you that fear God . . .' (*Acts* 13:16), and
again: 'Brethren, sons of the family of Abraham, and those
among you that fear God . . .' (*Acts* 13:26). That is, Jews and
those Yahweh-worshippers who had not been inducted past the
barrier of ritual into Israel proper.

These 'God-fearers' formed an intervening layer between
true Jews and pagans; the new religion may be regarded as
having been launched the moment the possibility arose of
adhering to a faith in Jesus without having to pass through
Judaism.

The constant transmosis that had been going on for generations between even Palestinian Jewry and the culture of the
Hellenistic world was to play a vital role in preparing the
ground for the new faith to strike root in, and having struck

root to be radically transformed by the pervasive influence of Hellenist thought.

These brief remarks on the Jewish Diaspora have led us to the Diaspora milieu – the Hellenistic world itself. In this vast subject I shall discuss a strand that concerns us directly: the prevalence of the forms of religious thought referred to as the 'Mystery religions'.

Around this time the eastern Mediterranean world was in a ferment of religious emotionalism. It teemed with cults, religious practices, and an enormous variety of superstitions. Altogether it was far removed from the apathy and scepticism sometimes attributed to it. Indeed, the cardinal trait of this ancient world, as far as the beginnings of Christianity are concerned, was its immense religious liveliness.

This religious intensity derived from the most diverse sources. Its keynote was syncretism – the mingling together of different beliefs and practices without regard to origin. The Hellenistic world was profoundly cosmopolitan, especially in the big cities. The ancient Oriental world had made itself competely at home beneath the umbrella of the Greek language. Both intellectually and institutionally there was a dense intermingling of tendencies derived both from Greece itself and from the Orient.

The components of the resulting religious complexity were thus traceable to the ancient religion of the Greek Olympus and to the swarm of Oriental cults that overwhelmed the Hellenistic world during the century before and after Jesus.

Though by this time the religion of ancient Olympus had lost much of its inward emotional value, it was superficially still alive, and under the inspiration of Augustus Caesar had actually undergone a restoration to its traditional forms. The cultivated classes were doubtless lukewarm in their conviction of its validity, but as a state-sponsored religion enjoying the benefits of a resplendent cult it may have had some patriotic or aesthetic hold over them: the common people were surely far more ardent in their belief.

There were also a great many attempts made by cultivated spirits to adapt the Olympian cult, felt to be somewhat sterile, to the new philosophical and emotional requirements of the epoch: the upshot of these attempts to reinterpret the ancient classical religion was a tendency towards the subordination of the multiplicity of ancient gods to a single divine essence (henotheism); this was an important factor in weakening resistance to those aspects of Christianity that were to emphasize the Jewish element of monotheism. Simultaneously, of course, the attenuated recollection of a variety of deities facilitated the divizination of Jesus.

Specialized deities were numerous and popular: they may not have enjoyed immense prestige, but they could always be called upon for a specific service, however trivial. A number of them, such as the Apollos of Delphi and of Claros, were famous for their oracles; Artemis of Ephesus, who was the inspiration of some venerated 'Mysteries', and Aesculapius, the healer, had particularly brilliant cults.

In addition there were vast numbers of 'demons', a word that at the time simply meant divine beings inferior to the gods and far more numerous. The universe, in fact, was thought to be teeming with them; each human being, as well as a particular locality, might enjoy the sponsorship of one of them.

Thus the ancient Greek religion had survived in brilliant forms of worship, however attenuated its emotional content had doubtless become. It also survived in the universal belief in miracles and magic, and their practice. For early Christian propaganda, with its emphasis on miracles, signs, and prodigies of all kinds, this was to prove very important; the ancient world was inherently receptive to such claims. It was also, because of its ancient and deeply rooted belief in oracular divination, receptive to claims of the fulfilment of prophecies.

The Oriental contribution to the complex *mélange* of cults and superstitions in the Hellenistic world was much richer and more variegated. The various Oriental religions that had been transplanted to the Hellenistic world differed from one another somewhat in their external, as it were, ideological expressions – in their myths, fables, legends, and so on. But they were closely akin to each other in their basic structures. These were all shaped by the attempt to interpret the phenomena of

nature. The Oriental deities were conceived of either vegeta-
tionally or astrally; they symbolized either the changes in the
seasons or the movements of the stars. This comes to much the
same, of course, since the sun determines the succession of the
seasons and their plant cycle.

During the half-century or so preceding the Christian era,
all these cults had made so many reciprocal borrowings from
one another that their original characteristics were no longer
discernible. It was just this process of intramural fusion that
was to provide the most favourable terrain for the new faith
introduced in Antioch.

Perhaps the most important point about all these complexly
intermingled Oriental religions was their emphasis on the individual. In contrast with the older classical religions, whose
emphasis lay on the preservation of social institutions, such as
the family, the state, or the city, the Oriental religions were
directed at the promotion of personal welfare. Having orgin-
ally begun as a corpus of rites designed to give aid to the sun
and the plant world in providing food, they had gradually been
transformed into a method of preparing people for the life the
food was meant to sustain. This transformation naturally implied the notion of salvation, which a growing apparatus of
myths and legends made emotionally effective as well as aesthe-
tically and intellectually attractive.

The syncretism referred to above as the cardinal trait of
Hellenistic religious life was due to the Greek love of variety.
However different these Oriental religions might have been
from the older forms of Greek religious thought, the Greek
thirst for eclecticism, the assimilation of elements taken from
everywhere and tailored to suit specific requirements, enabled
all these Oriental religions to live side by side with the cults
inherited from the Greek world proper, and eventually to fuse
with them in a complex transmosis. The Greeks, by contribut-
ing their own talent for speculation and ratiocination, ultimately gained most from this process, since the emotional
Oriental religions were far livelier and more stimulating.

The emphasis on the salvation of the individual (which of
course entailed universalism, in contrast with the partitions

mankind is divided into by the concepts of state, city, and so on) was also fortified by the existence in the Oriental religions of a man or manlike god as the object of worship. Osiris, Adonis, Attis, and Tammuz were some of these altogether anthropomorphic deities, who despite their power were perfectly accessible to their worshippers.

All these foci of interaction were naturally concentrated in the great cosmopolitan cities of the eastern Mediterranean, the commercial capitals like Alexandria, Antioch, Tarsus, and so on.

Now, during the period we are discussing there was a great yearning for personal immortality. The older religions, in their preoccupation with the human being in his collective capacity, as a member of a family, clan, state, city, and so on, paid no attention to the desires of the individual in isolation: neither classic Judaism nor classic pagan religion had much interest in what happened to the individual after death. Though some groups believed abstractly in the *fact* of immortality, their belief did not kindle any genuine emotional interest. Neither in the Hades portrayed by Homer nor in the Sheol of the Old Testament do we get the impression of any genuine life going on; they are indeed mere places of shadows.

But the vast social and political upheavals that were taking place during this stage of the Roman Empire, the dissolution of old forms of society, of ancient peoples and states, the uprooting of captive populations and the growth of slavery, had all wrenched the individual out of his formerly stable framework of life. It was doubtless this disintegration of the social fabric that, by putting the individual on his own, strengthened his dependence on new and more satisfying forms of ritual and, more specifically, generated a novel interest in speculations on life beyond the tomb.

It is in the elaboration of the 'Mysteries' of immortality, or salvation that we can see the most dramatic example of the fusion between the Greek and the Oriental attitudes. In these Hellenistic Mysteries the throbbing emotional mysticism of the Oriental cults was refined, structured, and rationalized by the Greek mind.

The Mysteries in general were rooted in the idea of immortality – in the belief that there was an afterlife that human beings could acquire knowledge of. This afterlife was of course far happier than life on this earth. The Greeks had come to this notion as a matter of metaphysical speculation via their dualism: once they had formed the concept that the human being was composed of two vital factors, material and non-material, and that the material, or corporeal, was destroyed by death while the non-material was *released* by death, they were prepared to go on to assume that the liberated non-material element – what in philosophical discussion became the soul – could survive independently of its material envelope.

The Greeks had had their own Mysteries before the fusion of their way of life with the religious thought of the Oriental world. Generally speaking, the Greek Mysteries resembled one another first in their assumption that the human soul was incapable of finding the road to salvation through its own efforts – which was why the Mystery was needed to begin with – and also in the practice of various degrees of initiation into the Mystery, usually by a liturgical process. With the possible exception of Orphism, which had a doctrine of salvation, the Mysteries generally were expressed in the form of a sacred drama: they had no metaphysics, but produced a dramatic spectacle that demonstrated the effectiveness of the various ritual practices. Similarly, they had no ethic, properly speaking, but were entirely preoccupied with rites of purification. The personal meritoriousness of the individual was not the important thing: what counted was the actual fact of initiation, which in and for itself was the source of salvation.

While these old Greek Mysteries were still influential around the beginning of the Christian era, they seem to have lacked the emotional intensity found in the Oriental cults; nor had the actual technique for achieving salvation been elaborated with adequate complexity.

It was during the century around the beginning of the Christian era that a real wave of religiosity, originating in the Orient, swept the Hellenistic world. Egypt produced Isis, Osiris, and Serapis; Syria, Adonis-Tammuz, Atargatis, and the various

Baals; Phrygia, celebrated for its religious fervour, extended the influence of its gods, Cybele, Attis, and Sabazius; Iran and Mesopotamia contributed Mithra, Ishtar, and so on. The whole of the Asiatic East seemed to pour its various religious beliefs, all straining towards the same goal, into the Hellenistic melting pot.

The Oriental newcomers and the Greek cults shared the same general characteristics: the individual was regarded as fundamentally incapable of securing his own salvation, which had to be accorded him by the grace of his god; if he failed to receive that grace and to become one of the elect he was cast out.

In the Oriental religions, as in the Greek, people were thought to consist of a persistent principle and of perishable matter. But since the nature of the connexion between the two was elusive there was a good deal of latitude in the manner of conceiving it. Some thought that the immortal soul ascended to wherever the happy live; others leaned toward the notion of resurrection of the dead in their purified flesh. That is, opinion wavered between a belief in the immortality of the soul and an expectation of the resurrection of the flesh.

Most important of all, the individual required the example, intercession, and active aid of a divine being whose cardinal function was to give him salvation – a Saviour. The ancient Oriental custom of looking upon rulers as terrestrial incarnations of divinity and as actual saviours was extended to the after-life as a matter of course.

The most frequent example of salvation given by these Saviours followed a pattern in which the divine being himself actually lived through the experience that the initiate was longing to have on his own account: the Saviour was to have lived, suffered, died, and *been resurrected*. Mystic communion with his Saviour gave the individual both a model for his own life and a guarantee of his immortality.

The techniques by which the initiate was enabled to commune with his Saviour, that is, achieve the mystical identification aimed at by the cult, constituted the corpus of rites, formulas, and other mystic operations characteristic of each cult. Each

Mystery of course had its own method of bringing about this identification of the individual with the suffering, the destiny, and hence the ultimate glorification of his Saviour: this method was based on omnipotent rites. The principal ones depended on the basic forms of communion – that is, in bed and at table.

In accordance with this implicit notion of conforming with the requirements of the divine cult in order to participate in the ultimate glorification of the deity, the idea had gradually gained ground that the best preparation was a holy life, that is, one purified by the subjugation of carnal desires.

From our point of view, what is of still greater interest is the fact that the elect, designated as such after various rites of initiation that separated the 'children' from the 'perfect' (with degrees between) could come from any social condition or any nation. This form of universalism was inevitable once the preoccupation of the older religions with collective entities gave way to the satisfaction of personal yearnings. Hence these mystic fraternities, which we should think would have been closed to non-initiates, could in fact legitimately hope to spread throughout mankind and thus become universal religions of salvation.

The recruitment into these mystic fraternities was taken care of on a private basis: each one of the elect, proud of his status, would propagate the faith as zealously as he could; also, each fraternity had its clergy, since the ritual and liturgy, of cardinal importance for the initiates, had to be properly administered.

One of the oddities about these Mysteries was the extreme tolerance they showed one another: the mere fact that each one of them by definition claimed to be the unique path to true salvation did not make them reject any other claim; many people, in an evident attempt to maximize their chances, joined a variety of cults, and theoretically, in fact, might join them all.

There is one point to be kept in mind here: the death of the Saviour, in these Mysteries, while indispensable as an example and a lesson for the salvation of worshippers, was not in and for itself the same as their actual *redemption*. The deity did not give his own life in order to compensate for the shortcomings of his devotees, but simply sacrificed himself in front of them as an edifying example.

Now, one of the most widespread and effective techniques of salvation was the assimilation of the divine substance by actual ingestion of the deity's body and blood. This was a cardinal element not only in the pagan Mysteries; it is one of the most ancient devices in primitive religious practice since the earliest records.

One example will suffice.

In the Phrygian cult of Cybele and Attis there was a ceremony called the Taurobolus (or Criobolus) that was part of the mystic initiation into the cult. A deep trench was dug within the area of the temple; the initiate went down into it and was covered by a grillework on which a bull (or goat) ritually had its throat cut. The initiate made a point of bathing all his members in the gush of blood.

By the beginning of the Christian era this and similar rites, which originally had nothing to do with the after-life of the individual but were dedicated to the power of Cybele and Attis, had acquired a purely spiritual content; they were conceived of as methods of achieving immortality. The explanation of this doubtless lies in the obvious identification of the trench with the realm of the dead; in going down into the trench the devotee is supposed to die; the bull (representing Attis) projects the principle of life itself by giving its blood, which the initiate absorbs, to emerge from the trench 'newborn'; milk was poured over him as though he were a newly born infant.

But he was not merely reborn as a man: at the moment of absorbing the vital principle of Attis he became *an* Attis, and was greeted as such.

Many of the Saviour and Intercessor cults, such as those of Mithra and the Syrian Baals, fortified this renewal still further by a sacred meal at which the faithful dined at the table of their god. They actually *ate* the god, represented by bread, sacred fish, wine, and so on.

Such, broadly, was the religious world in which Christianity was to make such a stir. I have thought it sensible to give this brief account of it because both the doctrine and the structure of early Christianity must be traced back primarily to the Hellenistic matrix it germinated in. The rupture between the new faith and its Jewish inspiration is of course well known; but most people take it for granted that though Christianity began on Jewish soil, was rejected by the Jews, and went on to fruition among pagans, there was nevertheless some organic continuity between the two stages in its formation. It is this assumption, indeed, that underlies the traditional interpretation of Christian history.

But this interpretation has only been made possible by the confusion and obscurity of the very first stages in the formation of the new faith.

The information given by our sources is not only meagre, but, more important, the final editorial revision gives us only the triumphant version of the events. In the struggle between Paulinism and its opponents, it is the Pauline view that serves as standard: that of its opponents is systematically obscured and falsified.

We see, in fact, that the very phrase 'Mother Church' is a usurpatory invention of the Church that generations later arose outside Palestine and obliterated the true story of the events by claiming for itself the primordial Jewish community of Jesus' followers as part of the 'apostolic tradition'.

Christianity by-passed the 'Mother Church' of Jerusalem, and we can see its genesis only through the prism of the tradition that, by conquering all its rivals, naturally claimed to be *the* tradition. Thus, in the struggle that must have occurred between the various components of the faith that eventually took shape, we hear only the victorious side.

No documents whatever have come down to us from the Jerusalem community; if its members wrote anything about themselves it has vanished. The Dead Sea Scrolls unfortunately disclose nothing of this period. As a matter of fact it is entirely likely that the community had no documents to leave; as far as we can see its central faith must simply have revolved around the feverish expectation of the Messiah's Second Coming. Since the Jewish believers in Jesus' Messiahship, assiduous in their Temple worship, had no reason to develop any theological novelties it is quite understandable that no need was felt to set down anything in writing. As the Second Coming kept postponing itself *sine die*, the desecendants of the original community either merged with the mass of pagans being converted to the later, non-Jewish faith in the Christ, or else fell back into the body of Jewry.

The divergence in the fortunes of the two branches of the faith in Jesus was doubtless inevitable: extinction was the portion of his theologically conservative Jewish followers, and unprecedented triumph for the eclectic and innovating proto-Christians proper.

All references to the 'Mother Church' were compiled and edited after the dispersion of the original Jerusalem community as a result of the Roman destruction of the Jewish state, and it is because of this *de facto* elimination of the 'Mother Church', and the consequent victory of Paulinism over its now forgotten rivals, that the New Testament as a whole must be looked at, not as history (though of course its historical elements are priceless), but as a cluster of documents, tendentious in their very nature, that are, in fact, the basic manual of the Church Triumphant as it was fixed toward the end of the second century.

The destruction of the Jewish state meant, of course, that the Jews who had been in Judea and Galilee lost their pre-eminence as a factor in the growing faith; the second generation of Christians found itself entirely thrown back for converts on to the masses of the Roman Empire. This made it necessary, on the one hand, to placate as far as possible both the Roman state and the Greek-speaking targets of conversion, and on the other hand it removed the inhibitory authority of the community that traced itself directly back to Jesus personally.

Indeed, if the facts of Jesus' actual existence had not imposed the fiction of the apostolic succession as a necessity in establishing the authority of the evolving Church, perhaps even this 'Mother Church', with its Jewish piety, unquestioning devotion to the Jewish ceremonial laws, and disbelief in the divinity of Jesus, would not have been mentioned at all. In terms of

the swiftly developing christology and progressive magnification of Jesus, the Jewishness of the 'Mother Church' was certainly something that had to be explained away or dissolved in
the confusion of a few piously disingenuous platitudes contriv-
ing to suggest that the Jerusalem community had been entirely
in harmony with the Christian Church that later claimed it as
the warrant of its own authority.

It is true that some of the *beliefs* of the 'Mother Church'
have come down to us in the earliest layers of the Gospels, in
the tradition of Jesus' davidic descent, and the various other
recollections of the Jewishness of Jesus' background. The
strength of this tradition, which fits in so awkwardly with the
universalizing, divinizing tendencies that were to magnify Jesus
on Hellenistic terrain, was doubtless due to the early Messianic
dogmatics that had grown vigorously enough in its Jewish
milieu to embed itself in the christology that later developed
in the pagan world.

But that is all we know of this branch of Jewish Messianism.
It was *accommodated* to the later christology. After the Jews
were dispersed, the faith of Jesus' Jewish followers became a
mere eccentric belief, unable to articulate any justification for
itself. Amid the general triumph of Hellenistic Christianity, the
living views of the Jewish believers in Jesus' Messiahship were
obliterated, except for their lifeless iconization in the Christian
tradition. After Jesus' death the belief in him among Jews,
rooted in nothing more than his Second Coming as the immediate prelude to the installation of the Kingdom of God, was
bound to wither away.

The destruction of Judea in A.D. 70 was overwhelming; it
had taken the powerful Roman Empire some four years to
reduce this tiny state; the fighting had been savage; the Jews
had displayed an unbelievably fanatical tenacity that could not
help impressing and infuriating the Romans. Josephus has given
partial estimates in different places of the losses sustained by the
Jews during this devastating war; they amount to 1,356,460!
This fantastic total, amounting to roughly half the population,
may of course be exaggerated, but there can be no doubt that
the devastation of the Jewish–Roman War calls for some similar

estimate. To the ravaging of the country and the slaughter of the population must be added the total destruction of the Temple, the politico-religious centre of world Jewry.

The disaster that wiped out the Jewish priesthood also destroyed the Sadducees as a party, and the Pharisees found themselves the *de facto* exponents of the religious and intellectual energies of the now defeated and dispersed nation. Thus for the first two centuries of the rise of the Christian faith, the Pharisees were identified with the Jewish people as a whole.

Before A.D. 70 Judaism had been indulgent to those who believed in Jesus but clung to the Jewish ceremonial; it reserved its hostility for Jesus' Hellenist followers, who wished to overthrow this ceremonial. After the national catastrophe, however, Judaism shrank back into itself; it became increasingly hostile to all forms of Christianity, especially since during this time Christianity itself was evolving along lines increasingly intolerable to Jewish monotheism. In order to bind together the Jewish people in the Diaspora that was now the sole framework of its existence, the Pharisees, accordingly, became increasingly exclusive as a matter of policy.

The rupture between the two faiths became unbridgeable: after A.D. 70 it was impossible to be both a Jew and a Christian. This alone was enough to seal the doom of so-called Judeo-Christianity. Without the ability to cast off all Jewish monotheistic restraints and magnify Jesus into a genuine and independent object of worship, as the Hellenistic branch of Christianity was managing to do with such éclat, it could only stifle in its own blind alley – too Jewish for Christianity, too Jewish to create a vigorous, independent sect in the teeth of Jewish tradition, and not Jewish enough, on the other hand, to melt back indiscernibly into the main body of Judaism.

These twin factors – the suppression after A.D. 70 of 'Judeo-Christianity', or the Jewish belief in Jesus as the Jewish Messiah, and the growing rigour of the Jewish attitude itself – forced Christianity proper to develop under exclusively Hellenistic influence.

Let us cast a glance at one stepping stone between the Jewish environment of Jesus and the later development of Christian theology. I have given some indication above of the way in which the original, still Jewish, faith in Jesus as the Messiah spread to Greek-speaking territory after the expulsion of the Greek-speaking Jews from Jerusalem; I have also referred to the logic of Jesus' magnification that stimulated the expansion of the newly forming religion.

The *general* Hellenistic receptivity to magnifications of Jesus was aided *specifically* by the concept of Jesus as the 'Son of God'. This idea served as the axis of the whole process of theologizing that swiftly transformed Jesus, the Jewish prophet and patriot, into the World Saviour and Lord of the Cosmos. It was the ultimate development of the relatively modest notion of the Virgin Birth, another contribution of Hellenism, which I have discussed above (pages 55–7).

Most Christians take this concept of Jesus as the Son of God for granted as having been implicit in Jesus' view of himself. But a moment's glance at the Gospels will show how it provided a matrix for the whole process of magnification. It was, indeed, the paramount magnification, and it laid the foundations of the Church.

For it we simply ask ourselves what the phrase 'Son of God' could have meant to a Jewish audience, in Judea or Galilee, during Jesus' life-time, we shall see at once that it could not even have been *understood* in its present-day sense.

The title 'son of God' was of course entirely familiar to Jews in Jesus' life-time and indeed for centuries before: *all* Jews were sons of God; this was in fact what distinguished them from other people. In II *Samuel* 7:14, for instance, we read, in God's words to David, 'I will be his father, and he shall be my son,' while in *Deuteronomy* 14:1 the chronicler says, 'You are the sons of the Lord your God.' Similarly in many other Old Testament passages (*Isaiah* 1:2, 63:8, *Jeremiah* 3:22, and so on).

More specifically the phrase was applied to eminent personages generally, and especially to kings, celestial emissaries, and so forth. It has even been thought that the verse from *Psalm* 2 used in the episode of Jesus' baptism, 'You are my son; today I have begotten you,' was part of the coronation ceremony of the Jewish kings of the Hasmonaean line.

During the postexilic period in Jewish history the word was further applied to any particularly pious man; ultimately it became common in reference to the Righteous Man and the Prince.

In all these cases of Jewish usage, the phrase was plainly a mere metaphor to emphasize a particularly close connexion between individual virtue and divine authority. The concept of any man's actually having been biologically *engendered* by the disembodied majesty of Yahweh, God of the Universe, would not only have been a grotesque extravagance in a Jewish milieu; it would actually have been unintelligible.

Nor is it possible to twist the plain metaphorical meaning of the phrase to make it signify only the Righteous Prince *par excellence*, the Messiah. It will be recalled that the Messiah was uniformly expected to be a human being, whatever the conception of his mission. It is, in short, generally conceded today by all liberal scholars that there is not a single clearly pre-Christian passage in Jewish literature in which the phrase 'son of God' can be regarded as referring to the Messiah.

The phrase could have acquired its literal sense of biological filiation only in the Hellenistic world, where the notion that a god had engendered a son of his own created no problems whatever. Divine parentage was, indeed, the least that could have been claimed on behalf of even a relatively mediocre public figure, to say nothing of a divinely sponsored object of worship. The very fact of 'the son of God' being expressed in the Greek language situated the concept in an altogether different framework from that of Jewish Messianism. For Greeks the phrase was no snag at all. Their conception of deity, essentially very supple and anthropomorphic, could easily be accommodated to the notion of a supreme God with an equally divine son. Neither the concept of biological fatherhood nor the transformation of Jesus Christ into a proper name like Julius Caesar would have been an obstacle to the Hellenistic reception of Jesus as the 'Son of God'.

The actual specific bridge to this broader christological conception, and the specific explanation of how it could have been attributed in all good faith to Jesus himself in his own Jewish milieu, is probably to be found on the one hand in Jesus' intense emphasis on the notion of the Fatherhood of God in general, and on the other in a purely philological accident.

A phrase often used of Jesus, perhaps in his own native environment by himself or his immediate disciples, is to be translated 'servant of God'. Now, the word used in Greek for 'servant' (*pais*) also has the meaning 'child'. It is used throughout the earliest Greek translation of the Old Testament, the Septuagint, to refer to those who are particularly in harmony with God's will; hence it is sometimes used of all Israel, Moses, the Prophets, King David, and so on. Thus the Greek phrase *pais tou theou*, 'servant of God', has exactly the same connotation as the Muslim name Abdallah – the 'servant of Allah'.

The mere fact that the same word in Greek means both 'servant' and 'child' and that a similar expression was used in reference to Jesus doubtless facilitated the transformation of this phrase 'servant' or 'child of God' to 'son of God', and thus gave a specific and, as it were, concrete aid to the magnifying effect of the early christology. The more restricted Jewish, or metaphorical, sense of 'son of God' survived among Jesus' Jewish followers simply as an equivalent of 'Messiah'; on Hellenistic terrain, where the concept was inherently far more elastic, it was well fitted to serve as a stimulus to the evolving christology of the first Christian generations.

13

A NEW RELIGION

HAVING set the stage by this brief account of the fiasco of Jesus' actual enterprise, the formation of the first community of his Jewish followers, the transposition of the Jewish faith to a Hellenistic terrain, and the subsidence of the Jewish community, let us look at the formation of the new faith – 'Pauline' Christianity.

Our sources for this are still *Acts* and Paul's *Epistles*, especially, of course, the latter. But the *Epistles* are far from providing us with a consistent, well-rounded exposition of Paul's faith. Indeed, nothing could be a better proof of the rivalry between contending 'Gospels' than the actual condition of these *Epistles*. Their very randomness, their often fragmentary nature, the uncertainty of authorship in a number of them, indicate that for some period of time they were *not* authoritative in Christian circles. They were doubtless only recovered, brought together, and cherished at a point when the tendency represented by Pauline Christianity in the life of the times had been successful. It was this that naturally inspired an attempt to rescue Paul's *Epistles* from oblivion; if they had been *authoritative* from the very beginning they would surely have been better taken care of.

It would be agreeable if we could study the germination of Paul's ideas in terms of his personality, but that eludes us almost entirely. The *Epistles* are the only source for his biography, except for the obviously stylized, tendentious references to him in *Acts* (whose second half reads like a Pauline account of the events); they often contradict *Acts* and in any case give us a thoroughly egocentric view of his activity. Indeed, Paul's actual purpose in writing the *Epistles*, which are not set pieces of dogmatic speculation but polemical *ad hoc* letters, substantially obstructs our view of the man.

It is best to disregard the voluminous speculation that has been devoted to Paul's evidently complex character, and simply consider his religious contribution. It should be emphasized that Paul himself was not, perhaps, the primary source of the views he expresses, whatever he may have contributed to them. It is likely that the initial elaboration of the primitive Jewish belief in Jesus' Messiahship had already begun in the Greek-speaking branch of the Jerusalem community, attaining fruition in Antioch after the transplantation there, as mentioned above, of the Greek-speaking Jews. But it is Paul's name that has come down to us as the proponent of the christological presentation that was ultimately successful. In any case the proportions of the personal contributions of others are obviously beyond our reach. Accordingly, Paul's name will often serve as the equivalent of 'Paulinism'.

I have given a sketchy outline above of the chief characteristics of the pagan 'Mysteries'; the reader will have noticed the resemblances to Christianity. The scholarly world has of course long been aware of the broad similarity between Christianity and many of the Mystery religions; few laymen realize just how striking it is. Orthodox opinion, of course, finds any comparison odious.

But the resemblances are fundamental: Christian communion carries us at once into the very heart of the Mysteries. There is no need to go into the technical components of this communion; they may be summed up as baptism, the Eucharist (the communal repast at the Lord's table), prayer, and ecstasy.

For our purpose it is enough to mention the Eucharist. Both in its basic concept and in its manner of execution it is unquestionably a piece of paganism.

It is true that the notions of alliance, expiatory sacrifice, and of a scapegoat for atonement are originally Jewish, but the actual core of Christianity is constituted by the idea of a magical communion with the Lord by means of his body and blood. This is totally pagan, as is the magical value assigned to the formula of consecration: 'This is my body . . . this is my blood.' Such ideas, as indicated above, were rampant throughout the universe of the Mysteries. For that matter the resemblance between the Christian baptism and Eucharist and the pagan rite of baptism in the blood of the deity and the eating of his body was noted from the very beginnings of the Christian faith, from Paul to Augustine (first century to the fifth century). It was a thorn in the side of the propagandists of the new faith, who were compelled to explain it away as the trick of a Devil determined to imitate Christ : the early Fathers reversed the sequence, claiming that it was the Christian Church that served as model to contemporary Mysteries. To be sure, it is not unlikely that evolving Christianity did influence some of the pagan faiths, equally bent on ensuring the individual's eternal salvation via the intercession of a deity, but all the principal pagan cults, all the basic myths, symbols, and effective rites preceded the birth of Christianity, and during Paul's own lifetime had found very widespread and ramified expression.

What is striking in the relationship between Christianity and the Mysteries is their identity both in the dynamic structure of the religion and in the modalities of its expression. It is more than a question of mere external resemblances between rituals, or of the abstract resemblance between mystical experiences as such.

Rituals derive their basic significance, after all, from the configuration of the religion. The dominant and meaningful element in both Christianity and the Mysteries was the view of human destiny that is expressed in the actual idea of personal salvation. Both Christianity and the Mysteries were faiths based on the concept of the indispensable mediation between the devotee and God himself of a divine Intercessor who has deigned to live as a man and to suffer a man's death in order to enable the otherwise helpless individual to achieve salvation by identifying himself with him.

Similarly with the question of communion : here the basic identity between the communion established by the Eucharist and the communion realized in the Mysteries is evident. Paulinism merely heightened the mythical intensity of this rite by enriching it with the concept of the devotee's being crucified *together with* his Lord. This expanded and intensified the mystical power of what in the Mysteries was merely a metaphor.

If paganism revolves around the fusion of essences between a devotee and a tangible deity, what Paulinism did was to deepen and enrich the paganism of the Mysteries. The dramatic power of the central concept of Redemption via the humiliating and hence exalting agony of the Lord on the cross transformed the fundamental Christian rite into a far more effective mystical accomplishment, within the same framework of salvation, than anything in the Mysteries proper.

But in both Christianity and the Mysteries the rituals derived their meaning from the structure of the religion, on the one hand, and the religion derived its emotional impact from the rituals, on the other, by means of the vital unity realized by their fusion. In both Christianity and the Mysteries the structure of both thought and feeling was identical.

This is the anatomy of Paul's theory of salvation:

A divine being, who has been in existence in godlike shape since before the creation of the Cosmos, has come down to earth, where he has been incarnated in Jesus, a physically normal man belonging to a certain people; this man then dies on the cross. This sacrifice is made in accordance with the eternal will of God and is intended, first, to reconcile the all-embracing Cosmos with the celestial Father by crucifying sin with Jesus' own body, thus annihilating it together with himself, and then to open up to all men the one true path to salvation.

In short:

The saying is sure: If we have died with him, we shall also live with him [II Tim. 2:11].

In content and structure this theory is obviously a myth. Its view of the significance of expiation has nothing in common with the old Jewish idea of the moral value of atonement; it revolves around the mystic, magical efficacy that belongs to the very nature of the death of a being simultaneously divine and human: it is his death, *because* he is such a being, that has the capacity of entailing the death of sin, and consequently the redemption and ultimate glorification of the individual.

Nor is it simply a question of our noticing resemblances: the first thing that strikes us about the Pauline Gospel is that it is *explicitly* presented as a Mystery. As late as the end of the second century and the beginning of the third century, Christian propagandists conceived of their faith along the lines of the other Mysteries prevalent in the ancient world, infinitely superior, to be sure, and not comparable in *value*, but nevertheless a Mystery. In the second century Clement of Alexandria made a point of counterposing the 'authentic Mystery' of Christianity to other Mysteries (which he regarded as satanic nonsense).

In this he was following the lead of Paul himself, who constantly used the word 'Mystery' to designate the core of his own revelation. He demonstrably conceived of the mission and role of Lord Jesus as analogous to the salutary effect of the gods of the various Mystery cults:

But we impart a secret wisdom of God, in a Mystery,* which God decreed before the ages for our glorification [I Cor. 2:7].

Also:

Now to him who is able to strengthen you according to my gospel and the preaching of Jesus Christ, according to the revelation of the mystery which was kept secret for long ages but is now disclosed and through the prophetic writings is made known to all nations, according to the command of the eternal God, to bring about obedience to the faith – to the only wise God be glory for evermore through Jesus Christ Amen [Rom. 16:25-27].

Now I rejoice in my sufferings for your sake, and in my flesh I complete what is lacking in Christ's afflictions for the sake of his body, that is, the church, of which I became a minister according to the divine office which was given to me for you, to make the word of God fully known, the mystery hidden for ages and generations but now made manifest to his saints. To them God chose to make known how great among the Gentiles are the riches of the glory of this mystery, which is Christ in you, the hope of glory. Him we proclaim, warning every man and teaching every man in all wisdom, that we may present every man mature in Christ [Col. 1:24-28].

'Hope of glory' means the hope brought by Christ of the devotee's being glorified like himself.

---

* I deviate from the conventional translation to make the meaning clearer.

Paul's version of the faith in Jesus Christ, accordingly, or his 'Gospel', is actually the framework of a Mystery. It is, moreover, the means of revealing that Mystery, since Paul is not only preoccupied by Jesus' person, the significance of his coming, and the role he plays, all of which might be a reflection of a general theology, but he specifically lays down the method to be followed by the devotee in order to *benefit* by this theology, that is, to achieve salvation.

This alone makes it a Mystery. For the essence of a Mystery is that it is a path to salvation: the particular method chosen to achieve salvation is a mere technical question.

Christianity differs, of course, from the Mysteries prevalent in the pagan world. Though the Oriental Mysteries revolved around the history of a deity and of his passion and resurrection, and guaranteed the immortality of their devotees by interpreting this history as constituting the path to salvation, they had no doctrine. The content of their revelation consisted of an apparatus of rites and formulas designed to enable the devotee to fuse with his deity. This fusion, by mingling the destinies of devotee and deity, guaranteed the annually renewed immortality of which the deity was the model.

The instruction in the Oriental Mysteries conveyed a hope and a model: it was not theologized. Most important of all, none of the Mysteries told the story of the deity's passion as though it had a redemptive value: the deity did not die in order *to make up for* his worshippers' shortcomings or sins.

But these are differences in content: the same *structure* for achieving salvation is characteristic of both Christianity and the Mysteries. Paul's doctrine revolves around the establishment of the path to salvation, whose substance is constituted by the dual doctrine of the Incarnation and Redemption.

In other words, the path to salvation as conceived by Paulinism consists of the Incarnation and the Redemption, and these are expressed by Paul himself in the language of the Mysteries.

At bottom, in fact, though Christianity differed from the Mysteries it was patterned after, what distinguished it was neither a structural nor an emotional nor a ritualistic novelty —

its unique distinction lay in its absorption of a *fact of life* – the actual crucifixion itself.

This is the deeper meaning of a passage already quoted (page 177):

For the word of the cross is folly to those who are perishing, but to us who are being saved it is the power of God. . . . We preach Christ crucified, a stumbling-block to Jews and folly to Gentiles

[I Cor. 1 :18, 23].

This theme of preaching nothing but Christ crucified is mentioned several times by Paul.

Its meaning is clear:

For Jews it was a stumbling block because of the grotesqueness of the notion that the Messiah, the Blessed One of Yahweh, could actually be tortured to death by evil-doers, when the whole point of his existence lay in his destroying them. This point of view was reinforced by the explicit curse laid by Yahweh on anyone 'hanging on wood' (*Deuteronomy* 21 :23).

As far as the pagans (Gentiles) were concerned, the problem was the absence in other Mysteries of this specific element of the redemptive crucifixion. The notion of Redemption itself might very well have been expected to prove attractive to pagans because of its depth, opulence, and mystical potential, but there was also a chance that its novelty, as well as the shocking extravagance of the cross as the path to Redemption, might have repelled them.

This is, incidentally, the best proof of the historicity of the crucifixion itself: the invention of such a grotesque idea would have been hazardous in the extreme.

In the event it was just this dramatic detail of the cross, charged with the profound significance and emotional power of the Redemption, that was to give Pauline Christianity its impetus. It remained a stumbling block for the Jews, to be sure – in fact they never surmounted it – but its success among the pagans was of course remarkable.

We have come round full circle once again: we took the execution of Jesus as our starting point for a study of the events that led up to it, and we came back to it again at the end, after finding it to be as simple a fact as it seemed: Jesus was killed as a rebel, and he was a rebel.

And now we have seen that it was Jesus' death that enabled his memory to survive at all, not merely in the sense in which Paul says his 'preaching is vain', as is the Christian faith if Jesus was not resurrected, but in the genetic sense of its having actually engendered the religious cult based on it.

Thus the enigma of Jesus' death in real life was ultimately explained by the fact itself, and in the realm of thought it was the manner of this execution that served as the germ of the speculation that became Christianity.

The crucifixion owed the vast power it generated to its very indigestibility. It was the outrageous impossibility of the cross, its baffling repulsiveness, the very perfection of its contradiction, that created a mighty thrust and transformed it into the starting point of Christianity not only chronologically but dynamically. A fact that could not be explained away *had* to be explained away: the contradiction *had* to be resolved. The compression caused by these impossibilities burst out in a powerful explosion.

The preparation for this ultimate explosion took place in two stages: in the Jewish milieu the faith in Jesus as Messiah depended on a vision of him as resurrected in glory appearing to his yearning followers; the second stage came about when the hope brought by his supposed reappearance was shifted to Hellenistic terrain, where a second and far more profound transformation became indispensable, since on pagan terrain the Messianic hope of the Jews meant nothing to anyone else.

Thus, while among the Jews the humiliating tragedy of the cross was excused by the resurrection of Jesus in glory, the magnification of Jesus that was launched in the pagan world demanded a far more ornate refurbishing of the drama of Jesus' agony to fit the theory evolving with the magnification.

The convulsive nature of this transformation is perhaps seen most directly in Paul's own psychology. True, even a tentative analysis of his character would be futile, but it must be evident that the motive force of his whole career is to be sought in the overriding tension between his Jewish monotheism and the emotional pull of the pagan Mysteries. His hostility to the developing cult of the worship of a fellowman as Saviour – if he has not overemphasized this hostility in order to capitalize on the contrast for the sake of a subsequent polemic – must be interpreted as reflecting an unavowed attraction by virtue of its very exaggeration. The intolerable tension between the two may have been explosively resolved when he suddenly perceived the possibility of having his cake and eating it – of retaining the fascination of the process of mystical fusion with a palpable deity, while at the same time not seeming to infringe on the prerogatives of Yahweh, the One God. Paul's vision of the Risen Christ on the road to Damascus may thus be a recollection of a historical but psychological fact: the Risen Christ proved a potent agent in the realization of this dramatic synthesis of Jewish monotheism and pagan idolatry.

The conception of a man-God as the scapegoat for all mankind, devised for the pagans on the model of the Mysteries they were familiar with, was the point of departure for the whole *specific* genesis of Christianity.

Paul's torment of spirit led him to the resolution of his personal tension by means of a conception that was both original and arrestingly simple: *the Lord had died because he had wanted to;* and he had wanted to because of the Divine Plan that had been in existence since the beginning of time.

In and for itself, of course, this notion is perhaps to be regarded as an echo of the Jewish habit of deducing consolation from catastrophe, but once this simple yet pregnant idea had germinated among the pagans, its Jewish motivation was irrelevant. It was borne abroad on its own power.

Once it was launched, the most repellent and mesmerizing aspect of the crucifixion – its baseness, as well as its cruelty – by virtue of the dynamic dialectic involved in its very conception, of the whole Divine Drama: it was in order to emphasize the supremely transcendent and glorious aspects of the divine project that the Lord and Saviour of the Universe had naturally chosen the *most* debased, the *most* horrible, the *most* repugnant of terrestrial deaths.

Thus we can see that while the fundamental Pauline doctrine retains the characteristic structure of other current Mysteries, which Paul and his followers felt themselves to be vying with, it contributed an element of genuine originality, not necessarily because of any personal genius but because in the logic of the circumstances the assimilation of the historic crucifixion imposed an explosive solution on the otherwise insoluble problem of the initial Jewish belief in a Messiah who had, in fact, failed.

We can see how inevitable the rupture with Judaism was. Paulinism was fundamentally an ancient pagan Mystery – streamlined, democratized, elevated, deepened, and dramatized. It was the cream, so to speak, of the Mysteries – a super-Mystery. Having absorbed their cardinal features, it gave a special mystic power to the intensely dramatic symbol of the redemptive crucifixion by localizing it in time and space. In doing this it was bound to magnify Jesus to the status of a deity, since otherwise the crucifixion could not have had its proper value. The substitution of Jesus for Yahweh is tersely conveyed in the following passage:

Therefore God has highly exalted him and bestowed on him the name which is above every name, that at the name of Jesus every knee should bow, in heaven and on earth and under the earth, and every tongue confess that Jesus Christ is Lord, to the glory of God the Father [Phil. 2:9–11].

The key phrase here is 'every knee must bow', which of course indicates the respect hitherto a prerogative of Yahweh's (*Isaiah* 45:23). The passage is revealing because the substitution is still incomplete, and in the juxtaposition of God to the 'name which is above every name' we seem to catch the process at the very crest of its confusion.

The divinization of Jesus naturally involved the liquidation of Jewish ceremonial, which was logically purposeless once the crucifixion had become the focus of the new cult. The Jewish Law was bound to be rejected if the crucifixion was to retain any salutary value:

Now it is evident that no man is justified before God by the law.... Christ redeemed us from the curse of the law, having become a curse for us – for it is written, 'Cursed be every one who hangs on a tree' – that in Christ Jesus the blessing of Abraham might come upon the Gentiles, that we might receive the promise of the Spirit through faith [Gal. 3:11–14].

For freedom Christ has set us free; stand fast therefore, and do not submit again to a yoke of slavery. Now I, Paul, say to you that if you receive circumcision, Christ will be of no advantage to you

[Gal. 5:1, 2].

We are a universe away from Jesus.

If Jesus came 'only to fulfil' the Law and the Prophets;

If he thought that 'not an iota, not a dot' would 'pass from the Law', that the cardinal commandment was 'Hear, O Israel, the Lord Our God, the Lord is one', and that 'no one was good but God';

If he actually considered himself 'sent only to the lost sheep of the House of Israel', and thought it wrong 'to take the children's bread and throw it to the dogs';

If despairing of the establishment of the Kingdom of God by divine intervention alone he took to action, and assaulted the lords of this world by violence;

If his undertaking was frustrated and he was executed as a rebel against the state;

What would he have thought of Paul's handiwork!

Paul's triumph meant the final obliteration of the historic Jesus; he comes to us embalmed in Christianity like a fly in amber.

The new faith, borne aloft by the successful synthesis of Paulinism, rapidly diverged from the religion of its supposed founder. But pagan in essence though it was, it retained three Jewish traits that, as compressive factors, added to its momentum.

The first was the monotheistic heritage of Paulinism. While Jesus, in becoming the axis of the evolving christology, supplanted Yahweh as the direct object of worship and of emotion, he never actually replaced him in Paul's theology, which in a confused and inexplicable sense (later to be resolved by the doctrine of the Trinity) kept Jesus slightly subordinate. On the other hand, the very fact of Jesus' elevation *towards* God implied that whereas in the Mysteries the full adept became *an* Attis or *an* Osiris, and so on, after performing the magical rites of communion, the Christian devotee could never dream that he himself had become *a* Christ. In the Mysteries the substance of the deity is eaten by the devotee, who thereby becomes the deity for the time being; in the case of Christianity it is the devotee who is absorbed by the deity: he 'puts on Christ'.

In another way it may be said that while Jewish monotheism held Jesus down a *little below* the concept of God, the pagan magnification of Jesus, conversely, put him *just beyond* the grasp of his devotees. Christianity effected a compromise between the all-encompassing claims of the ancient bodiless Yahweh and the homely accessibility of the pagan deities.

Pauline thought also extended the socioethical content of Judaism to the new faith; Paul was far more insistent on the constitution of a body of the faithful than were the Mysteries, with their fraternities of devotees. For Paul the Church had a real existence; it was a genuine entity, mystically established by the communion of the faithful 'in the Lord': indeed, if one thinks of Catholic Christianity it may even be said that it is the Church, mystically invested and unified by the indwelling Christ, that in fact constitutes the object of worship. Christ is apprehended by the faithful *via* the Church, which is not only the sole channel for the expression of the religion, the sole interpreter of the texts, and so on, but is an actual body of which Jesus is the head.

Jewish ethics survived in Christianity, furthermore, not merely in the sense in which the new religion inherited the ethical substance of Judaism, both of the Pentateuch and the Prophets, and indeed of the Old Testament as a whole, but because unlike the Mysteries the new cult was not satisfied with the mere fact of the salutary assimilation of the devotee to the deity. It insisted on the institution of an entirely new personal life in harmony with the life of mankind and of the whole Cosmos. In the Mysteries the devotee was actually able to regard himself as free of the constraints still incumbent on outsiders; in Pauline Christianity, on the contrary, the devotee's new life 'in the Lord' entailed a whole régime of strict moral requirements beyond the reach of outsiders.

But the Jewish trait that was perhaps to prove most effective in the actual spread of the new cult was the fundamental intolerance characteristic of a monotheism. The ordinary Mysteries were perfectly content to live together side by side, despite mutually exclusive claims that from a merely *logical* point of view would have implied the perniciousness of rivals. But in the case of Christianity mere logic was reinforced by a profound feeling of uniqueness: what made Christianity totally intransigent with respect to rivals was the emotional self-righteousness of the believers in the 'One True God', Yahweh, which Paul had doubtless inherited together with his other Jewish traits, and transferred to the new faith. There could be no question of its being merely one more Mystery *among* others: the propagandists of the new faith were bound to insist on the utter elimination of all 'false Mysteries' as coming from the Devil and infringing on the claims of the new Lord of the Cosmos.

While infusing the new cult with the social ethic and above all the purposefulness of life characteristic of Judaism, and making it the birthright of every human being as such, independently of the Jewish Law, Paul also made it absolutely exclusive: by making its emotional as well as its logical value absolute, Paulinism cut the ground away from under the Mysteries that had been so much at ease in one another's company.

But what was most Jewish of all, not so much in the structure of the new faith as in what may be called its moorings, was what has been suggested above – its historicity.

The Jewish revelation, unlike the timeless fantasies of paganism, linked to the eternal concordances of nature, is essentially a reflection on history. The various covenants between the Jewish people and Yahweh were conceived of as events in real life, which took place at certain times between certain individuals and a God who had manifested himself in the real world in a real way. History itself was meaningful only because it was the divine will manifesting itself: it was this, indeed, that made it history and not a meaninglessly trivial chronicle of no greater consequence than a gossip column.

Christianity took over from Judaism this sense of the intrinsic meaningfulness of history as the revelation of God's will, and so inherited its dynamic fusion of transcendental and historical events.

But of course it did something far more revolutionary, which in its dense interweaving of fact and symbol proved supremely compelling.

Starting out from the history-mindedness of Judaism, Paul intensified the thrill of communion with the resurrected deity by claiming that the Redemption was as much of an actuality as the crucifixion, that the two were, in fact, the identical act.

He not only reinforced the fluid speculations of the pagan cults by this emotionally intensified rite, but by claiming that the divine drama had actually occurred at a given point in time and space he bestowed on the new cult the incontestable superiority of an authentic event.

Thus, among other things, Paulinism turned the Jewish religious experience inside out.

Judaism took something that had happened in history – the evolution of Jewish monotheism – and made it mythical by personalizing its symbolical significance in the Biblical narrative.

Christianity did the opposite: it seized on a myth and maintained that it had really taken place.

For in being forced to digest the indigestible execution of Jesus, in being forced to assimilate this fact of life, Christianity did not of course allow it to remain a mere historical fact, inert and meaningless; it transcendentalized it.

And, by simultaneously maintaining that it had happened, it gave the myth the most important element a myth can have – the assurance that it is a fact.

SELECT REFERENCE LIST

Brandon, S. G. F., *The Fall of Jerusalem and the Christian Church*

Bultmann, R., *Le Christianisme Primitif*

Eisler, R., *The Messiah Jesus and John the Baptist*

Goguel, M., *Jean-Baptiste, Jésus, La Naissance du Christianisme*

Guignebert, C., *Le Christianisme Antique*
          Le Monde Juif vers le Temps de Jésus
          Jésus
          Le Christ

Loisy, A., *Les Origines du Nouveau Testament*

Robertson, J. M., *The Historical Jesus*

Schweitzer, Albert, *Die Geschichte der Leben-Jesu-Forschung*

Winter, Paul, *On the Trial of Jesus*

MORE ABOUT PENGUINS
AND PELICANS

If you have enjoyed reading this book you may wish to know that *Penguin Book News* appears every month. It is an attractively illustrated magazine containing a complete list of books published by Penguins and still in print, together with details of the month's new books. A specimen copy will be sent free on request.

Penguin Book News is obtainable from most bookshops; but you may prefer to become a regular subscriber at 3s for twelve issues. Just write to Dept. EP, Penguin Books Ltd., Harmondsworth, Middlesex, enclosing a cheque or postal order, and you will be put on the mailing list.

Some other books published by Penguin are described on the following pages.

Note: *Penguin Book News* is not available in the U.S.A.

THE PELICAN GOSPEL COMMENTARIES

The Pelican Gospel Commentaries mark a new departure in Bible criticism. Former commentaries have usually been of two kinds – either abstruse and academic, or over-simplified, fundamentalist, and out of date. These new paragraph-by-paragraph commentaries have been written by modern scholars who are in touch with contemporary Biblical theology and also with the needs of the average layman. They relate the teachings of Christ to the twentieth century, in the light of the latest archaeological, historical, and linguistic research.

The following volumes have so far been published:

SAINT MARK

D. E. Nineham, Professor of Divinity in the University of London

SAINT MATTHEW

John Fenton, Principal of Lichfield Theological College

SAINT LUKE

G. B. Caird, Grinfield Lecturer in the Septuagint, Oxford

THE DEAD SEA SCROLLS

John Allegro

This is a revised edition of the best popular account of the Dead Sea Scrolls.

In the early summer of 1947 an Arab shepherd stumbled on a cave near the Dead Sea and brought to light seven ancient scrolls. They proved to be part of the library of a Jewish monastic community which was in existence before and during the time of Christ. With the later discovery of the remains of hundreds more scrolls we have today an undreamt-of insight into Jewish Sectarianism of this all-important period. It is already clear that many of the characteristic ideas of Jewish Christianity were cradled in just such a religious environment.

John Allegro has long been connected with this exciting new field of research, both as an expert linguist and as trustee and secretary of the Dead Sea Scrolls Fund. In this new edition he has reappraised the discoveries, with their particular importance for New Testament studies, in the light of the very latest finds, and has discussed the possibility of future finds. Hitherto unpublished texts concerning the Essenes have been added to the book, which now includes a completely new set of plates.